W9-CBA-844

CONSUMPTION, IDENTITY, AND STYLE

COMEDIA

SERIES EDITOR: DAVID MORLEY

CONSUMPTION, IDENTITY, AND STYLE

Marketing, meanings, and
the packaging of pleasure

edited by

Alan Tomlinson

R

A COMEDIA book
published by Routledge
London and New York

First published 1990
by Routledge
11 New Fetter Lane, London EC4P 4EE

Simultaneously published in the USA and Canada
by Routledge
a division of Routledge, Chapman and Hall, Inc.
29 West 35th Street, New York, NY 10001

Printed in Great Britain by
The Guernsey Press Co. Ltd, Guernsey, Channel Islands

British Library Cataloguing in Publication Data

Consumption, identity and style: marketing, meanings,
  and the packaging of pleasure.
  1. Consumer goods. Consumption. Social aspects
  I. Tomlinson, Alan, *1950–*
306'.3

ISBN 0-415-01150-7
ISBN 0-415-01151-5 (pbk)

Library of Congress Cataloging in Publication Data

Consumption, identity, and style: marketing, meanings, and the
  packaging of pleasure/edited by Alan Tomlinson.
  p. cm.
Bibliography: p.
Includes index.
ISBN 0-415-01150-7. -- ISBN 0-415-01151-5 (pbk)
1. Consumers. 2. Marketing. I. Tomlinson, Alan.
HF5415.32.C66   1989
658.8--dc20   89-6317

Contents

v

CONTENTS

PART THREE
Consumer culture(s) and the market – some case studies

List of illustrations

Notes on the contributors

Sean Cubitt is a lecturer in the History and Theory of Art, Design, and Media at Middlesex Polytechnic and West Surrey College of Art and Design.

Stuart Ewen is Chair of the Department of Communications at Hunter College, and a Professor of Sociology in the Ph.D Program in Sociology at the City University of New York Graduate School. He is the author of *Captains of Consciousness* (1976), and co-author of *Channels of Desire* (1982). His most recent book is *All Consuming Images: The Politics of Style in Contemporary Culture* (1988).

Simon Frith is Research Director of the John Logie Baird Centre at the Universities of Glasgow and Strathclyde. He is the author of *Sound Effects: Youth, Leisure and the Politics of Rock* (1983), *Music for Pleasure: Essays in the Sociology of Pop* (1988), and (with Howard Horne) *Art Into Pop* (1987).

Dave Laing has worked in the popular music industry as well as writing rock biographies, critical analyses of popular cultural forms, and interpretations of radical theories of culture. He is the author of *The Marxist Theory of Art* (1978) and *One Chord Wonders: Power and Meaning in Punk Rock* (1985).

Graham Murdock works at the Centre for Mass Communications Research at the University of Leicester. He has written extensively on the political economy of popular culture, and on the economics of the moving-image industries. He jointly edited (with Peter Golding and Philip Schlesinger) *Communicating Politics: Mass Communications and the Political Process* (1986), and wrote (with Philip Schlesinger and Phillip Elliott) *Televising 'Terrorism': Political Violence in Popular Culture* (1983).

Deborah Philips is a contributor to *City Limits*, and was a co-founder of *Women's Review*. She now teaches at West London Institute, specializing in courses on fiction and women's studies. She has taught courses on popular culture for the Open University and a number of University Extra-Mural Departments. She is currently co-editing a volume of essays on women's experience of popular culture.

Jon Savage has written reviews and commentaries on the popular music industry for a wide range of publications, including the *Observer*, and the *Face*. He has also acted in a consultative capacity on television documentaries on style and popular culture.

Diana Simmonds worked as a writer for City Limits magazine when based in London. She is now Letters Editor and an arts writer for the Sydney Morning Herald in Australia. She is author of *Princess Di: The National Dish* (1984) and, with Robyn Archer, *A Star is Torn* (1986).

Grahame F. Thompson is a lecturer in the Faculty of Social Science at the Open University, where his strong interdisciplinary interests have contributed to innovative and influential initiatives such as the U-area course on Popular Culture. He is author of *The Conservatives' Economic Policy* (1986), and *Economic Calculation and Policy Formation* (1986). He also contributed to *State and Society in Contemporary Britain* (1984).

Alan Tomlinson works in the Chelsea School, Brighton Polytechnic, where he co-ordinates the Research Division and also acts as the Director of the Leisure Research Unit. He has edited and contributed to many volumes on sport, leisure and popular culture. He co-edited *Five-Ring Circus* (1984) and *Off the Ball* (1986) with Garry Whannel, and *Sport, Leisure and Social Relations* (1987) with John Horne and David Jary.

Helen Walker has taught social history and popular culture at the University of Sussex and has undertaken research for the Greater London Council and the London Strategic Policy Unit. She has published on the history of popular culture in the collection *Disorder and Discipline* (1987) and on twentieth-century mass leisure movements. She currently works as a planner for Brighton Borough Council.

Preface

This collection was conceived in the Winter of 1984/5. A number of pieces were written in 1985. They are none the less relevant for that. If anything, the general trends identified throughout this book have been consolidated and intensified.

Peter Ayrton, then of Pluto Press, was a stimulating editorial motivator at the beginning of this project. The collection owes much to his vision and insights. Dave Morley and Jane Armstrong acted swiftly and supportively in getting the project relocated on the Routledge Comedia list. I would also like to thank Mike Hall, John Humphrey, Grahame Thompson, and Garry Whannel for their stimulating and perceptive readings of a draft of the Introduction to the book.

With shifts in ownership in publishing, and Associated Book Publishers now a subsidiary of Thomson (who feature strongly in Grahame Thompson's contribution to this book) it is interesting to see the project itself as embosomed in this new level of integration in the leisure and consumer industries. I hope bookshops survive it all (or maybe Prose Parks or Word Centres lurk round the corner). In the absence of bookshops, perhaps some franchized Life Style Centre at one of Thomson's chartered airports would still find room for the odd non-fiction text.

Alan Tomlinson
Brighton, England
November 1987

1

Introduction
Consumer culture and the aura of the commodity

ALAN TOMLINSON

Some of the best people of our time speak now only in this dark language. Their grave voices have to compete with the jingles of happy consumption, the only widespread form of contemporary optimism.

Raymond Williams, 'Walking backwards into the future',
New Socialist, May 1985, p. 21.

whether the acute new awareness of self – its demands, its privileges, its rights – that had invaded the western psyche since the First World War was a good thing or a largely evil consequence of capitalist free enterprise . . . whether people had been media-gulled into self-awareness to increase the puppet-master's profits or whether it was an essentially liberalizing new force in human society.

John Fowles, *Daniel Martin* (Jonathan Cape, 1977,
BCA edition, p. 555).

The basis on which good repute in any highly organised industrial community ultimately rests is pecuniary strength; and the means of showing pecuniary strength, and so of gaining or retaining a good name, are leisure and a conspicuous consumption of goods.

Thorstein Veblen, *The Theory of the Leisure Class* (1899),
(Mentor, 1953, p. 70).

This is a book about the meaning of our lives as consumers. It is about leisure, lifestyle, and markets in today's consumer culture. In 1986 one measure of people's use of time in Britain identified

1

television watching as the major activity for both men and women outside paid employment and sleeping. On average, women watched slightly over three hours a day of television; men a little more.[1]

But if we look at the range of consumer activities and leisure spending in people's daily lives it is clear that much more goes on in the home, around and beyond the television set. Nearly one in three people in this survey (this is not an introduction to a television game show!) have an alcoholic drink at home; one in five or so regularly eat at fast-food restaurants (maybe to get back home for the favourite programme!) and one in thirteen bring the fast food home. Home entertaining is quite regularly engaged in by 6 per cent of the sample. Although this may not sound many, it represents several million people in Britain. That is a far from insignificant 'group' of consumers.

Out of the home, church or religious meetings vie with keep fit, individual sports, billiards, darts or visits to the pub as the most time-consuming regular activities. Running these close is 'taking a long walk for pleasure', though the tables do not show whether these are the same people as the 6 or 7 million who appear to go 'motoring for pleasure'. Going out to events in public – circuses, cinema, concerts, fairs, museums – is clearly in decline, only 1 in 50 or so people doing so with any regularity. Theme parks are constituting a new public leisure space, now more popular than most of these other more traditional 'going out' activities.

Alton Towers, the fun park set in the splendour of the Staffordshire countryside, attracted 2,250,000 paying visitors in 1986, the biggest paying attraction in the United Kingdom outside London.

The point about all this is that if even 1 in 50 can be encouraged to engage in an activity at all regularly, that constitutes a pretty big market. The market value of total leisure spending in 1986 was £56,242 million. The same figure, projected through to 1992, is put at £94,663 million.[2] That's a lot of growth, a lot of businesses, a lot of jobs. The British working population may have been seen, once, as the cast of labourers toiling away in the workshop of the world. More and more, British workers and earners are seen as prolific and discriminating potential consumers. It is the nature of this shift

2

which is the binding concern uniting the different contributors in this book.

Over a quarter of a century ago J.K. Galbraith observed, in his classic critique of modern consumer society, the need for a 'theory of social balance', for a combined concern with publicly provided services and privately produced goods. His vision of the imbalance at the heart of the postwar affluent society became one of the most widely quoted cultural comments of our time:

> The family which takes its mauve and cerise, air-conditioned power-steered and power-braked car out for a tour passes through cities that are badly paved, made hideous by litter, blighted buildings, billboards, and posts for wires that should long since have been put underground. They pass on into a countryside that has been rendered largely invisible by commercial art . . . They picnic on exquisitely packaged food from a portable icebox by a polluted stream. . .[3]

It's all there in this passage: family-based conspicuous consumption; indulgence alongside neglect, boom running side by side with blight; the intrusion of the copywriter into the natural environment. Galbraith was warning the advanced industrial world, the capitalist world, that if pursued as a major social objective, production would lead to modes of consumption taking place against a backcloth of neglect of public needs. He also implied that the desires and the needs of the affluent consumer were 'no longer evident' to the consumer himself. From different angles, other commentators in North America (Vance Packard in particular, in his sustained critique of the communications/image-building industries)[4] were offering critiques of consumerism, critical interventions, exercises in demystification.

Debates on the exploitative dimensions of contemporary capitalism have focused upon the experience of work, the nature of paid labour. The political dimensions of patterns of consumption have received little comparable sustained attention. Yet it is particular modes of consumption upon which many major productive processes now depend. Galbraith urged, quite rightly, the need to develop a balance between the public and the private, between state services and private enterprises. Without such a balance his scenario of the picnic excursion, of privileged plenty backgrounded by highly visible public deprivation, has come true many times over – most emphatically perhaps in atrophying regions of the North in Britain, where cultural heritage from Bradford to Merseyside is being effectively reworked as a set of tourist attractions. As Margaret Thatcher herself put it a few years ago: 'There's a great industry in other people's pleasure.' The top 'paying' and 'non-paying' United Kingdom tourist attractions are listed in Tables 1.1 and 1.2.

There is not a lot of fun in the freebies here. Blackpool nudges out the worthy self-improving activities dominating the rest of the list, winning for the carnivalesque over the cultural tone of our museums, galleries and monuments. But the list of paying attractions is interesting. Theme and fun parks pack the paying punters in. In York you *experience* the city's Viking history now, rather than just looking in on it via dead relics of the past. London still has four in the top ten – the grotesque Tussauds, the gory Tower, the dazzling plant life of Kew and the trapped wild life in the Zoo – but the major growth areas are the heritage experiences, the fun parks and all-in leisure environments.

Margaret Thatcher sees a great industry. In packaging people's pleasure, and constantly searching for the most lucrative novelty, this leisure and tourist industry prospers in a Britain in which the imbalance pointed to by Galbraith is as prominent as ever. Patterns of production have shifted, with typical forms of mass production giving way to flexible production catering for the market demands of a more fragmented

Table 1.1 Top 10 United Kingdom paying attractions for 1986 (number of visitors)

1.	Madam Tussauds	2,391,000
2.	Alton Towers (Staffs)	2,250,000
3.	Tower of London	2,020,000
4.	Magnum Leisure Centre (Irvine)	1,246,000
5.	London Zoo	1,190,000
6.	Kew Gardens	1,147,000
7.	Thorpe Park (Surrey)	1,060,000
8.	Drayton Manor Park (Staffs)	962,000
9.	Jorvik Viking Centre (York)	868,000
10.	Edinburgh Castle	832,000

Source: *Visits to Tourist Attractions*, British Tourist Authority 1986.

4

Table 1.2 Top 6 United Kingdom non-paying attractions for 1986 (estimated number of visitors)

1.	Pleasure Beach (Blackpool)	6,500,000
2.	British Museum	3,600,000
3.	National Gallery	3,200,000
4.	Westminster Abbey	3,000,000
5.	Science Museum	3,000,000
6.	Natural History Museum	2,700,000

Source: *The Economist*, 1 August 1987, p. 21.

social order. And the landscapes of worldwide capitalism have changed with steel-mills dominating Third World skylines and (with DAF using a United Kingdom advertising agency to launch its new truck) image-building and marketing the First World's forte, rather than manufacture. Fortunes are made in the new consumer and leisure industries. Sir Terence Conran, Richard Branson; these are the quintessential entrepreneurial giants of late capitalism, peddling interior design and cultural software for a new generation of lifestyle specialists. The captains of industry of the nineteenth century have little in common with these contemporary cultural brokers. If the Conrans and the Bransons are captains of anything, they are, in Stuart Ewen's telling phrase, captains of consciousness.[5] We are a consumer generation, in Galbraith's words again, 'synthesized, elaborated and nurtured by advertising and salesmanship'.[6]

The examination of patterns of consumption and leisure is a key contemporary task. For it raises hugely significant questions about what we believe and think, how we arrive at our beliefs, what we do, and how our actions express particular beliefs or values. Propagandists of the new right know this, which is why the apparent paradox of the new plastic usurer-culture is so perfectly in line with their views. Although the rhetoric of Mrs Thatcher conjures up the jam-jar cash economy of the kitchen, her economic growth is dependent upon spending before saving and her ideological hold is premised upon a notion of freedom in the marketplace.

As we near the end of the second millennium, we will no doubt see '2000' used as a dramatic landmark in the development of human civilization. But if '1984' symbolized debates about political freedom and citizenship, '2000' will come to symbolize issues concerning economic freedoms and consumerism. In Britain media institutions already offer an example of how things might move. Rupert Murdoch's takeover of *The Times*, for instance, led to the appointment of an editor whose editorial direction was, in Hugo Young's words, a drift from the notion of citizen as victim to a notion of citizen as consumer (*New Statesman*, 2 November 1984). We may have survived in 2000. Many of us may be free. But free for what? By then, worldwide, the sign of satisfactory survival might well be the colour television set and video, the personal transport system, the personal organizer, the personalized deodorant.

It is in the sphere of consumption – conspicuous leisure on the basis of adequate disposable income – that many will seek to express their sense of freedom, their personal power, their status aspirations. The effect of such a trend upon collective consciousness and cultural relations in particular societies cannot be understated. Popular culture and everyday life have always been of great concern to our political and economic masters. If popular culture can be reduced to a set of apparent choices based upon personal taste then we will see the triumph of the fragmented self, a constant lust for the new and the authentic among a population of consumer clones. That is why the issue of leisure, lifestyle, and consumption is a political one. If religion was, in Tawney's celebrated phrase, vital to the rise of capitalism, it is consumption which has become vital to its continuation and expansion.[7]

Markets have developed, throughout this century, which have radically altered the act of consumption. Take, for instance, mail order. Montgomery Ward and Co. began the mail order business in the United States in 1872, an opportunistic business initiative intended to constitute frontier pioneers as a consumer market. The more famous Sears, Roebuck and Co. issued its first catalogue in 1893, diversifying beyond Sears's and Roebuck's initial interest in jewellery and watches. From 200 pages of listings in 1893, it had expanded to over 1100 pages by 1900. The emphasis was very much on the honest sale, the good deal, the reliable source. The inside back cover (Figure 1) of the 1900 catalogue simply depicts the size and scale of the buildings from which the stock was dispatched. The front and back cover

Figure 1 Sears, Roebuck's five buildings, 1900

Figure 2 Front and back cover of Sears, Roebuck catalogue, Fall 1900

pictures were both the same (Figure 2), placing strong emphasis on value for money in the sticks as well as the city.[8]

Consumer goods were mimetically represented in the catalogue. Illustrations were simply faithful reproductions of what you would get for your money. If you wanted some gentlemen's suspenders, Sears Roebuck showed you what you'd get and also threw in a bit of advice: 'While we quote cheap suspenders, we do not warrant or recommend them. The better qualities are the cheapest in the end.'[9] From suspenders to leggings, rubber boots to toys, open lavatories to corsets, the emphasis was upon the integrity of the product, rather than its aura or its effect upon the consumer. Contemporary mail order catalogues might still stress value for money and consumer choice, but there is a fundamental difference in emphasis: the commodity has acquired, in late consumer capitalism, an aura beyond just its function. The commodity now acts *on* the consumer, endows him/her with perceived qualities which can be displayed in widening public contexts; consumption becomes a riskier business. It is the difference between buying an object mainly for its function, and acquiring an item for its style. Motor cars or jeans, for instance, are produced and consumed as more than functional means of mobility or clothing.

The role of the car in contemporary culture has altered in precisely this way. As early as 1949 Ford advertised its new model as 'a living room on wheels', with soft seats, modern fabrics and 'picture-window' visibility.[10] For the super rich and uninhibitedly status conscious, the car is only the raw material for the 'King of the Kustomisers', George Barris, to display his talents on. Barris painted Elvis Presley's Cadillac limousine with a gold murano pearl. Hub-caps and grille were gold plated. Even the telephone in the centre seat's pull-down section was gold. The interior of Liberace's Cadillac Eldorado included a piano keyboard motif on the seats and a musical score of his theme-song 'I'll be seeing you', with a miniature candelabra on its hood. Poor chicanos restyle second-hand models with brightly coloured carpets and chandeliers. The commodity itself is altered into an object of individual fantasy for the purpose of display.[11]

Shifts in production principles and advances in industrial technology brought the car into the mass market. Stephen

ALAN TOMLINSON

Bayley points to three key structural shifts: Henry Ford's application of Frederick Taylor's principles of scientific management; breakthroughs in design after the Second World War, which produced a technically sophisticated small car; and recent development in process efficiency in Japan which makes the perfect product an everyday reality.[12] Important changes in the production process might involve new techniques in selling, 'but the taste for symbolism, as ineradicable in human beings as the parallel appetites for love and sustenance, is going to stick around'.[13] It is this taste to which contemporary Japanese designers are seeking to appeal, with designers styling previously invisible parts such as suspension frames and engine bays. Buying a car has become, increasingly, a declaration of consumer choice on the level of symbols as well as cash. The amazing success of the Ford Cortina, launched in 1962 at a cost of £13 million, was certainly helped by its contemporary styling and continental naming:

> This new Ford was named after Cortina d'Aupezzo, the North Italian hill town that hosted the 1960 Winter Olympics. This gave the first generation of British tourists to benefit from cheap jet travel a tangible symbol of European awareness to park in their drives.[14]

Twenty years on, the Ford Sierra was launched with a new preoccupation with interior design, on the basis that the driver must be made to feel important. More recently, the city whizz-kid drives a Porsche. Production constantly seeks to respond to an identifiable consumer mentality, but also to redirect it and sometimes shape it anew. The marketing of the product has come increasingly to flatter the individual consumer, to fuel his or her aspirations, dreams, and fantasies; consumption resolves insecurity, offering status to the nouveau riche. The commodity becomes an object of passion, a source of potential distinctiveness, of constant renewal. Judith Williamson generalizes on this, equating consumer need with thrill and excitement:

> The power of the purchase – taking home a new thing, the anticipation of unwrapping – seems to drink up the desire for something new, the restlessness and unease that must be engendered in a society where so many have so little active

10

power, other than to withdraw the labour which produces its prizes.[15]

However much genuinely subjective passion for the commodity motivates the individual consumer, such subjectivity and consciousness is not unrelated to the process of packaging. Legends have been forged, fortunes made by producer-designers who have their fingers on the pulse (or throat) of the consuming public. And packaging, in the era of market segmentation, has become more and more sophisticated in its targeting, in its modes of address to selected markets. Benson and Hedges and Guinness perhaps, are the best British examples of 'understated' ways of really boasting about the elite status of the product.[16] But whether the commodity is targeted at a large mass market, or at the more lucrative high-earning and high-spending end of the market in a time when production structures are chasing a differentiated niche-market, it is still the aura of the commodity which the consumer is offered and attracted to or seduced by. It is, to paraphrase Roland Barthes, not what the object is or does, in any concrete sense, which gives it its attractiveness: rather, it is what it signifies.[17] In the middle of the 1980s there was perhaps no better example of this phenomenon than the advertising war over jeans.

In the late 1970s and early 1980s, after an all-time low in non-American sales of 501 jeans, Levi's began to tackle the image of the blue jeans. The 501s, baggier jeans with fly buttons, were earmarked for United Kingdom and European marketing. Tim Lindsay, of the British agency Bartle, Bogle, and Hegarty, identified three reasons why such a 're-launch' could work. First, 501s had a practicality about them which was in vogue. Second, the cut of the 501s offered a different style (familiar but different). And third, 501s 1950s image linked with a new generation of youth's view of that period as cool, mythical, stylish. Levi's put £10 million by to draw in new youthful buyers, whilst retaining fashion-conscious established buyers. Lindsay's agency created two television/cinema commercials: Nick Kamen undressing down to his boxer shorts in a fifties launderette, and washing his 501s; and James Mardle wearing his pair in the bath, to shrink them to the ideal fit. This was enough to catapult the unknown model Kamen to high-profile superstardom as

11

beautiful young man, actor, pop star or whatever. It was also enough to increase 501 sales from 80,000 in 1985 to 650,000 in 1986. For the follow-up campaign two story lines were chosen. 'Parting' had a young girl remembering her lost 'drafted' boyfriend by slipping on the 501s – symbol of civilian freedom and style – which he presents to her on parting. 'Entrance' featured Eddie Kidd, former motor-bike stuntman, as a hunky male wearing black 501s as he passes a 'No blue jeans' sign and enters a 1950s nightclub. The budget for these two productions was £500,000.[18]

In America, four expatriates from Marseilles run the Guess company, aiming for a more discriminating exclusive consumer. Guess jeans have aimed for the Calvin Klein designer jeans market, and now sell $250 million worth of merchandise annually, 95 per cent in the United States. The sales really boomed when a moody, provocative black and white approach was introduced in the advertising. In the words of one of the brothers: 'We wanted a difference, some drama, an emotional intense movement. We wanted Italian movie, Fellini atmosphere, *Dolce Vita*, 1950s St Tropez, Brigitte Bardot.'[19] These moments included ripped clothes, exposed bras, and cleavages. In Paul Marciano's words 'it is about sensuality and relationships between girls and guys'. Marciano's annual budget for Guess advertising is $20 million.

Guess's first two commercials, made by English director Roger Lunn, were inspired by a classic fifties film (Monroe, Montgomery Clift and Clark Gable in *The Misfits*) and a clever 1970s film depicting the fifties (Bogdanovich's *The Last Picture Show*, shot in black and white). In the third commercial Lunn spent £350,000 on a ninety-second film featuring Rolling Stone Bill Wyman's then little-girl friend, now wife, Mandy Smith, and a dissipated looking older male actor. Smith had already had an earlier modelling deal with Brutus jeans. Marciano took little persuading: 'She goes directly on Guess image. Meaning – sensual, attractive, provocative and youth.' In the commercial this couple arrive in late 1960s London to be hounded by press photographers. At no time in 'Paparazzi' do either of these lead players ever wear a pair of Guess jeans. The star endorses not the product, but the image around the product. 'Branding' is actually forsaken for the cultivation of desirable images. With a hounded sugar-daddy, you too could afford guess what.

With jeans as well as cars, we are now buying so much more than the object or artefact. We are buying into the imagery that surrounds the object. Cars, Peter York has commented in his review of the Marsh/Collett and Bayley books, must:

Share the stage with a lot of other choices now – so many other things to buy. The notion of 'lifestyle' supposes a fine-stitch tapestry of many small choices with brands attached – a Filofax here, a Tizio lamp there. In these terms, a car's just another *accessory* – though a hugely important one – and it has to fit in.[20]

Our personal identity is created out of elements created by others and marketed aggressively and seductively.

This is the key to what have emerged as the dominant modes of consumption, based upon an individualized sense of selfhood and well-being and the notion of free choice. But if we think we are free when our choices have in fact been consciously constructed for us, then this is a dangerous illusion of freedom. And if in paid work with money to spend we define ourselves as free human actors in a drama in which we can all have the choice of a part, we by Inference define all of those without parts too as free. Those who are not able to consume are simply the weak-willed, unable to exploit their freedom!

There is a double danger in this illusion of freedom. First, consumer choice is highly constructed. Second, millions unemployed by anyone and uninvited by Visa are, simply and brutally, excluded from the sphere of freedom. Freedom of goods for some goes hand-in-hand with subordination for others. Critics of consumerism must always remember this. It is a privilege to critique women's romantic novels in the pages of the increasingly glossy 'left' periodicals; it is an exclusion and a deprivation not to be able to afford a second-hand Mills and Boon because that is the price of a loaf.

Many contemporary critiques of consumerism can sound pretty elitist, detached, or supercilious. A strand of British cultural commentary of real interest here is that in which the upwardly mobile (often northern) working-class male bewails the effects of mass culture upon the indigenous and self-created culture of the working-class he has left behind. Such writing often speaks of consumerism as a Corrupting Other, a Distorting Influence on working-class consciousness. The condemnatory tone does say a lot, though, about the scale of transformation in popular culture, everyday life, and types of consumption.

J.B. Priestley discussed the implications of new ways of consuming half a century ago.[21] On his *English Journey* he saw that new forms of mass production were breaking down long-established cultural boundaries, images, and uniforms. Two 'older' Englands – one of cathedrals, minsters, manor-houses and inns, the other the nineteenth-century industrial England of old heavy industries and class-specific institutions – were giving way to a third England. This new England, very much American influenced, was in Priestley's view 'essentially democratic':

> You need money in this England, but you do not need much money. It is a large-scale, mass-production job, with cut prices. You could almost accept Woolworths as its symbol. Its cheapness is both its strength and its weakness . . .
>
> This is the England of arterial and by-pass roads, of filling stations and factories that look like exhibition buildings, of giant cinemas and dance-halls and cafes, bungalows with tiny garages, cocktail bars, Woolworths, motor-coaches, wireless, biking, factory girls looking like actresses, greyhound racing and dirt tracks, swimming pools and everything given away for cigarette coupons . . .
>
> It is an England, at last, without privilege. Years and years ago the democratic and enterprising Blackpool, by declaring that you were all as good as one another as long as you had the necessary six pence, began all this. Modern England is rapidly Blackpooling itself.[22]

It is also, to jump a few decades in argot, a more individualistic new England; an England in which 'Jack and Jill are nearly as good as their master and mistress', in which they simply 'get on with their own lives'.[23]

Priestley's main point was a simple one. Through forms of mass consumption, previously deferential social groups were throwing off the shackles of subordination. Priestley was right to emphasize this element of choice. Factory girls could certainly choose to idolize Greta Garbo rather than Queen Elizabeth; young men could pay homage to Herbert Chapman's Arsenal rather than the Royal Family. But Priestley reminded his readers too that the openness of such choices is limited.

He found the new cultural democracy a 'bit too cheap', too much a 'trumpery imitation' of pretty dubious originals. It was also imposed by 'elaborate publicity schemes' and depressingly monotonous, the outcome of media build-up and opportunistic marketing. Priestley recognized a classlessness in this new England, but also a dullness, an over-Americanized mass culture not of the people's making: 'You feel that too many of the people in this new England are doing not what they like but what they have been told they would like.'[24] Priestley regretted the loss of spontaneous expression in this emergent culture.

This view of the consumerist tendency in British culture has been echoed by a succession of post-Second World War cultural critics. Richard Hoggarts's atmospheric depiction of the collective values of traditional working-class life in *The Uses of Literacy* was in essence a plea for cultural freedom in the face of centralization and technological progress. If inner freedom were lost, he concluded, 'the great new classless class would be unlikely to know it: its members would still regard themselves as free and be told that they were free'.[25]

Hoggart highlighted the juke-box boys in milk-bars listening to nickleodeons and flipping through publications full of 'sex in shiny packets', in his attack on new forms of mass culture. They represented for Hoggart no more than 'a peculiarly thin and pallid form of dissipation', the modern equivalents of Samuel Butler's mid-nineteenth-century ploughboys; occupants of a 'myth-world' made up of 'a few simple elements which they take to be those of American life'.[26]

This theme has been a common one, particularly for writers who have moved up and out of working-class contexts. Jeremy Seabrook believes that 'the old coercive forces of poverty and want' have been replaced by the new tyranny of an 'insatiable and joyless consumerism'.[27] His work on working-class culture has been a consistent effort to indicate alternative sets of values for a culture that has lost its way and has fallen in too readily with consumerism:

> Because consumerism is felt to be based upon people's deepest wants and aspirations, and because it appears to incorporate the idealism of the early socialist pioneers, its morality and philosophy are felt to be generally a good thing; some of its effects have not been considered very deeply.[28]

Its main effect, for Seabrook, has been a 'subtle and less readily discernible bondage'.

Seabrook also sees the working-class young as symbolic of the contemporary crisis of values. He sees them as 'trapped, functionless and without purposes', locked into an acquisitive culture of yearning for material possessions – the 'primary determinant' in their lives a 'lopsided insistence on buying, getting, having' in a time of 'drugged somnolence, an even greater subjection than has been known before'.[29]

A recurrent theme in such commentators is that of seduction: the marketplace, the plaza, the mall, the media seduce working people away from some nobler, more idealistic, and always more collective sense of their destiny. Gutted of its substance, to paraphrase Seabrook, the working class becomes increasingly dependent upon commodities – a 'tragic vision', in Huw Beynon's words, overemphasizing hopelessness rather than anger or persistently creative resistance.[30]

Jeff Nuttall, searching for the roots of the northern stage and film comic Frank Randle, used the concrete urban redevelopment of the 1960s as a symbol for the burial – the 'passing over' – of a culture:

> The city centre is concrete and there is only one. A legion of spotty boffins who see themselves as civic thinkers are paving my country over because they think that this is the way the window must be dressed for those smartly shod angels who bear the economic miracle over the sea. A legion of men no-one has ever seen is disguising my country as Dusseldorf. I am journeying anonymous through the rising tide of concrete in search of a man, a memory, that will act as a talisman against an age that is somehow trying to cancel me out.[31]

The consistency of interpretation amongst these commentators is unmistakeable. White middle-aged and (at least now) middle-class males usually find in images of more traditional working-class life a set of values which the new subject in contemporary history – consumerism, often emanating from the United States – has displaced. Why are they so concerned, these Richards, Jeremys, Jeffs? Perhaps their own sense of loss and dislocation colours their interpretations: it is often a sad, dislocated, elitist, and perhaps menopausal, critique. Consumer culture can be exciting, novel, convenient and fun; it can be energizing rather than enervating. And it will not, with the significance of the service sector in the British economy and the relocation of manufacturing bases in dynamically developing centres in the Third World and some parts of the European Common Market countries, simply go away. Consuming can be a passionate experience, an expressive act. It can also appear vulgar, selfishly indulgent, and sadly bathetic.

Jonathan Raban has recognized this, from the 'guiltless style of splashing out' by the 'fast and flash' in American-style country/sailing clubs in Essex:

> The women at these tables all appeared to be modelling themselves on famous vamps in 1940s movies. They went in for platinum hair, rouge, mascara, monogrammed cigarettes and skirts with slits to the top of their thighs. While the men talked property and killings, the women dropped brand-names like Hong Kong, Antigua, the Seychelles and Pierre Cardin,[32]

through to the conspicuous consumption of yacht owners in the dining-places of Lymington:

> People were scoffing chicken liver pate with walnuts and knocking back Chateau Langoa-Barton at £22.50 a bottle. They were not hushed. Their boisterous gold-card voices rang out over the tables, and they talked in the new slang of space and computers. 'We have lift-off on the Swanley deal', 'I find the Volvo pretty user-friendly'. . .[33]

Raban also noted another less public yet central side to consumer culture, keeping in touch with the marketplace in the lonely and isolated privacy of the home. A tax-exiled architect in the Isle of Man displaces his own emptiness onto his wife:

> You know what she does? She spends half her life writing off for catalogues of kitchenware . . . mixers and whiskers and food processors and stuff like that . . . then she spends the

other half reading the bloody things. Reading catalogues! She's probably doing it now. They come by every post. The kitchen's jammed solid with machinery. She never uses it. And she goes sending away for those catalogues; reads them aloud too, right down to the voltage specifications. If you ever want the *Which* guide to food processors, I'm your man.[34]

There are certainly enough catalogues to keep this going. *Innovations* by mail order which come through most of our doors with instant availability by credit card include some of the most superfluous consumer goodies imaginable. The electronic bug-killer or the sonic pest repeller; the battery controlled alarm-clock pill carrier; the toothbrush with the asymmetric 'neck and thumb' scoop which cleans teeth, gums and 'gingival crevices' all at the same time; the rest-rite neck pillow and the mains-operated foot-massager. Tenuously para-medical in kind, many of these presage a phase in consumer culture of sheer super-fluity.

Priestley saw some important aspects of an England moving towards this consumer culture. Hoggart attacked that culture with all the Puritan self-righteousness of the respectable work-ing-class grammar school boy. Seabrook mourned the passing of a craft culture and the easy and all-pervasive progress of consumerism. Nuttall saw it as a vacuous alternative to deep-rooted lived and regional values. Raban, coasting in and out of parts of contemporary Britain, captures its diffusion, on differ-ent levels. Even where consumer culture has been held at bay, it is clear that the hope of economic regeneration lies in that very culture: 'Rye had found that there was a profit to be made out of its own dereliction ... The marketing of a whole country as an historic facade is being ingeniously managed by the PR indus-try.'[35]

Social theory, rather than cultural commentary, has produced a number of theories which seek to account for the rise of consumerism. But general categories alone, such as the univer-sal market, consumer capitalism, post-modern culture, are too wide to convey the ideological complexity of the contemporary politics of consumption.[36] For any debate on consumerism must be about stages of cultural transformation, about fundamental shifts in values, about confusions over class, regional, genera-tional and gender identities. Theory which has had something to say about consumption, has too frequently operated at the most general and therefore abstract of levels.

Marx, obviously, could hardly ignore consumption if he was to develop an overriding theory of capitalist production:

> Production is also immediately consumption .... The act of production is therefore in all its moments also an act of consumption .... The product only obtains its 'last finish' in consumption .... Production ... produces not only the object but also the manner of consumption, not only objectivity but also subjectivity. Production thus creates the consumer.[37]

Marx noted that there is no production without a need and that it is the act of consumption which reproduces the need. There are different scales of need though. Marx instances hunger. Eating cooked meat with a knife and fork is not the same manner of consumption as bolting down raw meat with hand, nail, and tooth. One could go further in identifying different 'manners' of consumption which this relation produces. Foodies in fashionable restaurants, young people in McDonalds, schoolchildren eating hot school dinners, these are all aspects of a developed consumerism, and their respective prominence as a mode of consumption indicates which direction the consumer culture is actually moving in. Individualized school packed-lunch boxes and single cartons of juice represent the triumph of a particular kind of consumer practice over a more collectivist mode of public provision. It is in the manner of our consuming, and in the nature of the distributive mechanism between the acts of production and consumption, that we see what is specifically modern about consumerism/consumption. And in scrutinizing these mechanisms we can identify vital shifts and ideological processes. Richard Johnson, on this theme, offers the example of the Mini-Metro, an object produced, marketed by 'market researchers, capital's own cultural accountants' and consumed by the practical consumer. But the Metro symbolized much more than merely individual consumer choice:

> The use of similar strategies for selling cars and weakening workers' collective power suggests considerable accumulations (of capital, power and meanings).... The Metro

became a little paradigm, though not the first, for a much more diffused ideological form – 'the nationalist sell'.[38]

Marx's notes on consumption certainly illuminate some aspects of the circulation of contemporary commodities. It is vital too to consider the ways in which goods come to be defined as either 'necessary' or 'luxury' goods, for differentially placed social groups and classes. Perhaps the biggest issue which could be developed out of his thinking and contemporary development of his thinking would be that of need: if the act of consumption reproduces a perceived need, then a highly constructed need (we all need to eat, but do we need to dine out flourishing our credit cards?) may well become internalized, perhaps even naturalized. The question of what need is in consumer capitalism can hardly be addressed without a sense of how relations of privilege and power are often exhibited in displays of status, and overlap with the pleasurable and the subjective.

In Jean Baudrillard's words the real effect of consumption has been to herald 'the passage from use value to sign value', in a new period which has taken us beyond a 'Faustian', 'Promethean' or even 'Oedipal' phase of production and consumption, 'to the narcissistic and protean era of connections, contact, contiguity, feedback and generalised interface that goes with the universe of communication'.[39]

Baudrillard's is a yuppie political economy, premised on a model of an affluent consuming public. He also leaves us with an image of the human consumer as appendage to the commodity-object, in technical rather than psychological relation to the commodity – in some kind of phase beyond exchange and use, in 'a *sacrificial logic* of consumption, gift, expenditure, potlatch',[40] somehow beyond the realms of any rationalized economy of exchanges. Baudrillard's view of consumer culture reduces the human subject to the victim, the uncritical recipient of signs and messages which seem to emanate from some supra-human realm. It remains a major characteristic of consumer culture that it constructs needs (presents at Christmas, the most recently topical toys); it does this by creating new types of perceived use-values, what Baudrillard, quoted above, might call the sign-value. It is undeniable that consumption is anchored in a dynamic of sign/image construction and their interpretation;

but it would be premature to abandon the category of need in pushing towards an analysis. For this would be to dismiss the consumer's expressed passion and lived subjectivity as virtually inhuman. And for every consumer there remains, potentially at least, a producer – a wage earner. For the vast majority wage-labour is the sole means of entering consumerdom.

Mike Featherstone has highlighted Baudrillard's depiction of consumer society as 'characterised by the dominance of the commodity-sign' as a central feature of such a society/culture. Certainly the Guess jeans advertising strategy discussed above assumes this. His second point is that a modernist core in consumer culture imagery collapses 'traditional reference points in pursuit of new juxtapositions which will reactivate memories and stimulate desires'.[41] Meanings and images overlap and intermesh in key new ways: if Nick Kamen's so famous, why not get him to sing? And get famous to a classic American song, Nick, confirming American dreams as the source of so many of our desires. Third, in Featherstone's definition, the everyday world offers the consumer the potential for expressive outlets; this produces a 'greater aestheticisation of reality'. We wear 501s or Guess jeans for style. If they don't retain their stylishness, we'll look elsewhere. We read ourselves, we apply ourselves to the reworking of commodities into *our* lifestyle.

Fewer and fewer people in contemporary capitalism work at making things. More and more people work to make impressions. As Mike Featherstone says:

> Consumer culture does not . . . encourage a grey conformism in the choice of goods . . . rather it seeks to educate individuals to read the differences in signs, to decode the minutiae of distinctions in dress, house, furnishing, leisure lifestyles and equipment.[42]

Mass production has created mass (but not homogeneous) consumption. The current problem for the productive process is how to meet the new demand for fragmentation. In all of this, any adequate political economy of capitalist culture must recognize the centrality of the aura of the commodity, and the process whereby this is both produced and consumed.

So far in this introduction I have pointed to discernible patterns of contemporary time-use and major shifts in modes of consuming; impassioned but sometimes flawed critiques of the consumer culture; and some contemporary critical frameworks for theorizing the consumption process. This book offers some sustained discussion of revealing cases and themes, without which all the fancy theoretical frameworks will themselves remain the most floating of signifiers. But it is worth looking at predominant contemporary models of the consumer act and process, and at currently prevalent market research interpretations of the lifestyling consumer. Richard Johnson has called market researchers capitalism's cultural accountants. That's a rather dry description of them. There's an element of the soothsayer to them too, in their combination of objective observation and futurology.

There are very few areas of human behaviour, at this stage in the development of western expert culture, without their own knowledge brokers. Professional pundits on marketing are in no short supply, offering up a range of models of buying behaviour. From Alfred Marshall comes the explanation of our consumer acts as essentially economic and rational behaviour. A stimulus-response model is imported from the experimental psychology of Pavlov, with the stress on drive, cue, response, reinforcement. Motivation theory derived from Freud's work on human drives and instinct provided a third framework, one which became the butt of Vance Packard's assault on the marketeers. Galbraith too was contesting this approach in his seminal critique of consumer society. The work of Thorstein Veblen, exploring the relationship between social standing/prestige and conspicuous consumption has offered marketing theorists a more sociological framework. Michael J. Baker discusses these approaches and then offers his own list of six key concepts which help explain how buyers choose; all this before outlining his own 'composite' model of buyer behaviour.[43] Here is Baker's model 'expressed notationally', and, to do him no injustice, in full detail:

$$P = f [SP, (PC, EC, (T_A - T_D), (E_A - E_D), BR)] \text{ where}$$

P = purchase

f = a function (unspecified) of

SP = selective perception

PC = precipitating circumstances

EC = enabling conditions

T_A = technological advantages
T_D = technological disadvantages
E_A = economic advantages
E_D = economic disadvantages
BR = behavioural response

The first point to be made is that this is a sequential process model: PC is equivalent to *awareness*, EC to *interest*, $(T_A - T_D)$ and $(E_A - E_D)$ represent evaluation, and BR dictates the action taken which, of course, is not always to purchase but may be to reject the proposition or to defer judgement. Neither of these is precluded by the model, which is concerned solely with positive purchase outcomes.

Secondly, the precise nature of the function is not specified, for the simple reason that it is not known and that it is unlikely, to say the least, that any single functional form could capture the interaction between the other variables in the model.

SP or selective perception is a new variable in the model. In earlier versions the influence of this factor was subsumed within BR, which occurs at the end of the process. By placing SP at the beginning as a factor mediating the other variables it is possible to communicate that this is a process model and that selective perception will determine whether or not one will even become aware of a purchase opportunity (EC) besides conditioning the information selected for evaluation and the interpretation placed on it.

Finally, the behavioural response may be almost automatic as, for example, when the preceding evaluation indicates that one option is clearly to be preferred. Alternatively, it may be an extremely difficult and protracted stage when the preceding analysis has failed to suggest the choice before all others – a common occurrence in many markets.[44]

What the 'notional' depiction of this model achieves (beyond being a useful mnemonic) is not at all clear, though the ruse of the formula is to sell speculation as science, as a kind of rationalized economics. Baker wants it all ways, to account for all possible outcomes that might arise in buyer behaviour, with some abstract and generalized model of the 'buyer'. But, at least – unlike, it seems, his earlier models – he now recognizes that there is a place for 'selective perception', though it is not at all clear whether this is a self-generated or imposed selectivity of perception in the consumer. For Baker has no sense of the centrality of the processes of signification in the marketing process, and in the dynamics of consumption generally. His model says nothing about the contribution that images might make to the sphere of the ideological. When he talks about packaging he offers up pictures of outstanding packaging – John Player Special cigarettes, Ritz crackers, Coke bottles, Mars bars, Kit-e-Kat.[45] Why are such examples outstanding? For Baker, because their 'simple designs and vivid colours attract the shoppers' attention'. This truism, this triumph of the trite, surely misses the essential point. Outstanding packaging purveys particularized meanings, connotes chosen values:

JPS King Size: black/gold, high-tec, Grand Prix connexions

Ritz crackers: a gem of polysemy here; crackers about this biscuit; ritzy; a luxurious snack

Coke: youthful fun and cosmopolitanism (sponsors of gymnastics, Olympic Games)

Mars: exotic (other planets) and durable (the god of war) – no wonder it can help you work, rest and play – now finds its perfect sponsorship deal with the London (People's) Marathon.

Kit-e-Kat: an onomatopoeically irresistible appeal to the domestic pet, bolstered by claims about scientifically informed caring.

It is not just the packaging or wrapping that has kept these products as market leaders. It is the millions of pounds and dollars that have been poured into the construction of the image around the commodity, so that current and projected markets see those objects as their own. It is the aura of the commodity that allows the consumer to buy passionately at times, to express subjective desire within the objectively cold impersonal relations of consumer capitalism.

American Express sends a magazine to its 'card members' – members, note, not holders – as if entry has been gained to some sort of exclusive club. Just look at the picture opposite from the September 1987 copy of *Expression*:

Figure 3 Front cover illustration, *Expression: The Magazine for American Express Cardmembers*, Sept. 1987

Look at the verbally stated themes: money, stress, power, success. Access is symbolized in the key – the key to what? Big luxurious cars, Concorde flights throughout the world – smart classless suits, ageless haircuts, and a quiet assured all-male confidence. And inside the pages of this slick mechanism for reinforcing consumer status the signifiers of consumer power are there: features on squash, new Ferrari models and, wait for it, Rumbelows, where the old HP grab-now-pay-later usury comes under the neat little euphemism 'Options 3'. Managing Director Ian Gray arrived in 1985 and launched Rumbelows from just another seedy-looking high-street rental business into a high-profile retailer moving increasingly into out-of-town sites. And of course, what better evidence of these aspirations than the 'decision to take the card'. As Gray says, trampling the remnants of Rumbelow's cosier smaller-scale image into the high-street dust:

> Quite frankly, we would not have expected American Express cardholders to want to shop at the old Rumbelows, but now we think that's changed . . . We really believe that our range of products, with top names like Hitachi, Sony and Grundig, coupled with our stylish and attractive store design, give us a lot of appeal for the more upmarket consumer.[46]

With increased choice, and the sense too of consumer awareness generated by the Ralph Naders of the world and the *Which* guides to consumer decision-making, the marketeer has begun to move more and more seducingly, flattering the punter, coaxing in the consumer. The act of purchase or consumption then becomes an invitation rite – *yes*, you choose X rather than Y. And of course that's because you're quite as discerning and in-the-know as those other discriminating consumers whom you're now joining.

In the construction of lifestyle on the basis of consumerism, the Henley Centre now talks of a contemporary 'savvy' culture, in which the 'connoisseur consumer' is nobody's fool. The individual now seeks new 'position possibilities' by using particular knowledge, skills and possibilities:

> We believe such positions are increasingly preferred to the other position statement possibilities because 'savvy curren-cies' lack a common 'numeraire' by which everyone can be

reduced to a single and common base (hence, savvy positions are 'immeasurably' better than others).[47]

In this Newspeak of leisure futurology, the message is: the market is heterogeneous; there is no lowest common denominator of consumption. Everyone is potentially different; everyone's special.

The 'connoisseur consumer', then, doesn't so much as keep up with the Joneses as keep away from them. 'Savvy society', Tyrrell goes on, produces connoisseurs at all levels. A bottle of Frascati can be bought for £2.50 from ASDA and served up boastfully with the correct food. Savvy is the employment and display of informed choice. It now informs choices about lifestyle. You would not need to be style-slick to show savvy:

> Lifestyle is all about knowing the style-code, and the fewer the people that know, the slicker the lifestyle . . . the lifestyle pyramid: the more you know the style, the fewer are the people that can de-code your own lifestyle, and the higher your place in the pyramid. This is the cornerstone of modern marketing.[48]

Elite or exclusive style may be inaccessible to many, forever just out of reach, but savvy can be displayed anywhere on the pyramid during this 'late 20th century . . . era of self-gratification and self-fulfilment'.[49] For thinkers at the Henley Centre the emergence of lifestyle is more than mere media hype: it represents a profound rupture from traditional and long-established bonds and affiliations, on the level of both consciousness and action:

> We believe that increasing free time, the growth in discretionary spending power (for the 'haves'), more sophisticated technology, more sophisticated people and an apposite response from people like Terence Conran, Rodney Fitch, Peter York et al. have all conspired to emancipate increasing numbers of people from a life dominated by the imperatives of the production system (i.e. their jobs, class, subsistence income) to one dominated by the possibilities of consumption.[50]

Consumption and the construction and display of self add up to a new freedom here. Tyrrell lists four implications of this emancipatory scenario. First, people become motivated by

27

lifestyle, there is less correlation between class and status. Second, consumer sovereignty shatters establishment deference and any respect for traditional authority or labels. Third, the connoisseur consumer takes his/her interests seriously, exercising an informed and genuine discrimination. Fourth, people relate less to technical/production criteria, more and more to criteria relating to their style of life. Tyrrell earmarks here what I have called the aura of the commodity throughout this introduction:

> we no longer want to shop in 'hardware and electrical shops', but in the 'Cookshop'. We find the 'Body Shop' strikes more of a chord than 'Chemist'. We don't want to eat 'meat', 'dairy produce', 'fresh vegetables', etc., but we do relate to 'food on the move', 'Snacking', 'Convenience', 'The Deli Counter' etc.[51]

This has been a major development. Looking for a wallbank (or cashline) south of the Humber bridge recently, I had to go to a little town which could have been anywhere. It was as if shops and businesses were no longer run by human beings. Get your bread at 'Crusts'; nip in for a haircut at 'Blow' or 'Snippers'; have a snack at 'Nosh'. This is beyond doubt: spending has become intensively thematized. This whole analysis of the style/status relation, of the shift from function to lifestyle, of the precedence for self-identity of consumption over production, leads the Henley Centre to chart out 'strategic maps and locations' of and in consumer culture.[52] The hierarchy of consumer needs is becoming less rigid, less closed in their view, so that a move is identifiable towards more fragmentation.

Henley Centre communicators see and predict expanding opportunities for this connoisseur consumer. The squeeze for space at the top of the pyramid is giving way to a new openness of possibilities in the widening out of the onion shape. Most significantly, in this model, the merely functional is reduced, and the scope for lifestyle choices and needs considerably expanded.

Growth areas of consumerism include video watching and home dining, a move from the collective to the individual or more individualized mode of consuming, with instant experience on hand. Projecting trends, the Centre predicts a permis-

FROM HIERARCHY TO FRAGMENTATION

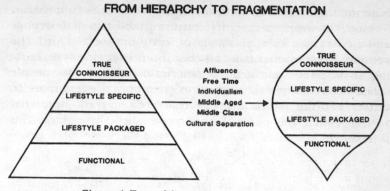

Figure 4 From hierarchy to fragmentation
(*Source*: see note 52)

sive economy, prompting still further discretion; a reinforcement of trends to have and have more; a culture nearly
over the edge, but always giving a new edge; a stress on 'what
things mean', as much as on cost or size. In 1960 we had the
baker and the grocer, the tailor and the sports shop, the
nutritious food or cosmetics shop. By 1980 these functional
offerings had given way to 'functionally atomized lifestyle
offering' – Sainsbury, Next, Boots. By 2000, the Henley Centre
predicts, we could be making our choices in 'personal appearance shops'. Marketing research, in the form of the sophisticated modelling of Henley Centre, locates the individual in
these position maps; an 'optimal brand portfolio' will locate the
individual (or the targeted segment of the market) along the
lines of a 'functional cutting edge' or a 'lifestyle leading edge'.

These astrologers of consumer culture prioritize individualism over collectivism, status over class, consumption over
production. The Henley Centre begins to recognize the skill of
the consumer, the selectively interpretative readings that the
consumer can make of what is on offer. Neither Michael Baker
nor Bob Tyrrell, of course, develop a critical dimension to their
modelling, or any sense of the role of ideology in contemporary
consumption. Theirs is a 'science', a practical applied science of
the market. As with many such sciences, it is of course inherently
ideological.

Why should all this matter? It matters because our response to the aura of the commodity can position us in very important ways. It is incontestable that meaning and consciousness are vitally linked to the relations of consumption, and that we respond to images in many aspects of our everyday lives. In this sense the politics of consumption are central to the dynamics of social and cultural change in contemporary capitalism. Six themes at least illustrate this, and are of recurrent importance throughout this book.

First, in Margaret Thatcher's Britain there are many people disenfranchised from the consumer culture. The expressive dimensions to consumer leisure remain for them a pipedream, yet one seemingly just around the corner; the market appears as, in Stuart Hall's term, an 'expansive popular system however excluded from it you might be'.[53]

Second, the selling of personality is interwoven with debates on values. Politics in Britain has become dominated by images – the Iron Lady, the shabby Foot, the eloquent Kinnock, the dashing (though dethroned) Doctor (Owen). Robert Elms argues that 'until we throw off the shabby yoke of middle-class guilt and the rigid conservatism of old-style socialism, we will not win the style wars. And that is one battle that we cannot dodge.'[54] And it is not enough, he notes, for Neil Kinnock to make 'a fool of himself' in a Tracey Ullmann video. The central problem here is that if Elms is right, is the battle then waged primarily in terms of form rather than content?

Third, with the structure of global capitalism as it is, the left needs to recognize the pervasiveness of the market. Peter Kellner has argued that markets in themselves need not be anti-socialist. They could be sources of real information, whereby genuine consumer preferences are then expressed. They could 'actively facilitate the exercise of consumer choice' and reconcile 'freedom of individual action in the marketplace with State power'.[55]

Fourth, as implied already, form and content become blurred, but often at the expense of content. A-Ha can make a million by capturing the teenybopper market, without ever having performed in front of a live audience. This is the victory of the model pioneered by The Monkees in the slipstream of The Beatles in the 1960s. If you stay in vogue, reminding audiences of your contemporaneity, you might stay successful. As Jon Savage says of Freddie Mercury and Queen, the 'precise mastery of form and studio' of their recordings cannot come through in stadium performances, where 'Queen have nothing to communicate except their success: sadly, this makes them quite contemporary.' Or, in Paul Gambaccini's words: 'The Reagan-Thatcher period has been a consumer, rather than a creative, period.'[56]

Fifth, the individualized modes of consumption redraw the map of acceptable boundaries of public/private. This is where an historical dimension is vital, to see where large publics are now acceptable – in orchestrated media events like Live Aid and Sport Aid, but not in the more spontaneously useable spaces of our everyday environments. Consumer culture is not a vibrant or at all spontaneous street culture: it is a culture of the spectacle.

Sixth, the more the market addresses different groups as exclusive groups, the more the Henley Centre models, for instance, might come to be predictive not just descriptive. Youth as community, for instance, becomes replaced by youth as a category constructed by the market. There is a rhetoric of freedom at the heart of the approaches of marketeers, an emphasis upon the choices that are open to the consumer. But whatever the seduction of the commodity, the attraction of its aura, consumption remains a social and economic construction. Terence Conran, a key figure in Britain's contemporary consumer culture, is not just an image maker. He runs a highly organized business in which any surprises or doubts at the point of distribution have been more and more successfully integrated into a newly flexible production-end. Many of our individually consumed purchases and pleasures are production led. Technology, design and marketing have become highly organized elements in a production managed for reliability and continuity as much as for fashion, style and the novel.

The 'we's' so beloved of the Henley Centre, snatching at style and status on credit, would do well to remember this. Any network of Marks and Spencer or Benetton is more than a freely chosen lucky dip for the affluent punter – it is a slick capitalist operation with a successful overall production strategy. This is clearer than ever in the transformation of some of our most traditional and innocent and often casual pastimes and pleasures. It is not any inherent character or attraction of an activity that guarantees its buoyancy in everyday life. Rather, it is the marketing strategies of market-men and media-programmers that determines much of our consumption. Look, for instance, in the early days of the Star Wars battles for control of the media, at the move against televised presentation of popular working-class sports by the controllers of the United Kingdom commercial television networks.

In May 1988 Channel 4 television in the United Kingdom announced its decision to omit snooker from its 1988–9 schedules. Although the Channel's fifty-one and a quarter annual hours of afternoon coverage of the green-baize duels regularly attracted 4 million viewers, Chief Executive Michael Grade was unambiguous on the thinking behind the decision: 'Snooker helps boost our viewing figures but it damages the image of the channel . . . . We will replace it with programmes for people who hate snooker',[57] he told the snooker player and journalist Clive Everton. Any potential bid by the ITV networks to go for the top snooker contracts was now, with Channel 4 no longer offering any scheduling slots in partnership, on the rocks.

A couple of months earlier Channel 4 had broadcast a series of discussion programmes on sport, one of which explored the sport-media relation (*Running Late*, 9/10 March 1988). Adrian Metcalfe, the Channel's own commissioning editor for sport, was sitting next to Barry Hearn, the snooker (and embryonic boxing) impresario, manager of many top snooker stars, including Steve Davis, MBE to be. When the programme showed the number of hours devoted to sports on television, the cash-till eyes of Barry Hearn twinkled still more. Introduced in the programme as the 'undisputed Mr Big of snooker', Hearn presented his usual line on the game as '*Dallas* with Balls', and admitted that 'we've got to break a leg not to make money . . . it's laughingly easy'. But he also conceded that fresh formats, novel events, were needed to make the sport look less predictable in its televisual forms; and that 400 hours of televised snooker in standardized form is 'more than enough'.

Figures for 1986 revealed that snooker headed the top ten of television sports, in hours of coverage per year (see Table 1.3).

These figures made quite an impression upon – but did not impress – Adrian Metcalfe: 'Nobody in this country wants to watch 400 hours of snooker . . . . Britain is dead in terms of more

Table 1.3 Top 10 TV Sports in hours of coverage, 1986

Top 10 TV Sports	Hours
1 Snooker	394
2 Cricket	336
3 Horse racing	276
4 Soccer	262
5 Tennis	189
6 Golf	149
7 Athletics	131
8 Bowls	112
9 Boxing	58
10 Equestrianism	56

Source: *Running Late*, Channel 4, 9/10 March 1988.

snooker on television.' Broadcast late at night, snooker was in Metcalfe's view a sedative not a stimulant: 'You just sort of nod off and these big objects move .... That's what it is. It's Mogadon.' Within a couple of months, and hot on the heels of Cliff Thorburn's suspension and fine for producing traces of cocaine in a drug test back in February, the sport was axed from the United Kingdom's ritziest channel. Metcalfe hadn't been joking.

More recent figures, for 1987, show that snooker fell behind cricket in that year. The saturation point seems to have been reached in 1986, the year following the remarkable World Championship Final of 1985 in which the Steve Davis versus Dennis Taylor match was watched by record-breaking audiences.

But, two years on, something beyond audience vicissitudes is behind some of the shifts in scheduling policy. Much of the regular snooker audience (daytime and late-night) is made up of over 55s and over 65s with only 4 per cent of 16–24-year-olds tuning in regularly. The consumer youth market did not feature prominently among this particular audience. Audience research shows too that upmarket AB classes who did tune in to snooker on television tended to watch the public broadcasting channels, so perpetuating a snobbish avoidance of commercials and advertising.[58]

In the early summer of 1988 Independent Television (ITV) announced its decision to drop coverage of darts, bowls, and gymnastics, arguing that 'these sports are too downmarket, appeal only to older people and have little attraction for the advertisers'.[59] Having already cut wrestling out of its schedules, ITV here amplified its developing policy of transmission of copy-easy, upmarket, advertiser-easy sports. Traditional and/or working-class sports less easy to programme, however gripping in their soap-operatic focus on states and emotions, are clearly less and less attractive to the commercial channels. It is in the public broadcasting sector that the large audiences generated by many of these sports will continue to be catered for.

Snooker's success is linked with a process of gentrification, common to the world of entertainment and crime as well as that of sport – in all these worlds we see the working-class lad turned into the showbiz gent. As well as producing super-rich individuals, the snooker boom has attracted millions of participants at the grass-roots level, and this in turn has affected the reshaping of many pub lounges and bars throughout the country. In 1965 there were only 161 clubs affiliated to the Billiard and Snooker Control Council; by 1980, 3,860.[60] By 1983 snooker/billiards had become the most frequently played sporting activity amongst adult males, the sixth most popular among women.[61]

As Gordon Burn's writings on snooker throughout the 1970s and 1980s have shown so superbly,[62] once he entered the world of boom-time snooker – indeed some would say actually created this world – Barry Hearn has never been far from the action in a world of increasingly rich pickings. Hearn's Svengali grip on Davis has provided a model for new partnerships such as that between the young Scot Stephen Hendry and his manager Ian Doyle.

Hearn's success and prominence are a celebration, Burn rightly argues, of the values at the core of Thatcherism. He has been able to succeed in different spheres – accountancy, then fashion, before moving into property speculation and gaming machines, then on to sports management and snooker as showbiz. His string of successes embodies the kind of popular capitalist enterprise beloved of Margaret Thatcher, the kind on which she believes the renaissance of Britain depends.

Barry Hearn-Land is a Thatcher dreamland: no nationalized industry, the dominance of the market, lower taxes, minimized government intervention, and a downgraded welfare net for those who are disenfranchised in dreamland. As Gordon Burn so rightly says, Hearn's type of society celebrates the restoration of self-help Victorian values, in its modern-day form – a society along the free-market, free-enterprise lines of Hong Kong.

The relation between our everyday pleasures and the politics of the age is a binding concern over and above the six themes which inform this volume. And this will inevitably lead us to the question of ideology. What is the status of our feeling of freedom, of our selected subjectivity, if it is so heavily constructed for us? This collection looks at general trends and particular case-studies. We have tried to develop informing case-studies, so that the eloquent conceptualizations of general theorists might have more to go on. All of us become at some point, and for however little time, what we buy. The key question surely is this: how far are we able to recognize the aura that we buy our way into, and so retain the sense that this is not the only way, the natural state of things? And for how long will such a constructed consumer choice be acceptable as the major determinant of personal freedom?

NOTES

1 The Henley Centre for Forecasting, *Leisure Futures: Forecasts of People's Use of Free Time and their Leisure Spending*, Spring 1987, p. 00.
2 ibid., p. 17.
3 J. K. Galbraith, *The Affluent Society* (1958), Harmondsworth: Penguin, 1962, p. 207.
4 The most prominent of these is probably *The Hidden Persuaders*, first published in 1957, reprinted with a new introduction and epilogue nearly a quarter of a century after its initial appearance. Packard sees the same processes at work, with refined techniques applied to the 'skills of luring' in a business that is now 'a forty-odd billion dollar industry'. Vance Packard, *The Hidden Persuaders*, Harmondsworth: Penguin, 1981, pp. 9, 10.
5 Stuart Ewen, *Captains of Consciousness: Advertising and the Social Roots of the Consumer Culture*, New York: McGraw Hill, 1976.
6 Galbraith, *The Affluent Society*, p. 14.
7 R. H. Tawney, *Religion and the Rise of Capitalism: A Historical Study* (1926), Harmondsworth: Penguin, 1938.
8 Sears, Roebuck, and Co., Inc., *Consumers' Guide* (Fall 1900), Northfield, Illinois: DBI Books, 1970.
9 ibid., p. 541.
10 Peter Marsh and Peter Collett, *Driving Passion – The Psychology of the Car*, London: Jonathan Cape, 1986, p. 11.

11 ibid., pp. 132–3. See also Martin Pawley, *The Private Future – Causes and Consequences of Community Collapse in the West*, London: Pan, 1974, pp. 50–6, where the car is discussed as an example of the 'pathology of privacy'.

12 Stephen Bayley, *Sex, Drink and Fast Cars: The Creation and Consumption of Images*, London: Faber & Faber, 1986, p. 101.

13 ibid., p. 103.

14 ibid., p. 88.

15 Judith Williamson, *Consuming Passions: The Dynamics of Popular Culture*, London: Marion Boyars, 1986, p. 13.

16 See Deyan Sudjic, in *Cult Objects*, London: Paladin Granada, 1985, ch.6, 'Putting pack art onto the shelves' for some interesting examples of the art of successful packaging.

17 I offer no excursions into semiotic discourse here, just a key reference. See Roland Barthes, 'Myth Today', in *Mythologies* (1957), London: Paladin, 1973, pp. 109–59.

18 The details of the Levi's 501 advertisements are from Hugh Sebag-Montefiore, 'The bottom line', *Sunday Times Magazine*, 1 February 1987, pp. 60–5.

19 Matthew Gwyther, 'Mandy keeps us guessing', *Observer Magazine*, 26 July 1987, pp. 26–9. The following quotes from Marciano are from this piece.

20 Peter York, 'Crash of a sex symbol', *The Observer*, 23 November 1986, p. 57.

21 J. B Priestley, *English Journey – being a rambling but truthful account of what one man saw and heard and felt and thought during a journey through England during the Autumn of the year 1933* (1934), London: Heinemann, 1968.

22 ibid., pp. 401 and 402.

23 ibid., p. 402.

24 ibid., p. 403.

25 Richard Hoggart, *The Uses of Literacy* (1954), Harmondsworth: Penguin, 1958, p. 287.

26 ibid., p. 204.

27 Jeremy Seabrook, *The Everlasting Feast*, London: Allen Lane, 1974, p. 237.

28 ibid., p. 8.

29 Jeremy Seabrook, *Unemployment*, London: Granada/Paladin, 1983, pp. 8–11.

30 Huw Beynon, 'Jeremy Seabrook and the British working class', in Martin Eve and David Musson (eds), *The Socialist Register 1982*, London: Merlin Press, 1982, pp. 285–301.

31 Jeff Nuttall, *King Twist: A Portrait of Frank Randle*, London: Routledge & Kegan Paul, 1978, p. 2.

32 Jonathan Raban, *Coasting*, London: Collins Harvill, 1986, p. 297.

33 ibid., p. 168.

34 ibid., pp. 71–2.

35 ibid., pp. 209 and 211.

36 On the universal market, see Harry Braverman, *Labour and Monopoly Capital*, New York: Monthly Review Press, 1974. On post-modernism see Fredric Jameson, 'Postmodernism and consumer society', in Hal Foster (ed.), *Postmodern Culture*, London: Pluto Press, 1985, pp. 111–25; and 'Postmodernism or the cultural logic of late capitalism', *New Left Review*, 146, 1984. On consumer culture see *Theory, Culture and Society – Explorations in Critical Social Science* 1 (3): 1983 (special issue on consumer culture).

37 Karl Marx, *Grundrisse: Foundations of the Critique of Political Economy* Harmondsworth: Penguin, 1973, pp. 90, 91, 92.

38 Richard Johnson, 'The story so far: and further transformations', in David Punter (ed.), *Introduction to Contemporary Cultural Studies*, London: Longman, 1986, p. 285.

39 Jean Baudrillard, 'The ecstasy of communication', in Foster (ed.), *Postmodern Culture*, pp. 127, 133.

40 ibid., p. 126.

41 Mike Featherstone, 'Consumer culture, symbolic power and universalism', Paper read at the Conference 'Mass Culture, Life Worlds, Popular Cultures in the Middle East', Universitat Bielefeld, 7–9 February 1985, p. 4.

42 ibid., p. 9.

43 Michael J. Baker, 'Buyer behaviour', in *Marketing Strategy and Management*, London: Macmillan, 1985, Ch. 5.

44 ibid., pp. 130–1.

45 ibid., p. 272.

46 Quoted in Gaythorne Silvester, 'A little revolution', *Expression, the Magazine for American Express Cardmembers*, September 1087, p. 32.

47 Bob Tyrrell, 'Changing motives: what will animate people as we move into the 21st century?', discussion paper, Henley Centre for Forecasting, undated.

48 Toby Young, 'The fall of the house of style', *New Society*, vol. 73, no. 1179, 2 August 1985.

49 Bob Tyrrell, 'The way people will spend their time: some key influences', in Henley Centre for Forecasting, *Leisure Futures*, Winter, 1985, p. 19.

50 ibid., p. 22.

51 ibid., p. 22.

52 Examples of these 'strategic maps and locations' are taken from Henley Centre for Forecasting, *The Business of New Lifestyles: Chart and Forecast Material*, booklet prepared for Day Conference at the Cavendish Conference Centre, 20 February 1986.

53 See Alan Tomlinson, 'Playing away from home: leisure, disadvantage and issues of income and access', in Peter Golding (ed.), *Excluding the Poor*, London: Child Poverty Action Group 1986, pp. 43–54; and Stuart Hall, 'The culture gap', *Marxism Today*, January 1984, pp. 18–22.

54 Robert Elms, 'Style wars', *New Socialist*, no. 38, May 1986, p. 14.
55 Peter Kellner, 'Can markets be socialist?', *New Statesman*, 2 November 1984, pp. 7 and 8.
56 Jon Savage, 'Style bandit', *The Observer*, 20 July 1986, p. 22. Gambaccini was quoted in James Erlichman, 'The day the music died', *The Guardian*, 24 November 1987, p. 29.
57 Cited in Clive Everton, 'The game is bad for our image, says Grade as Channel 4 put their cues away', *The Guardian*, 17 May 1988, p. 17.
58 Peter Fiddick, 'Whose eye on the ball?', *The Guardian*, 18 September 1987.
59 See Shyama Perera, ' "Downmarket" sports fear loss of cash lifeline as ITV axes minority coverage', *The Guardian*, 2 June 1988, p. 3.
60 Sports Council, *A Digest of Sports Statistics 1st Edition*, Sports Council Information Series no. 7, London 1983, p. 10.
61 Central Statistical Office, *General Household Survey 1983*, London: Her Majesty's Stationery Office, 1985, Table 10.9., p. 201.
62 Gordon Burn's work has appeared in the *Sunday Times Magazine*, other national newspapers' colour supplements and magazines, reviews, *The Radio Times*, *The Face*, and many in-house publications on the world of snooker. His writing constitutes an illuminating evocation of the atmosphere of boom-time snooker, presenting its main characters, and exploring its central tensions. His book *Pocket Money: Bad Boys, Business-heads and Boom-time Snooker*, London: Heinemann, 1986, describes and dissects the phenomenal transformation of snooker from disreputable working-class street-culture to lucrative marketing outlet for the leisure and consumer industries.

Part one

Trends in consumption and leisure

2

Marketing dreams
The political elements of style

STUART EWEN

'Style, hard to define. . .but easy to recognize.'
(Magazine advertisement for Hathaway blouse, 1983)

'We are surrounded by emptiness but it is an emptiness filled with signs.'
(Henri Lefebvre, *Everyday Life in the Modern World*, 1971)

'The given facts that appear . . . as the positive index of truth are in fact the negation of truth . . . . (T)ruth can only be established by their destruction.'
(Herbert Marcuse, *Reason and Revolution*, 1941)

Each week on USA network television in 1984, a taut-faced woman named Elsa Klensch hosts a programme titled 'Style'. While the prime focus is on the new designer collections, and transports us to major fashion shows around the world, there is more. Some features centre on the homes of the people in the world of fashion design: castles in the countryside near Rome; converted farmhouses in rural Connecticut; fabulous playpens overlooking Paris. Still other items deal with the daily lives of people employed in the world (one dare not call it *industry*!) of fashion. We follow a tawny Milanese mannequin through her regular two-hour body and facial treatment at Sergio Valente. We observe a busy New York model, roller-skating and taking tap-dance lessons; sharing her intimate longing to 'make it' in the musical theatre. Accompanying commercials blend right in, telling us of the slimming value of Tab cola, or of the way that Henry Grethel clothing will lead us into accidental and

41

anonymous romantic encounters with beautiful women – or men – in elegant hotel rooms.

We see that style is about beautiful, mouth-watering surfaces; but we see more. Beyond displaying surfaces, the uninterrupted message of the television programme is that style makes up a way of life, a utopian way of life. The people we view apparently inhabit a universe of infinite bounty. They wear dresses costing thousands. They live in castles. Their encounters with interior designers lead to unrestrained flights of fancy. Their desires, their fantasies, are painlessly translated into objective forms. There are no conflicts. There is no mention of cost. There is no anxiety about affordability.

If this way of life is marked by a succession of material objects, it is a life which curiously seems to float beyond the terms of the real world at the same time. This is essential to the magic of style, its fascination and enchantment. Part of the promise of style is to lift us out of the dreariness of necessity.

At the other end of the tunnel of television, however, sits the viewer: cheaper clothes; no castles, bills piling up; no stranger to the anxieties of desire placed within the constraints of possibility. The viewer sits, watches, embedded in the finite terms of daily life. From this vantage point, the viewer is engaged in a relationship with style. It is a relationship which offers a pledge, a pledge repeated across the panorama of American consumer culture again and again. Everyday life in its details (clothing, house, routine objects, and activities) can, through the sorcery of style, be transformed. Without ever saying so explicitly, the media of style offer to lift the viewer out of his/her life and place him/her in a utopian netherworld where there are no conflicts, no needs unmet; where the ordinary is – by its very nature – extraordinary.

So we see something else. If style constitutes a presentation of a way of life, it is a way of life which is unattainable for most, nearly all, people. Yet this doesn't mean that style isn't relevant to most people. It is very relevant. It is the most common realm of our society in which the need for a better way of life is acknowledged on a material level, if not met. It constitutes a politics of change, albeit a 'change' that resides on the surfaces of things. If the 'life-style' of style is not realizable, it is, at the same time, the most constantly available lexicon from which many of us draw the visual grammar of our lives. It is a behavioural model that is closely interwoven with modern patterns of survival and desire. It is a 'hard to define . . . but easy to recognize' piece within our current history.

Precisely because style deals in surface impressions, it is difficult to concretize, to discern its definitions. It forms a chimerical, yet highly visible corridor between the world of things and human consciousness. Yet investing profane things with sacred meanings is an ancient activity, a universal preoccupation. This, in and of itself, does not define style; nor does it situate style within the particular conditions and contradictions of contemporary life. It is within these conditions and contradictions that we proceed toward an understanding of the role and power of style within our lives.

Within our modern consumer society there are three general arenas in which style plays a conspicuous role. First, style has become a critical factor in definitions of the self. As one enters, or falls into encounters with other people – intimates and strangers alike – style is a way of stating who one is: politically, sexually, in terms of status and class. Style is a device of conformity, or of opposition. Style conveys mood. Style is a device by which we judge – and are judged by – others. It is worn on the surfaces of our bodies; it organizes the space in which we live; it permeates the objects of our daily lives; it is often mistaken for subjectivity. To 'have a lot of style' is an accolade of remarkable personhood.

Second, style has a major impact on the way we understand society. Social institutions are continually mediated by the mirages of style. In the process, substance becomes unrecognizable. Large corporations, employing the lives and energies of thousands, and often exerting power on a global scale, invest millions to cultivate a palatable corporate image and style. Politicians, up to the president, rely on style to build and maintain 'democratic' constituencies. Style overlays the world of goods. Style places an aura around the world as it is, and offers an influential rendition of what many see as 'social change', as history.

Last, and firmly rooted in the previous two areas, style has come to comprise a basic form of information within our society. Style is a powerful element of consciousness about the world we inhabit. Insofar as this information is ephemeral and emerges from a lucrative trade in surfaces, it fosters a state of ongoing confusion. At the heart of this confusion between evanescence and substance, lies the way we comprehend reality itself.

These three arenas of style – self, society and information – have developed dramatically within twentieth-century American life. They are underpinned and continuously shaped by vast industries whose basic product is style. Together they compose the political contours of the contemporary moment. The rise of style, however, can not be comprehended in its own terms. While it is common to present history as an endless parade of changing styles, a catalogue of surfaces only conspires in a process of mystification.

To understand the growing presence and importance of style within our society, it is necessary to do something that style implicitly abhors: we must penetrate the surface of the image and place it within the social and historical setting of its development. If style speaks to the general definitions of society, self, and information, then we must assume that modern modes of existence have altered people's experiences in these inter-related realms in substantial ways.

In the rest of this chapter, I would like to briefly suggest some of the ways that style may be seen in the light of these transformations.

STYLE AND SELF

The development of consumer capitalism in America was fuelled by more than entrepreneurial genius; from the mid nineteenth century on it was fired, also, by a series of massive migrations providing a cheap work force. For people coming from rural agrarian or small town artisanal roots, the move to urban industrialism posed a shock of world historic dimensions. People were uprooted from familiar patterns of work, family and community, and from customary ways of understanding the world. Often coming from places where the number of people encountered was small and familiar, they now entered a terrain in which 'others' included countless strangers. Social life itself had been transformed from something known and set by custom, into something that was increasingly anonymous; where custom was inadequate to provide measures and lessons of survival.

Within the shadow of this relocation, two important developments posed a crisis of *self*. First, life became an experience of repeated encounters with the unknown. As Raymond Williams has argued, people began to learn not only that 'others' were strangers, but that they, themselves, were often seen as 'strangers'.[1] The very terms of the experience required, as part of the rules of survival and exchange, a sense of *self as alien*. Entering into a job market no longer meant participation in a venerable circle of craft. Work was increasingly unskilled, and as one applied or interviewed for a job, one knew how important it was to make a good 'presentation'. This new world required a sense of self that was malleable and sensitive to the power of the surface. Addressing the historical transformation of identity, Warren Susman has described this as a shift from the importance of 'character' (intrinsic self) to the importance of 'personality' (a mouldable, extrinsic self).[2]

Similarly, patterns of courtship were affected. Rooted in a past of patriarchal authority and arrangements between families, now relations of love, sexuality, and matrimony were drawn from the world of strangers. This required new tools of negotiation. Life, and the sense of self within it, were becoming – more and more – market activities. Here we see a second change in the definition of self. As people became what Raymond Williams calls 'mobile individuals' they experienced a break from old patterns of hierarchy and authority, rooted for many in feudalism. This was both disorienting and promising, posing the possibility of greater autonomy, of democracy. The industrial society that emerged was filled with contradictions. If many aspects of it were cold, monotonous and grim, by the late nineteenth century, American capitalism was revealing a peculiar and seductive genius as well. If the machine supplied a modern context for misery and exploitation, it also contained an ability to reproduce – on a mass scale – images and symbols of luxury and abundance, of privilege and franchise. Things once limited to the province of an upper class now became reproducible, if only as surface images. These images were often appended to inferior goods, but their 'look' was drawn from the repositories of 'style', of upper-class life. Initially in the garment industry, and by the early twentieth century in many areas of the consumer market, people who had previously been denied access to images of sumptuousity now held them in reach, for a price. Style had been transformed from a prerogative of the few, to an amusement of the millions.

Within a milieu of strangers the necessity and appeal of style were dramatic. If one was repeatedly made aware of *self as other*, of one's commodity status, style became a powerful medium of encounter. Immigrant and migrant workers learned, as a basic lesson of Americanization, to be 'presentable'. The emerging marketplace of consumer goods provided instruments for the construction of a self, to be seen, to be judged, to penetrate the wall of anonymity. In worlds of work and love, status and aspiration, the assembly of 'self' was becoming compulsory for ventures in society. The appeal of 'style' was not a matter of aesthetics alone; it was also a functional acquisition of metropolitan life. The legendary tie-in between style and the city is not without reason. Style provided an extension of personality on a physical plane (body, home, etc.), an attractive otherness, a 'phantom objectivity' (to borrow a phrase from Georg Lukacs) to be weighed in the eye's mind.

Also, as these first mass-produced styles mimicked the accoutrements of wealth, they transformed anonymity into an odd kind of advantage. One appeal of style was its ability to create an illusory transcendence of class. While hierarchy and inequities of wealth and power were – in many ways – increasing, the free market in style offered a symbolic ability to be one's own namer; to become a 'lady' or a 'gentleman', a 'Sir' or a 'Madam'. While mass produced and often shoddy in manufacture, style seemed to subvert an ancient monopoly over the image that had predominated in the cultures out of which many of these 'greenhorns' were drawn. If style was essentially a matter of surface and mystification, it was a surface that offered a democratic charm.

For these new recipients of style, and for us, their progeny, style has become part of the common vernacular of self-expression and perception. Alongside this development, there has arisen a vast array of cultural guides (books, magazines, films and the star system, television programmes, advertising) which serve as 'useful', everchanging charts of navigation.

One last point on *style and self*. As style entered the popular imagination, it was not merely reflected in people's lives. It entered their language. It was used and altered by people. Its meanings, its uses became increasingly volatile. Drawing from the spectacle of American culture in the twentieth century we find a myriad of examples: the flapper look, the zoot suit, the crash pad, the geodesic dome, dungarees, dashikis, 'sex, drugs, and rock 'n' roll'. Even for those who would challenge the substantial issues of life in a consumer culture, style has become an essential, inescapable instrument of cultural and political discourse. The ability for renegade styles to be reabsorbed into the consumer market may also make it an instrument of cultural and political containment.[3]

STYLE AND SOCIETY

Within contemporary consumer cultures there are a number of ways in which style presents people with ways of seeing and comprehending society. The proliferation of style across the landscape of American life, for example, is often cited as tangible evidence of democracy; choice and variety in images is sometimes equated with choice and variety in ideas. The ultimate 'qualification' for political leadership, as well, has increasingly come to reside in the vaporous area of style. The social relations of power and the process of historical change are also refracted through the prism of style.

The relationship between style and social power is not a creation of twentieth-century consumer culture in particular. This alliance has a long history. Before the rise of a mass market in style, style was already a visible embodiment of power relations.

Within the contexts of European feudalism, for example, style and consumption among the nobility marked their special status within society. Their clothing set them off, palpably, from the common lot of humanity and demonstrated their power over others. Sumptuousness and elaborate cutting and layering of cloth revealed the expanse of material that went into constructing their apparel. In certain cases the clothing of the nobility used over 1,000 yards of cloth in a single garment, many times the amount of material necessary to dress an extended family of commoners. In a world where material scarcity and hard work were the common definition of life, such excessive images connoted a power over others: the employment of enormous forces of detailed labour for the purposes of body decoration; the enjoyment of waste and leisure in a context where most lives were spent in arduous squalor.[4]

The association between image and power did not end with feudalism, it only shifted some of its attentions. In the late eighteenth and early nineteenth centuries an imagery, a style, emerged that spoke to the new power relations of an incipient industrial capitalism in Europe. The orderly symmetry and stark efficiency that we, in the twentieth century, associate with modern architecture and industrial design, finds a precursor in certain new structures of that era. Michel Foucault has discussed the rise of 'panoptic institutions' and 'panopticism' in architecture during the period.[5] Literally meaning 'all seeing', panopticism served as a style model for a broad range of modern institutions: prisons, schools, offices, and factories. The term, deriving from Jeremy Bentham's innovation in prison design (Panopticon), describes an architecture that was designed to serve, above all else, as a mechanism of power. Describing such structures, Foucault notes that using no other instrument save 'architecture and geometry. . .[panopticism] acts directly on individuals; it gives 'power of mind over mind'. The panoptic schema makes any apparatus of power more intense. . .'[6] Making innovative use of backlighting, central observation posts, and spatial unity, panoptic architecture offered an imagistic rendering of an unequal social relation; it embodied the priorities of observation, surveillance, and discipline. Its intended result was efficient social control; it diminished the ability of an individual (worker, student, prisoner) to act unseen.

In the twentieth century, where style has increasingly entered the utopian idiom of a mass consumer market, such explicit statements of the apposition between form and function would be ideologically damaging to the mythology of progress. While much in the realm of modern style is inspired by the factory or other institutions of panoptic industrialism, explicit depictions of social relationships tend to be muted, mystified. A building may make people feel that their humanity is threatened or diminished, but it is only a feeling. A dramatic example of the aestheticization of social relations can be seen in the work and ideas of Le Corbusier, a powerful influence on the look of things today. The variations on his theme can be heard across the broad canyons of modern style, architecture, and design. Industrial designers Norman Bel Geddes, Henry Dreyfuss, and Raymond Loewy – whose combined efforts shaped the look of countless consumer goods, from telephones to toasters – all were touched by his spirit, if not by his particular style.[7]

In many ways Le Corbusier's manifesto, *Towards a New Architecture* (1923), is a call for an architectural style rooted in the priorities of panopticism: the social relations of observation, surveillance, discipline, and efficiency. His place of stylistic departure is rooted in the factory and the business office. His fascination is with the 'capacity for achieving order and unity by measurement. . . .'[8] In this regard he stands firmly in the tradition of scientific management, time-motion study, etc. His concept of organization is derived from the machine and his imagination is disciplined by 'cold reason'.[9] Yet if Bentham's Panopticon was, overtly, a structure of power and coercion, in Le Corbusier's work (or in much of modern design), this function has been reduced to a matter of style. Drawing from the social forms of industrialism, his vision is thoroughly aestheticized, divorced from any overt association with coercion or conflict. Le Corbusier takes from the look of the factory, but ignores the oppressiveness of factory work. For him the factory is simply a part of 'the most noble quarters of our towns'.[10] By separating the 'nobility' of form from the social content of the factory, surface is separated from its substance. As applied to architecture or industrial design, panopticism now becomes the repository of utopian visions of transcendence, of pure freedom, its opposite.

What is revealed is the definition of 'functionalism' in a world of consumable style and manipulated meanings. Surely the function is not usability. Most 'functional' furniture, for example, is less comfortable than the old styles it replaced. The function in 'functionalism' is, primarily, ideological. It transforms the imagery of social control into an imagery of transcendence. Relations of power in society are transformed, by style, into things of beauty.

Le Corbusier, himself, seemed aware of style as a device for neutralizing the possibility of social conflict. Despite a rhapsodic tribute to the factory, he was also aware of the industrial world as one which gave rise to 'violent desire' and 'alarming symptoms'. His response was to erect a new style, not to change social structure. This is repeated in the ongoing activities of the advertising industry which solves problems, as it were, on an imagistic level. For Le Corbusier, desires must be met by style, lest they be met on the level of society. As he said so succinctly in closing his manifesto: 'Architecture or Revolution. Revolution can be avoided'.[11] The deflection of social concerns through the channels of style has become an earmark of the culture within which we live.

Similarly, the process of history has come, increasingly, to be represented in the theatre of style. The essential quality of a consumer society – predicated on obsessive/compulsive buying, waste, and the continuous cultivation of markets – has made changing styles a cardinal element of economic life. In furniture, in housing, and – systematically – within fashion and automobile design, we confront a visual representation of passing time. What we see here is of great significance. As style becomes a rendition of social history, it silently transforms history from a process of human conflicts, an engagement between social forces, into a market mechanism. As this happens, history disintegrates as a way of understanding the world, it becomes an incomprehensible catalogue display. It shifts from the realm of human subjects engaged in social relations, motivated by interest, circumstance, and experience, to the realm of objects, discrete commodities to be bought and sold. Popular historical retrospectives capture decades in terms of how things looked. Memory is capsulized in 'depression glass'. The past can be evoked through the assembly of style. Hollywood is very good at this. Even people become understood in these terms. Roosevelt, Bogart, and Hitler; each captures the style of the thirties and forties in a different way. Together they embody the spirit of a decade! Society is, once again, divested of conflict, depicted by a history of consumable objects. Style can code our understanding of the past; it can also give shape to our expectations for the future. Much of our daily experience reinforces the notion of people as saleable objects; such versions of past and future assume a certain validity, if not truth. In the words of George Orwell: 'Who controls the past controls the future. Who controls the present controls the past'.[12]

If style offers a rendition of society as defined by surfaces and commodities, the media by which style is transmitted tend to reinforce this outlook. The genesis of commercial photography, for example, has evolved a worldview that is lifeless and object-oriented. For the still camera the most controllable subject is one that freezes well, that can be ripped out of time, motionless. The idealized human becomes the plastic human, able to maintain a perpetual smile, not one whose beauty requires a lingering familiarity. Similarly, rooms or living spaces are conventionally photographed devoid of people, devoid of evidence that people have been there: stark, uncluttered (or stylistically cluttered), no intimation that there is any significant action outside the frame.

People involved in the creation of style are occasionally candid about what they do. In an interview, James B — a photographic stylist whose work appears in major ad campaigns, retail and wholesale catalogues, and 'shelter' (home decorating) magazines, discussed the definitions of his work:

> I create the image that people want to see. It's up to me to fake people out . . . to, in a sense. . . . Basically you lie to people. You create . . . you create a picture and then they adapt to that picture. You can bring people up in taste level, you can bring them down in taste level just by what you create, what you put into it . . . . And it's just pulling together elements which work with whatever you're trying to sell.[13]

What B — describes is an ongoing dynamic of the consumer culture. After a brief acknowledgement of what 'people want to see', he arrives at the heart of the matter. Style is a process of creating commodity images for people to emulate and believe in.

Here the stylistic representation of self and society come together. As frozen images – in ads or style magazines – become the models from which people design their living spaces or themselves, extreme alienation sets in. One becomes, by definition, increasingly uncomfortable in one's own skin. The constant availability of alternative styles to 'adapt to' thrives on this discomfort. The marketing engines of style depend on anomic subjects seeking to become splendid objects. The extent to which objects seem so promising may be but an index of the extent to which the human subject is in jeopardy; destined only to be defined as a consumer.

STYLE AND INFORMATION

In a society where image-management is a strategy of commerce, industry, and politics, style becomes a basic form of information. It is as a form of information (or mis-information) that style places us on slippery ground. Where style has become a visible world of 'facts', easily appended as a facade to almost anything, it has emerged as a powerful element in the evolution of modern consciousness, creating what Herbert Marcuse once called 'a closed universe of discourse'.[14] The ability to stylize anything: toothpaste, clothing, roach spray, food, violence, other cultures around the world, ideas, etc., provokes a comprehension of the world which focuses on its easily manipulated surfaces. Most notably, as the evanescent becomes increasingly 'real', reality becomes increasingly evanescent.

Like the authoritarian language 'Newspeak', in Orwell's *1984*, style is capable of holding two contradictory ideas simultaneously without any apparent conflict or opposition. As a form of information, style creates a consciousness which is seductively at war with much of our experience. As a form of information, style discourages thought.

> WAR IS PEACE as camouflage battle fatigues join the iconography of high fashion.
> FREEDOM IS SLAVERY when manacles or 'slave bracelets' are worn as the shiny accoutrements of liberated sensuality.
> IGNORANCE IS STRENGTH as a young woman in a Calvin Klein jeans commercial proudly announces 'when you lose your mind, it's great to have a body to fall back on'.

As style gains as a powerful – if not customary – form of information, it vies for legitimacy with the world of lived experience. Within this battle, those very agencies which claim responsibility for providing us with knowledge and information about the real world become increasingly stylized. As style becomes information, information becomes style. Nowhere is this more evident than in the arena of television news.[15] Sets are styled to create the look of a command centre, to offer an imagistic sense of being 'plugged-in' to what is happening, to convey authority. Journalists are selected and cultivated for their looks, their screen presence. The Christine Craft affair, where an anchorwoman was taken off the air because she couldn't fit the right image mould, is a case in point. In a business where anchorwomen are expected to appear both cool and attractive, beauty does – indeed – become truth.

Within this context the news, itself, is beyond comprehension. Stories are presented as a series of jagged bits. Segues between tragedy and farce are the glue that holds the whole thing together. The interconnectedness of facts, their relations in the world, are never developed. The highly stylized news program offers the only principle of cohesion and meaning. Again, surface makes more sense than substance. The assembled facts, as joined together by the familiar and authoritative personality of 'The News', becomes the most accessible version of the larger reality that most Americans have at their disposal. Consciousness *about the world* is continually drawn away from a geopolitical understanding of events as they take place *in the world*. Style becomes the essence, reality becomes appearance.

If the news helps to promulgate an ongoing cognitive confusion, closely related are the dominant channels of political influence. As far back as the presidency of Andrew Jackson, when the vote was extended beyond the propertied classes, political stylemakers have negotiated between the objective power and interests of ruling elites on the one hand, and rising popular democratic aspirations on the other. Social inequalities of wealth and opportunity are transformed, within the hoodoo of political promotion, into a consensual notion of 'common interest'.

Since the end of the Second World War, the stylization of politicians and political ideas has become commonplace. Within a burgeoning consumer culture, electoral politics have become one more market of consumable items. Advertising agencies regularly participate in the packaging of governmental policies for public scrutiny and consumption. A whole field of media consultancy has emerged to advise candidates and office holders in matters of leadership style. Within a theatre which, at every turn, obscures underlying realities, the manufacture of political fictions becomes the norm. In the resulting realm of superficial meanings, democracy itself becomes style. Political involvement assumes spectatorship.

This fractured consciousness is relied upon by those in power. Public politics has devolved to the status of style. Nowhere can we see this more clearly than in the presidency of Ronald Reagan. Reagan was trained for political life as a Hollywood actor and, later, on television and in the field as a spokesman for the General Electric Corporation. Given the contemporary parameters of politics, he is the logical president. His background has provided him with a repertoire of proven images and appeals. At times we can close our eyes and hear the honest tones of Spencer Tracy. When an aura of simple trustworthiness is called for, he can draw upon his folksy Jimmy Stewart routine, replete with a shake of the head and an implied, 'aw, gee'. As the executioner of social programmes he becomes the 'last angry man', true to his own sense of justice, painfully misunderstood. As a militarist he assumes the pose of the indignant good guy, out to right the world's wrongs. In defining America's enemies, world struggles for power are couched in the familiar idiom of 'Star Wars', or some medieval costume drama. We are implored to join a heroic struggle against the 'Evil Empire'. The plots are all familiar, tried, and true. The Hollywood narrative supplies a stylistic model for political consciousness.

This commitment to a politics of image permeates administrative responses to criticism. While the deregulation of business allows for greater profits and reduced attention to industrial health and safety, the argument that Reaganism favours the rich is characterized as a problem of 'perception'. As thirty years of civil rights legislation is systematically dismantled, the conviction that Reaganism is insensitive to minorities is addressed, likewise, as a problem of 'perception'. By reducing all social issues to matters of perception, it is on the perceptual level that social issues get attended to. Instead of social change, there is image change. Flexibility at the surface masks intransigence at the core.

The impulse to dissociate images from social experience is, as we see, reiterated throughout the various strata of our culture. The repetition of this dynamic, affecting our sense of self, society, and information, has created a world in which style has emerged as the predominant arena of meaning. The danger is this; as this world encourages us to accept the autonomy of images, 'the given facts that appear' imply that substance is unimportant, not worth pursuing. Our own experiences are of little consequence unless substantiated and validated by the world of style. In the midst of such charades, the chasm between surface and reality widens; we experience a growing sense of disorientation.

Though it is easy to think of style as a merely 'frivolous', a 'put-on', or an 'attitude', its universal application tells us something different. In its endless incarnations, style has overwhelmed the perspective of modern consciousness. It is a recognition of this dynamic that will allow fruitful discussion and analysis to proceed.

NOTES

Reprinted from Jefferey Bucholtz and Daniel Bertrand Monk (eds), *Beyond Style: Precis 5*, New York: Rizzoli, 1984. Parts of this chapter appear in *All Consuming Images: The Politics of Style in Contemporary Culture*, New York: Basic Books, 1988, particularly in chapters 1, 7, 9, and the concluding chapters to the book. Also, I want to thank Elizabeth Ewen for her intellectual guidance and editorial suggestions in the writing of this chapter.

1 Raymond Williams, *Culture and Society, 1780–1950*, London: Chatto & Windus, 1958, pp. 299–300.
2 See Warren I. Susman, ' "Personality" and the making of twentieth century culture', in John Higham and Paul Conkin (eds), *New Directions in American Intellectual History*, Baltimore: Johns Hopkins University Press, 1979.
3 A very good discussion of 'renegade styles' may be found in Dick Hebdige, *Subculture: The Meaning of Style*, London and New York: Methuen, 1979. Also in this regard, see the Public Broadcasting System's hour-long documentary, 'Style-wars', originally broadcast on 18 January 1984. The Hebdige book deals with the rise of 'punk' culture in Britain; the 'Style-wars' video is about the 'bombing and burning' subculture of graffiti writers, breakers, and rappers in New York City. Both the above are extraordinary.
When I use the term 'renegade style' I view such developments as very distinct from the term 'style' as used throughout this chapter. 'Renegade styles' are attempts to do battle with the

dominant imagery and market patterns of society, to assert an imagery which is defined in one's own terms. 'Style' as used here is about marketplace images. Certain confusions arise as the 'style' market (fashion industry, art galleries, etc.) absorbs images from the battlefield of 'renegade style'. When this happens, 'renegade style' is no longer renegade. It no longer undermines the dominant image market. It has been colonized into the realm of 'style'. A discussion of this process regarding fashion may be found in the essay 'History and clothes consciousness', in Stuart Ewen, Elizabeth Ewen, *Channels of Desire: Mass Images and the Shaping of American Consciousness*, New York: McGraw Hill Inc., 1982, pp. 233–51.

4 Aristocratic patterns of clothing are discussed in Ewen and Ewen, *Channels of Desire*, pp. 110, 117–28.

5 Michel Foucault, *Discipline and Punish: The Birth of the Prison*, New York: Random House, 1977, pp. 199–207.

6 ibid., p. 206. The interior quotation is from Jeremy Bentham.

7 For an interesting discussion of the rise of industrial design in the United States see Jeffrey Meikle, *Twentieth Century Limited: Industrial Design in America 1925–1939*, Philadelphia: Temple University Press, 1979.

8 Le Corbusier, *Towards a New Architecture*, translated from the 13th French edition by Frederick Etchells, New York: Dover Publications, 1927, p. 143.

9 ibid., p. 109.

10 ibid., p. 54.

11 ibid., pp. 288–9. For a historical discussion of the development of advertising, and of the imagistic solution of social problems, see Stuart Ewen, *Captains of Consciousness*, New York: McGraw Hill Inc., 1976.

12 George Orwell, *1984*, New York: Buccaneer Press, 1989, p. 32.

13 The interview comes from oral history research reported in *All Consuming Images: The Politics of Style in Contemporary Culture*, New York: Basic Books, 1988.

14 See Herbert Marcuse, *One-Dimensional Man*, Boston: Beacon Press, 1964, p. 84ff.

15 The power of style can be seen in other agencies as well. A similar argument could be made about newspapers, for example.

3

HOME FIXTURES
Doing-it-yourself in a privatized world

ALAN TOMLINSON

'Home is where the heart is' sang the sanitized Elvis in the early 1960s, 'and my heart is anywhere you are . . . anywhere you are is home, home, home. . .'. Twenty years later, in 1982, Soft Cell's dirge on family life focused more on the problems of communication within the family. In Marc Almond's bleak vision of familial disharmony parents sit silently at the table, rowing again, always blaming the kid(s). Mother's learned her lesson well, though Almond spits the word 'lesson' out and it sounds as much like 'weapon'; and fathers simply never understand;

When children have the upper hand. . .

They say that home is where the heart is
But home is only where the hurt is
                    (Soft Cell, 'Where the Heart Is', 1982)

Even this sounded like a melodious encomium on family life next to Public Image Ltd's caterwauling flipside to 'Flowers of Romance' of the previous year. Here the 'blind lead the blind' in liking 'security in luxury':

Home is where the heart is
The daily paper on the carpet
My body burns . . .
                . . . (Screams)
(Public Image Ltd, 'Home Is Where the Heart Is', Virgin
        Music Publishers Ltd/Warner Bros Music Ltd, 1981)

ALAN TOMLINSON

Home is a complicated and often messy repository of competing interests. It might not seem so at first. For people edging away from it the idea of home can seem very reassuring. These are the jottings of a young adult male on 'home', at the beginning of a degree course in a new town: 'Home always was family home but now more house in Brighton. Like going home because it's very uncomplicated. See my mates, go to football, get fed, keep warm. Dislikes – coming home pissed, no freedom.' Not so uncomplicated after all! Home is often a cramped context for clashes over use of space, forms of expression, attitudes to time-use. Yet despite all the problems of household dynamics, it is a major focus for forms of contemporary consumption.

In the half-decade between mid-1980 and mid-1985 consumer expenditure soared, despite record levels of unemployment in Britain. A CBI estimate pointed to a 9 per cent increase in consumer expenditure in real terms: 'we increasingly tend to sit in our centrally heated homes, with the video blinking beneath the colour TV, while the washing spins in the tumble drier and the convenience food pack heats up in the microwave'.[1]

The image we are offered here is of the autonomous consuming unit, a self-sufficiency of consumption within the home. And, if the home has indeed developed in this way, with the mobile living-room on wheels the major mode of mobility outside the home, then the self-containedness of the home itself is the embodiment of the triumph of privatization. Home-based consumption represents the retreat from the public realm of community, according to Martin Pawley:

Consumer society fragments, and universal consumer society fragments universally...

Just as the small suburban house and its attendant life-style represented a means of escape from the system of community obligations ... so it is also the incubator of an even more fragmentary and microscopic social unit which will eventually succeed it – the private individual ...

The *real* basis of social stability has become paradoxically dependent on continued progress towards autonomy through increased consumption. Within the breast of the private citizen today lurks not a yearning for an older, simpler pattern of community obligations, but a desperate desire for a commodity-induced nirvana to obliterate fears of a future seemingly blocked by insoluble crises in the form of overpopulation, resource exhaustion, pollution or nuclear war.[2]

The persuasiveness of Pawley's case should not blind us to his own streak of puritanism here. He allows little room for the experience of pleasure, and sometimes radical renewal, in the act of consumption. The privatized self retains some social dimensions, still inhabits a social world, a household; and is still inscribed in particular class dynamics. The privatized self is Janus-faced, not always the desperate victim of Pawley's vision. Privatization, as a type of fragmenting consciousness, can be considered around several central themes. Arthur Brittan lists four of these: 'The dissolution of totality . . . consumerism and the insatiability assumption . . . embourgeoisement . . . familialism.'[3]

The first of these themes – dissolution – refers to the break-up of community bonds. The second theme is concerned with the developing tastes of the consumer which know no limits, so that personal accumulation of consumer durables becomes the dominant form of pleasurable living and, on the level of the social, absolutely central to the logic of contemporary capitalism. Brittan's third theme is that of embourgeoisement, the idea that a central process in postwar industrial society has been the erosion of old class barriers to the extent that everybody is now becoming more and more middle class, particularly in terms of lifestyle: the optimistic version of this thesis, clearly prevailing in the models of copy-writer and market researcher, sees the affluent society as 'the promised society in which the "private" individual is free to retreat into the confines of his house and garden'.[4] A critical version of this thesis simply equates privatization with alienation, consumerism with corruption of older, more noble collective values. The fourth theme, the family, raises questions about the effects of the split between public and private: as the family has become increasingly a unit of consumption rather than production, in the industrial epoch, and as women, especially, have been encouraged to run this unit, family life has incarcerated the individual in her/his private world.

Privatization, the fragmentation of consciousness and the atomistic nature of much of our contemporary social relations, are major themes in any discussion of the politics of consumption. Brittan concludes that 'privatisation is not an imaginary phenomenon, although it is almost impossible to obtain accurate information about the extent to which "consumerism" is in fact a dominant aspect of contemporary consciousness'.[5] Maybe it's not now so difficult, ten years on and a decade into Thatcherism. Brittan's second and fourth themes, the dynamics of home-based consumption, are the subject of the rest of this chapter.

In a recent analysis of 'leisure spending priorities since 1978' three features were highlighted. First, despite economic difficulties people have continued to give leisure spending a lot of priority. Second, the two main foci for such spending were entertainment in the home and holidays abroad. Third, there has, since 1983, been a swing back towards spending on leisure activities away from the home. But a really major feature of the early 1980s was the acquisition of new consumer products for the home. Video-cassette recorders were acquired by almost one in five of United Kingdom homes by the end of 1982; and sales of new television sets increased by over 50 per cent, people replacing their early seventies sets or picking up a portable for more flexible use.[6]

Video is open to a number of different uses. Material can be pre-recorded, or obtained from the corner video library or the specialist rental outlet; it can be recorded at home by the user, from the television itself; or it can be recorded (with a video-camera) for playback. The most pervasive uses have been for viewing rented films, and recording programmes from television schedules for later viewing, with feature films featuring most regularly here.[7]

In 1977 there were only around 5,000 VCRs in British private homes. By 1981 this figure had risen to 1.5 million. By the early summer of 1984 – the year of the Summer Olympics in Los Angeles – it was estimated that 30 per cent of households in Britain rented or owned a VCR. By 1987 the market was approaching, in the Henley Centre's view, saturation point: at the end of 1986, VCR ownership stood at 38 per cent (more than double that of home computers). But the Centre could still predict, confidently, home-based leisure activities as the most buoyant leisure sectors in the period up to 1992: audio, home computers, video, d-i-y goods and gardening. Although markets remain always unpredictable – ask Sinclair, Acorn and Commodore about the home computer boom – one-fifth or so of the population without VCRs in 1986 'considered it important that they should get one in the future'.[8] By the mid-1980s film-watching was almost totally a home-based, small-screen affair, with 97 per cent of film-watching done via broadcast television or video-film hire, outside the cinema.[9] If the cinema could be seen as a symbolic site of commercialized but collectively experienced leisure, the growth of the VCR has been an index of the increasing grip of the privatized context in which leisure is now consumed.

The Henley Centre has described the home itself as a leisure centre and has seen the population of the household as a multi-active cellular family, a classically organic model, situating discrete parts as essential elements of wholes. Whilst the VCR offers a technology capable of bringing the family together, early work on viewing patterns and VCR use suggests that its effects are much more splintering. Children, spouses together, spouses alone, different modes of viewing have emerged around particular types of programme.[10] With a set perhaps in the children's bedroom, the kitchen as well as the lounge, different mini-audiences can pick and choose the time and place of viewing, literally at their leisure.

This is how the cellular household lives as, in the Henley Centre's evocative phrase, 'the Oxo family meets the Next generation'. In the cellular household everybody is a lifestyle leader, choosing 'leisure the Lacoste way'. In their picture of 'the home as an activity centre' Henley Centre commentators present suitably androgynous figures labouring away at different forms of pleasure: someone typing on the computer keyboard in a study-bedroom; someone working out to an exercise tape in a bedroom; someone sitting with the family dog in another bedroom containing both television and radio-cassette player; someone slumped into the sofa in the lounge watching the television/VCR; and someone standing over the hob across from the microwave in the kitchen (cooking for one?).[11] In the cellular household the social unit gets smaller and smaller. In their picture of the cellular household at work and play the

Henley Centre pundits picture the connoisseur consumer as recluse, leisure as a specialist monadic activity. It is cellular in another sense too, then perhaps inadvertently punned by the Centre: the individualistic consumer inhabits an anchoretic utopia – or hell.

In general terms, household expenditure in Britain in 1984 showed that, after eating and drinking out, the biggest 'leisure spending for the most well off households was on reading materials, audio-visual materials, d-i-y equipment and holidays. As Table 3.1 shows, no other activities featured particularly significantly. And more affluent households spent more on everything.

An average of one-sixth or one-seventh of family expenditure going on leisure expenditure – much of it in-house – is an enormous outpouring, a huge number of individually motivated consumers ready to express themselves in the mass market.

The home has always been a focus for some forms of social activity. But its physical characteristics have been developed throughout this century to accommodate the widening needs of the different family members. The popular family house – in either the public or the private part of the market – became the main model. It might be semi-detached or terraced but the two-storey three-bedroomed house emerged as the twentieth-century prototype.[12] And in such houses, in Gordon Cherry's view, inter-war life was at times compartmentalized, linked to emerging forms of consumption, but resonant with familiar patterns:

> The inter-war generation may be reasonably considered as perhaps the most family-minded and home-centred one in history . . . Radio had perhaps the greatest impact, with sets now being purchased on a massive scale. This provided for family leisure time, but more often than not male and female roles were clearly defined: the man was the wage-earner and the woman was the home-maker. The husband worked in the garden and did home-improvement jobs and had popular periodicals to help him. A woman's evening domestic occupation was also guided by magazines. Suburban leisure was increasingly home-based: even the innovation of the football pools in 1922 may be understood as a domestic activity, unconnected with attending matches.[13]

United Kingdom

		Gross normal weekly income of household					£s and %
	Up to £100	Over £100, up to £150	Over £150, up to £200	Over £200, up to £250	Over £250, up to £300	Over £300	All households
Average weekly household expenditure on (£s):							
Alcoholic drink consumed away from home	1.71	3.70	5.42	6.64	7.76	10.90	5.30
Meals consumed out[a]	0.97	2.18	2.52	3.73	4.30	7.66	3.18
Books, newspapers,magazines, etc.	1.41	2.02	2.29	2.84	3.05	4.06	2.42
Television, radio, and musical instruments	2.06	2.85	3.93	6.10	6.48	7.85	4.36
Purchase of materials for home repairs, etc.	0.60	1.45	2.06	2.40	3.85	7.53	2.66
Holidays	0.94	3.05	4.42	3.35	6.45	10.88	4.28
Hobbies	0.03	0.02	0.08	0.05	0.08	0.23	0.08
Cinema admissions	0.02	0.07	0.06	0.10	0.14	0.21	0.09
Dance admissions	0.04	0.08	0.09	0.22	0.18	0.30	0.13
Theatre, concert, etc. admissions	0.04	0.10	0.18	0.22	0.29	0.53	0.20
Subscriptions and admission charges to participant sports	0.07	0.20	0.47	0.61	0.78	1.48	0.53
Football match admissions	–	0.03	0.07	0.07	0.06	0.10	0.05
Admissions to other spectator sports	–	0.02	0.03	0.02	0.04	0.08	0.03
Sports goods (excluding clothes)	0.04	0.11	0.26	0.39	0.58	1.72	0.47
Other entertainment	0.10	0.21	0.22	0.37	0.46	0.64	0.30
Total weekly expenditure on above	8.05	16.09	22.10	27.09	34.50	54.18	24.08
Expenditure on above items as a % of total household expenditure	*11.8*	*13.5*	*15.1*	*15.5*	*16.8*	*18.5*	*15.8*

Source: Central Statistical Office, *Social Trends No. 16* (1936 edition), London: HMSO.
Note: [a] Eaten on the premises, excluding state school meals and workplace meals.
n.b. Although some of the totals in this table are slightly incorrect, this in no way undermines the discernible patterns, or indeed my argument.

A major shift in the perception of the home in this period elevated hedonism above holiness. If Victorians designed home-based recreations as 'alternatives to the risks of public entertainment, to inculcate moral values and individual security',[14] the inter-war period this century produced housing and homes which recognized a felt social need for newly affordable leisure functions.

Centrally important here was the decreasing inhibition about design: the dwelling was to be an expression of personal taste, a personalized project. After the First World War old urban and suburban houses were too large and cumbersome, not conducive to new domestic technology and a nightmare to run without expensive domestic servants. Commuting increased in practicality with improvements in bus, train and car transport. One observer wrote in 1919 that 'one does not lose caste these days by moving into a smaller house'.[15] Though not strictly in line with the prevailing model of the 'popular family home', the bungalow embodied these trends: 'the bungalow was small, compact and had no stairs. Not only did it reduce areas to be cleaned; without the presence of servants, the need for social space separating employer from employed also disappeared.'[16]

Housing, producing new types of social space, also represented ideals which we would now call elements of a lifestyle. The bungalow stood for an idea of health, open-air life and leisurely social life: a verandah for eating and relaxation, a cautiously al fresco everyday lifestyle. If you got the bungalow of your dreams you really might have 'dun roamin'.

Between the wars in Britain the ideology of the home was redeveloped around a 'spirit of ambiguity' concerning town/ country and individual community. Suburban consumers wanted, first, a sense of the past built into their homes, whilst craving new labour-saving appliances. Second, they aspired to a cosy internal environment, but alongside an expansive outlook towards the great outdoors. Third, the suburbanite was concerned to express his/her individuality, but without forsaking the role of street-dweller or community member. A fourth ambiguity in their suburban culture was expressed in a thrifty approach to spending and consuming, which ran alongside the desire to display affluence. Finally, the suburban dweller wanted a practical house, but with a hint of modernity.[17]

The developing suburban ideals were in stark contrast to the community-based values of the contemporaneous council estate. Ian Bentley comments on the internal layout of the council estate:

Even *inside* the houses, one main living room often served as a through route to other rooms: unable to be closed off for completely private use, it emphasised the high value which designers placed on reinforcing a sense of community even within the family group.[18]

By contrast, 'Dunroamin' stood for 'individualism, private ownership and social mobility', and offered a model appropriate to the diversification of everyday activity – a forerunner of the Henley Centre's cellular household.

Commercially provided leisure was dominated in the 'Dunroamin' years by the cinema. By 1934 3.8 million people could at any one time have sat in Britain's 4,305 operative cinemas. From then until the eve of the Second World War a new cinema opened up every three to four days.[19] Throughout all this, suburbanites continued to form part of that public audience, but also transformed the private sphere of leisure and consumption.

The 'Dunroamers' at home were engaging in a range of new consuming activities,[20] with a significant switch from human labour (servants were found in only one in twelve houses by the end of the 1930s, a decline from a figure of one in five just after the Great War) to domestic technology. By 1938 75 per cent of households were on electricity grids, and hire purchase was available. The elements of a privatized consumer culture were coming to the fore in the quasi-rural Arcadias of suburbia. Reaching out to this dispersed public was the new type of mass circulation magazine. *Woman* was founded in 1937 and achieved weekly sales figures of 750,000 within a year. As women consumed the romantic stories, domestic tips and features of *Woman*, and operated as unrelieved line-managers of the new domestic technology, men and children grasped the leisure opportunities of the new housing. The piano – bastion of familial leisure in the late Victorian household – was replaced by the gramophone, and the foundations of the popular music industry were laid in jazz and big band/crooner booms of the 1920s and 1930s respectively.

But the biggest impact of all on the leisure patterns in the home came from broadcasting. Licences for individual radio sets were held by 75 per cent of households by late 1939. The BBC itself popularized radio during the wartime years, in a reluctantly populist concession to the people's taste: the Forces Programme of the war years became the Light Programme, and the Third Programme was then introduced for 'serious' listeners. But in the inter-war years British homes had the limited choice of the Regional Programme and the National Programme (the latter became the Home Service at the beginning of the war); and 'serious fare' made up much of the broadcast output. Serious music made up 17.31 per cent of total output in 1938, only 8.84 per cent by 1942. Variety and revue (keep the war workforce, the Home Front, happy) took up 14.84 per cent by 1942; it had only been 5.76 per cent in 1938.[21] Reith's vision of broadcasting's mission prioritized edification over entertainment. The populist mobilization of consciousness during the war undermined this project, but even so, in the pre-war years: 'the radio brought the Victorian dream much closer – sophisticated entertainment within the home became the norm, often a real escape from the harshness without and, paradoxically, the relative poverty within'.[22]

Semi-detached or detached escape hatches and privatized modes of consuming mass products and services, much more availability of credit – the outline of the consumer culture was solidifying.

In some working-class contexts the combination of poor housing and squalor denied these changes: in such cases 'the street, and not the home, was the centre of leisure'.[23] But such public leisure was increasingly labelled as undesirable, and repositioned as marginal under the double pressure of urban renewal and intensifying ruthless forms of policing. Sir Percy Sillitoe, for instance, got the European Ju-Jitsu Champion, Harry Hunter, to train his force in self-defence; sent police into the heart of working-class territories such as the pub, the street and the neighbourhood; and experimented with new methods to intervene in the Sheffield Gang wars before moving on to clean up the Gorbals in Glasgow.[24] The public street-culture of the Gorbals,[25] the Edwardian gangs like the Scuttlers of Manchester, The Peaky Blinders of Birmingham, the Great War's

Redskins of Glasgow and Napoos in Manchester[26] – those cultures spoke a different language of leisure. But this was a language increasingly marginalized as the contours of consumer culture continued to be redrawn within new boundaries of conformity. By the 1920s 'new influences like jazz music, the cinema and the growing fashion industry began to change the old youth cults. Street fighting remained important but image and sexuality took an even greater significance than before'.[27]

In the 1920s, the Bowler Hats in Birmingham's Small Heath Area would block the Monkey Run, the main road, and would be feared at local dance halls. But they did not carry razor blades in the peaks of their caps (as did the Peaky Blinders), and they pre-figured the more modern consumer. Even in the street, then, the more public culture of the working-class was not immune from the influences of developing consumer markets.

The relentless march of consumerism in the postwar period has confirmed the ascendency of suburban values, with analysts throughout the last quarter of a century recognizing that 80 per cent of all leisure time is spent in or near the home. The most recent sustained survey on the nature of home-based leisure focused on 523 households in Nottingham, covering private detached houses, council semis, owner-occupied semis, terraced houses and council flats. Of all 'leisure events' recorded in this survey 86 per cent took place in the home. 'The home dominated the life-styles of all social groups, and especially women, single parents, people of retirement and pre-retirement age, the professional class and the unemployed.'[28]

Conspicuous in their out-of-home absence from this list are young people and employed working-class adult males, still seeking excitement and escape in the public spaces of the youth market and long-established male preserves. Despite wide-ranging car ownership, much out-of-home activity remained very local – over a third of such events took place within a mile of home. But most revealing of all in this survey: 'activities were predominantly solitary, even for people living in large households. Half of all events, and 39 per cent of all time were spent alone. Leisure was more social than life in general. Life in the home was especially solitary: 42 per cent of time at home was spent alone'.[29]

Undeniably, the home has become a primary site for an

unprecedentedly privatized and atomized leisure and consumer lifestyle. With hi-technology applied to old concepts such as mail order, it is even possible that long-established forms of sociability – the walk to the bank, the visit to the shops – could be shifted into the home. And as the home fills up with leisure equipment servicing the needs of dispersed household members, it moves towards a new function. The Puritan notion of the home saw it as a 'little kingdom', the Victorian concept stressed 'Home as Haven'.[30] The Late Modern Elizabethan concept constructs the 'Home as Personalised Marketplace'. It is where most of us express our consumer power, our cultural tastes. And it is in this privatized postwar home that home-maintenance and d-i-y have flourished as major leisure-time activities.

This was not so much the case in the inter-war period. Any adaptations to architecture or environment at that time remained 'normally discrete, controlled and respectable', without the boldness of the 1960s do-it-yourself movement.[31] Home decorating might have been revolutionized by plywood in that period,[32] but sophisticated power tools remained unavailable until the 1950s and the 1960s. And from the 1960s onwards your leisure could be profitable: working on the home as freely chosen leisure could prove a good investment, particularly in more economically affluent regions of the country, where a nifty little extension could put you well ahead of the already inflated market.

Home maintenance and d-i-y is no minority activity. In 1983 one of the United Kingdom's major national surveys indicated that 51 per cent of all males aged 16 and over had done some d-i-y in the four weeks before the interview took place. Among women, 24 per cent had also been active in this area.[33] With 68 per cent home ownership predicted in 1990, and a rise in the number of 25–44 year olds in the population, the d-i-y and associated gardening markets offer one of the growth markets for home-centred consumption. There has been a 9 per cent real growth in spending on d-i-y goods from 1981 to 1986, with £3,161 million being splashed out on such goods in 1986.[34] Home-based consumption, home ownership and autonomy in decorative display – these are intensifying trends in Margaret

Thatcher's Britain, where the selling off of public housing stock has encouraged some working people to abandon their traditional values. Sell off your council house after buying it then doing it up; retire early; move to the retirement suburb.

Here we see Margaret Thatcher's rhetoric of the freedom of the market translated into practice: the escape from the public sphere into that 'closed-in, self-contained style which is the essence of suburbia'.[35] The retreat from public to private in the sphere of housing reveals the ascendancy of the privatized unit: the triumph of a particular kind of spatial ideal based upon separation and self-containedness. It may have taken almost a century, from the 1780s to the 1860s, for the 'crystallization of the ideas of privacy and domesticity' among Britain's middle-classes.[36] In Thatcher's version of postwar consumer Britain the diffusion and consolidation of these ideas may be achieved in a much shorter time than that. The home as the base for a consumer-based privatized culture will have achieved this fundamental transformation in consciousness.

Do it yourself, then. Build your own cultural environment. Thematize all your spare time activity. Express your familiarity with and ease in the consumer culture by the choices you make in this sphere: and, also, with d-i-y, make some canny investment decisions.[37]

The metaphor of the jobbing individualist is open to some dazzling and flashy interpretations. For David Punter it is a preparation for a future of disruption where survivalist skills will prevail and 'we will have to reabsorb into ourselves the skills of survival and demonstrate that the spirit of Crusoe still lives within the bourgeoisie ... from handsaw to complex power tool', the middle classes 'cannot resist the phallic'.[38] But d-i-y is a pragmatic, economic, and culturally expressive activity, quite as much as an unconscious articulation of contemporary crises. It is not a predominantly middle-class, male, and phallocentric activity. And the d-i-y phenomenon is not class or gender-specific. It is not only the hi-tech specialist who does the carpentry: it is the bus-driver, the nurse, the postman.

We leave our home bases in late twentieth-century consumer culture on scheduled tasks of consumption, organized leisure excursions: to the publicly designated 'amenity woodland' on the manicured edges of the New Town; to the Theme Park with no themes; to the latest thrill ride in the grounds of what used to be simply the Zoological Gardens. We do this in units decreasing in size, in our mobile living-rooms, when we choose. Raymond Williams has called this 'mobile privatization'.[39] We meet people along the way, but not many, and we know them not as people but as functions: the supermarket check-out girl; the (always only one!) smart-suited informant in the d-i-y warehouse; the smiling salesperson who is desperate to move on to the next pitch. And then we retreat back home, to adorn our environments in our 'highly individualist' way. We do our own thing, millions of us, over and over again. In Richard Sennett's view, we live a 'feeling of "community" in unthreatening sameness':

> Abundance . . . increases the power to create isolation in communal contacts at the same time that it opens up an avenue by which men can easily conceive of their social relatedness in terms of their similarity rather than their need for each other.[40]

> Thrown back upon the reserves of those few close to us in 'an intimate society', we stumble traumatized towards 'the end of public culture',[41] in which the high-pitched wail of former Sex Pistol Johnny Lydon/Rotten's Public Image is the chilling soundtrack to our post-modernist script.

> Parts of this soundtrack come too from the car. Roland Barthes saw cars, in the 1950s, as

> almost the exact equivalent of the great Gothic cathedrals . . . the supreme creation of an era, conceived with passion by unknown artists, and consumed in image if not in usage by a whole population which appropriates them as a purely magical object'.[42]

As we drive our cars around the outskirts of our suburbs to our megastores and warehouses they are not so much cathedrals as carriages transporting us and our wares to and from the new cathedrals of consumer Britain – the B & Q, Payless and MFI warehouse. Windowless, standardized, passionately designed as the most functional of forms, they lay out the possibilities before us, the anonymous unattended punters – the soft cell, security in luxury, home fixtures.

NOTES

1 'The Consumer Home' (New Society Data base), *New Society*, vol. 75, no. 1202, 10 January 1986, p. 84.

2 Martin Pawley, *The Private Future: Causes and Consequences of Community Collapse in the West*, London: Pan Books, 1975, pp. 36, 88 and 179.

3 Arthur Brittan, *The Privatized World*, London: Routledge & Kegan Paul, 1977, p. 56. Chapter 3 on 'Privatisation and fragmentation' offers a comprehensive and lucid discussion of the work of social theorists on these themes.

4 ibid., p. 66.

5 ibid., p. 74.

6 Bill Martin and Sandra Mason, 'Spending patterns show new leisure priorities', *Leisure Studies*, May 1986, 5 (2), 233–6.

7 Eric Gates, 'Video: the growth of a new leisure industry', in Judy White (ed.), *Leisure: Politics, Planning and People* Volume 5, *The Media and Cultural Forms*, Leisure Studies Association Conference Papers no. 26, Brighton Polytechnic LSA Publications September 1986, pp. 80–95.

8 Henley Centre for Forecasting, *Leisure Futures*, Autumn 1986, p. 58. Previous figures on video are culled from Eric Gates' article and from copies of the Henley Centre's *Leisure Futures* up until Summer 1987.

9 J. Howkins, 'Mr. Baker: a challenge', *Sight and Sound International Film Quarterly*, Autumn 1983, p. 227, quoted in Ann Gray, see note 10 below.

10 Ann Gray, 'Behind closed doors: women and television in the home', in Helen Baehr and Gillian Dyer (eds), *Boxed In: Women on Television*, London: Routledge & Kegan Paul/Pandora, 1987.

11 Henley Centre for Forecasting, *The Business of New Lifestyles: Chart and Forecast Material*, booklet prepared for Day Conference at the Cavendish Conference Centre, 20 February 1986.

12 Gordon E. Cherry, *Leisure and the Home*, London: Sports Council/Social Science Research Council, 1982, p. 17.

13 ibid., pp. 33 and 34.

14 Alun Howkins and John Lowerson, *Trends in Leisure, 1919–1939*, London: Sports Council/Social Science Research Council, 1979, p. 13.

15 Gordon Allen, *The Small House and Cottage*, cited in Anthony D. King, *The Bungalow: The Production of a Global Culture*, London: Routledge & Kegan Paul, 1984, p. 168.

16 ibid., p. 68.

17 Ian Davis, 'A celebration of ambiguity: the synthesis of contrasting values held by builders and house purchasers', Paul Oliver, Ian Davis and Ian Bentley, *Dunroamin: The Suburban Semi and Its Enemies*, London: Barrie & Jenkins, 1981, ch. 3, pp. 77–102.

18 Ian Bentley, 'Individualism or community? Private enterprise housing and the council estate', in Oliver *et al.*, *Dunroamin*, ch. 4, pp. 104–21. The quotation is from p. 114.

19 Paul Oliver, 'Suburban values and the role of the media', in Oliver *et al.*, *Dunroamin*, ch. 5, pp. 122–35.

20 Most of the following detail on inter-war leisure is from 'At home', in Howkins and Lowerson, *Trends in Leisure 1919–1939*, sect. 4, pp. 13–19.

21 David Cardiff and Paddy Scannell, ' "Good luck war workers!" Class politics and entertainment in wartime broadcasting', in Tony Bennett, Colin Mercer and Janet Woollacott (eds), *Popular Culture and Social Relations*, Milton Keynes: Open University Press, 1986, pp. 93–116. The details are from p. 94.

22 Howkins and Lowerson, *Trends in Leisure, 1919–1939*, p. 17.

23 Stephen G. Jones, *Workers at Play: A Social and Economic History of Leisure 1918–1939*, London: Routledge & Kegan Paul, 1986, p. 77.

24 J. P. Bean, *The Sheffield Gang Wars*, Sheffield: D & D Publications, 1981.

25 For an account of the extraordinarily public culture of the working-class neighbourhood – the one in which the boxer Benny Lynch grew up – see John Burrowes, *Benny: The Life and Times of a Fighting Legend*, Glasgow: Fontana/Collins, 1984.

26 These were some of the gangs thriving around the turn of the nineteenth and twentieth centuries, asserting territorial rights (primarily male), toughness, and a sense of clothing style. These are discussed in Steve Humphries, 'Peaky Blinders and Scuttlers', BBC Radio 4, 25 August 1987.

27 ibid.

28 Sue Glyptis, 'Leisure and the home: leisure patterns and lifestyles in Nottingham', in Sue Glyptis (ed.), *Leisure and the Over Fifties and Leisure in the Home*, proceedings of a Seminar held on 10 December 1986 at Loughborough University of Technology, Leisure Studies Association Newsletter Supplement 1987, p. 23.

29 ibid., p. 23.

30 Leonore Davidoff and Catherine Hall, "Home Sweet Home", in 'Victorian values: historians take issue with Mrs Thatcher', *New Statesman*, 27 May 1983.

31 Oliver *et al.*, *Dunroamin*, p. 88.

32 Howkins and Lowerson, *Trends in Leisure, 1919–1939*, pp. 17–18.

33 See Table 10.2, ch. 10 on 'leisure' in The Central Statistical Office, *Social Trends* No. 16, 1986, edition. London: Her Majesty's Stationery Office, p. 160. The survey cited is the 1983 General Household Survey.

34 Henley Centre, *Leisure Futures*, Summer 1987, pp. 60–1.

35 J. M. Richards *The Castles on the Ground: The Anatomy of Suburbia* (1946), London: John Murray, 2nd edition, 1973, p. 3.

36 F.M.L. Thompson, 'Introduction: the rise of suburbia', in F.M.L. Thompson (ed.), *The Rise of Suburbia*, Leicester: Leicester University Press, 1987, p. 14.

37 Rosalind Coward, 'Ideal Homes', in *Female Desire*, London: Paladin Books, 1984, pp. 61–71, writes well on home restoration as economic investment.

38 David Punter, 'The unconscious and contemporary culture', in David Punter (ed.), *Introduction to Contemporary Cultural Studies*, London: Longman, 1986, p. 259.

39 Raymond Williams, *Towards 2000*, London: Chatto & Windus, 1983, pp. 188ff. Williams calls his neologism 'an ugly phrase for an unprecedented condition'. He first defined the phrase in his book on *Television: Technology and Cultural Form*, London: Fontana/Collins, 1974.

40 Richard Sennett, *The Uses of Disorder: Personal Identity and City Life*, Harmondsworth: Penguin, 1973, pp. 97 and 48.

41 Richard Sennett, *The Fall of Public Man*, Cambridge: Cambridge University Press, 1977, particularly ch. 11 on 'the end of public culture'.

42 Roland Barthes, *Mythologies*, Paris: Editions du Seuil, 1957; repr. London: Paladin, 1973, p. 88.

Part two

The visual media and consumption

4

Television and citizenship
In defence of public broadcasting

GRAHAM MURDOCK

Watching television is most people's major leisure activity and the main source of the information, images and arguments through which they make sense of the world. Virtually all households, except the very poorest, have a set and almost half (46 per cent) have more than one.[1] In the average home, a set will be turned on for between 4½ and 5½ hours a day (depending on the time of year) and the average person over the age of four will watch around 3 hours a day, which accounts for just over a third (35.1 per cent) of their total 'free' time. The next most popular activities – visiting friends, relaxing or napping, and doing hobbies – take just over 8 per cent each. Centrality is not the same as influence, however. Research shows that viewing is almost never passive. People interpret, evaluate, dismiss, and argue back at the screen on the basis of their social experience and their involvement in other media. The problem is that cultural forms that were previously separated from the television system are being increasingly tugged towards it, reinforcing its command over experience and debate.

A sizeable slice of the British film industry is now financed directly by television companies, and even those films which are not are mostly watched on the small screen. Similarly, the rapid rise of the rock video as a key promotional device has led to the progressive televisualization of the music industry, or at least that half of it that is geared to the single and album charts. Nor are the print media exempt from television's centripetal pull. The news pages of the tabloid papers often carry as many stories about television personalities and stars as they do about political events and economic affairs, sometimes more. According to one count, in January 1987 they carried eighty-one stories related to television soap operas alone.[2] Book publishing too is increasingly tied to the small screen both through the titles directly linked to programmes and through the push to sales that an author's appearance on a chat show or arts programme confers. In addition, income from television exposure, and the sponsorship it brings in its wake, is becoming increasingly important to more and more sports.

As a result of television's progressive annexation of the media and leisure industries, it organizes the circulation of meaning not only through the range of programmes made especially for the small screen but also by providing a major point of access to other cultural activities. The net result is an increasingly television-saturated and television-centred cultural formation. Consequently, the way the television system is organized and the implications of this for its ability to engage with the range and complexity of contemporary experience have far-reaching consequences for the vitality of democracy.

At the heart of this issue is the relation between television and citizenship. Full and effective citizenship requires access to the range of information, insights, arguments, and explanations that enable people to make sense of the changes affecting their lives, and to evaluate the range of actions open to them both as individuals and as members of a political community. Without these resources, they are excluded from effective participation. They become the victims not the subjects of change, unable to pursue their rights and press for their extension. Precisely because of its cultural centrality the television system has become a key site on which the struggle to secure and develop resources for citizenship takes place. Once this is recognized, we are bound to ask how current and impending changes in this system are likely to affect its capacity and willingness to deliver and develop these resources. But before we examine this question in detail, we need to define what we mean by 'the television system' a little more carefully.

THE TWO TELEVISION INDUSTRIES

Up until recently in Britain, this was not an issue. 'Television' was synonymous with broadcasting in the sense that everything that appeared on the domestic screen was produced or purchased by the BBC or by one of the ITV companies. This duopoly was broken in the early 1980s with the rapid growth of the video recorder market and the advent of new commercial cable services.

Domestic video cassette machines have been available since 1971, but the market didn't really take off until 1981, Royal Wedding year. In a rerun of the pattern followed by the first generation of postwar television sets, when penetration soared in Coronation year, Prince Charles and Lady Diana's nuptials gave a massive stimulus to VCR demand. By the end of that year, there were an estimated 1.3 million machines in circulation, as against just over half a million twelve months before. Since then, the VCR market has expanded rapidly, helped by the falling price of machines and extensive rental facilities, and by 1986 the number of adults living in a household with a VCR was variously estimated at between 44 per cent and 51 per cent,[3] though this average disguises some marked class differences. Contrary to popular mythology, the higher your income the more likely you are to have access to a video cassette machine. VCRs are used for two main purposes. First, they enable viewers to record broadcast (or cable) programmes (particularly feature films) for later viewing. This option, known as time-shifting, is easily the most popular use of the VCR and although it scrambles the broadcasters' carefully constructed schedules, it does not challenge their command over the small screen. The real threat comes from the third or so of VCR owners who use their machines to watch recently released feature films or other non-broadcast material hired from the local video store.[4]

Although the history of cable in Britain is almost as long as the history of broadcasting, with the first systems opening in Hull, Ramsgate, and Clacton in 1928, its emergence as an independent industry, separate from broadcasting and in competition with it, parallels the rise of video. Up until the early 1980s cable's sole function was to relay broadcast signals (initially radio and later television) to areas where off-air reception was poor or impossible or where buried cables were preferred to roof-top aerials on environmental grounds. Apart from a handful of experiments with community access channels in the 1970s, cable systems operators were barred from providing additional services. This situation changed in 1981, when the first Thatcher government gave operators in thirteen locations permission to offer their customers one extra subscription channel. These modest experiments were never intended as anything more than a stop-gap, designed to get some sort of commercial cable industry underway while a full policy was being drawn up. This happened very quickly. The Information Technology Advisory Panel set up by Mrs Thatcher outlined an initial plan in March 1982 and the government published its own proposals in a White Paper just over a year later following a hastily conducted inquiry under Lord Hunt. The following year, a new regulatory body, The Cable Authority, was in place and ready to award the first franchises for purpose-built broadband systems to add to the existing network of limited capacity and rapidly ageing systems in mostly working-class areas. The resulting industry differs from conventional broadcasting in several ways including its programming.

Historically, broadcasting has been geared primarily to making programmes for national distribution, with a modest amount of regionally oriented production as a secondary aim. This national cultural project has been protected by stringent voluntary restrictions on the amount of overseas material that can be shown on BBC and IBA controlled channels, though the definition of 'home' production has now been extended to cover programming made within the European Community. In constrast, cable systems operators are in the business of marketing channels which have been designed to appeal internationally. This follows logically from the fact that they are currently delivered to local cable networks by low powered satellites whose beams cover continental Europe as well as the United Kingdom. Not surprisingly, the companies best placed to take advantage of this distribution system are the major multinational media groups. Consequently, the list of leading cable programmers features some very familiar names including Rupert Murdoch, who operates the general entertainment service Skychannel which reaches around 11 million homes throughout Europe, and Robert Maxwell, who is a major partner in the main film channel available in Britain, Premiere, and operates the European end of the American rock video channel MTV, in partnership with the American company Viacom.

As yet, cable only reaches around a quarter of a million

homes, mostly connected to old systems which offer only a limited number of channels. However, in areas where new multichannel systems are available, cable has made sizeable inroads into broadcasting's share of the television audience with one 1986 survey showing 44 per cent of total viewing going to cable services, led by Maxwell's main film service and Murdoch's Skychannel.[5] The imminent launch of medium- and high-powered satellites which allow customers to by-pass the cable operators and pick up signals directly with a small dish antenna will reinforce this threat by making access to satellite-delivered programming much more widely available. It will also accelerate the present movement away from a television system centred around national broadcasting, towards one dominated by trans-national imagery.

The 1980s then, have seen the division of the television industry into two. On the one side, stand the established broadcasting organizations – the BBC, the ITV companies and Channel 4 – working with varying concepts of public service. And on the other side, stand what we can call the new television industries, of video, cable and DBS (Direct Broadcasting Satellite), conceived and operated purely as commercial enterprises. But how are we to evaluate their respective performances? What criteria should we use? More importantly, can we arrive at an alternative definition of public broadcasting which is capable of defending and extending the cultural resources required for citizenship? I want to argue that we can, and must, and that we should base our case around the concepts of diversity and accessibility.

DEFINING DIVERSITY AND ACCESSIBILITY

A diverse programming system needs to meet four basic conditions:

First, it must provide people with the full range of information that they need to make considered personal and political judgements and to pursue their rights effectively. In particular, it must provide adequate and disinterested information on the activities of the major public and private agencies that have significant power over people's lives.

Second, it must engage with the greatest possible range of

contemporary experience, both personal and collective, and excavate the historical roots of present conditions.

Third, it must offer the broadest possible range of viewpoints on these experiences and the greatest possible array of arguments and contexts within which they can be interpreted and evaluated.

Finally, it must encourage these understandings to be expressed in the widest possible range of voices and forms and take positive steps to encourage innovation in presentation and visual style.

Listed baldly like this, these aims may seem worthy enough but overly po-faced, and have little to do with pleasure or entertainment, which are after all what most people watch television for, most of the time. This is a misunderstanding. Providing resources for citizenship does not have to smack of the lecture room. Some of the most effective contributions have come from iconoclastic comedy and from dramas that combined popularity with new ways of engaging contemporary experience. Advocating diversity entails using the full resources of television to develop programme forms that will offer a variety of pleasures as well as a variety of insights.

Diversity in this sense is not at all the same thing as plurality, although it is often treated as though it was. Proponents of plurality argue that opening up more channels is the best way to guarantee greater diversity of programming. but more does not necessarily mean different. It can equally well mean more of the same or the same product marketed in a number of different forms. Indeed the economic dynamics of the new television industries push them powerfully towards exactly these options and away from genuine diversity. One reason is that video, cable, and satellite broadcasting are primarily distribution systems. Their main business is repackaging existing programming. They do not initiate major production to any real extent. Moreover, because they are run as commercial enterprises, dependent on customer payments and/or advertising, they are mainly concerned with providing more of the kind of programming that has already proved popular on existing broadcast channels, or which attracts audiences advertisers are interested in reaching, such as young people, affluent professionals, and housewives. Hence, satellite-delivered programming tends to be of two main types. One type follows the video industry in taking the most popular elements of broadcast programming, such as sports, news, rock videos, and feature films and offering them as separate options. Others, like Skychannel, provide mixed programming with the accent firmly on relaxation.

These additions do expand consumer choice in the sense that they allow people to watch more of the kinds of material they already like, but they do not extend the overall diversity of provision. On the contrary, the economics of transnational television operate to marginalize or exclude certain kinds of programmes that play an important role in providing resources for citizenship, such as investigative documentaries and innovative contemporary drama. Cable operators are not interested in these areas because there is no economic reason for them to be, and they are not bound by the same public service requirements as broadcasters. As the White Paper on cable makes very clear, the government considers it has 'a duty to enable new technology to flourish and fulfil its potential unfettered by unnecessary restrictions'.[6] It believes, consequently, that 'it is not necessary, or even appropriate, for cable services to be required to achieve in their programmes a wide range and balance, or high quality, in the way that has been thought right, in the public interest, on the BBC/IBA services'.[7]

In other words, cable should be seen as a business and nothing should be allowed to interfere with its successful expansion, including local programming, which many optimists had rightly seen as one of the system's most interesting possibilities, and a genuine addition to the overall diversity of television-delivered programming. But technological potential is not the same as economic reality. As The Cable Authority made clear in its first Annual Report, they 'concluded at an early stage that the most important of its statutory duties was to promote cable services' by supporting cable operators in attempts to establish a viable business.[8] To the extent that local services can advance this aim by building good will in the community they are to be welcomed but the Authority warns that 'it is unrealistic to expect substantial amounts of money to be devoted to [them] until a successful business has been established' (para 81–2). Some cable operators may extend their local programme provision but there is no real incentive for them to do so in the forseeable future, apart from public relations, and many will probably settle for a minimal commitment.

In addition to criticizing the new television industries for extending plurality at the expense of diversity, supporters of the current public broadcasting system frequently defend it on the grounds that it produces 'quality' programmes. Michael Tracey speaks for many commentators when he argues that 'the point about public service television and why we need it is that it is a system which is more likely to produce 'good' programmes than a heavily market-oriented television system'.[9] Alasdair Milne, the BBC's ex-Director General goes even further, arguing that under his administration, the Corporation had only one purpose: 'the making of programmes as good as we can achieve'.[10] Unfortunately, 'good' is a very difficult concept to pin down, not least because it is used in debate in two rather different senses.

The first champions such concepts as 'cultural excellence' and 'the need to protect the creative spirit',[11] and opposes the descent into formula juggling and stereotype that follows the move from personalized to mass production. Against the spectre of 'wall to wall *Dallas*' it celebrates the work of Denis Potter and the other designated auteurs of broadcasting, who are able to mark their productions with their own inimitable stamp and produce work that challenges established expectations and common sense judgements rather than confirms them. While this kind of programme making certainly has a place in any television system devoted to extending diversity, it is not synonymous with it, since once institutionalized, the idea of authorship can all too easily operate to exclude perspectives and voices that fall outside its orbit. A genuinely diverse programme system needs to find ways of allowing these voices to speak for themselves, whether or not the results conform to the canons of 'good' programming. Sometimes they will, often they will not, particularly if they are involved in deconstructing established forms of presentation.

This argument applies even more forcefully to the second major meaning of 'quality', which equates 'good' with professionalism. On this definition *Dallas* is a 'quality' programme because it is good of its kind in the sense that it is very professionally put together. Conversely, programmes which fail to meet the prevailing norms governing how particular types of production should look, are all too easily dismissed as amateurish, poor quality, and worst of all, boring. Here again, it is not difficult to see how notions of professionalism can be employed as an exclusion mechanism. Against this, a diverse programme system needs to operate with a more pluralistic set of judgements and not measure every production by the standard yardsticks.

Alongside diversity of production, a broadcasting system oriented towards citizenship must be able to guarantee universal access, both geographically and socially. That is to say, the entire output should be equally available to everyone regardless of their income or where they live. There should be no additional charges for access to the more expensive programmes or those aimed at minorities. This principle of universal access has always been at the heart of public broadcasting in Britain and must be defended, particularly since it has been comprehensively jettisoned by the new television industries.

Having defined these two central principles of diversity and accessibility, we are now faced with the problem of specifying what institutional arrangements are best able to underwrite them.

PROFESSOR PEACOCK'S FLAWED UTOPIA

One option, which has attracted a great deal of influential support in recent years, advocates that the television system should become a publishing business whose range and direction is determined primarily by the 'free' play of consumer demand. Since the recent Report of the Committee on Financing the BBC, chaired by Professor Alan Peacock, offers the most sustained case for this position to date, it provides a useful vantage point from which to examine it.[12]

Although the Committee was originally set up to look into alternative ways of funding the BBC, with particular reference to the possibility of the Corporation taking advertising, it soon broadened its purview to take in the whole future of television services, and became, in effect, a mini Royal Commission. After sifting the available evidence, it concluded that:

British broadcasting should move towards a sophisticated market system based on consumer sovereignty. That is a system which recognises that viewers and listeners are the best ultimate judges of their own interests, which they can best satisfy if they have the option of purchasing the broadcasting services they require from as many alternative sources of supply as possible. (para 592)

As they point out, this goal requires certain key conditions to be met. First, there needs to be a rigorous policy to prevent monopolistic concentration among programme providers and to ensure that the greatest possible number of producers are able to enter the market. Second, programme making must be controlled solely by the general laws relating to obscenity, libel, incitement to racial hatred and so on. All additional controls applied specifically to the circulation of audio-visual material should be abolished. Third, all services must eventually be provided on a subscription basis so that viewers can register their demands directly.

As they candidly admit however, this kind of market system cannot guarantee full diversity of programme production and consequently there 'will always be a need to supplement the direct consumer market by public finance for programmes of a public service kind supported by people in their capacity as citizens and voters but unlikely to be commercially self-supporting in the view of broadcasting entrepreneurs' (para 133). These programmes include: news, current affairs and documentary programmes which 'contribute to responsible citizenship'; 'critical and controversial programmes, covering everything from the appraisal of commercial products to politics, ideology, philosophy and religion'; and popular programming which experiments with different forms of presentation 'to the ones which viewers would have demanded unprompted' (para 563–5). But if the market-led system they propose is incapable of underwriting genuine diversity and providing the range of resources for citizenship which they admit are essential, why build the whole television system around it and confine public broadcasting to a residual role financed by a combination of government funding, private subscriptions and corporate patronage? The American Public Broadcasting System is in exactly this situation in the United States and the results are not encouraging. Since President Reagan cut the amount of federal money going to PBS in his first budget leaving Corporate America to make good the shortfall, programme production and acquisition has become more and more reliant on sponsorship from major companies, with mounting problems for editorial control and overall diversity.[13] A public television system capable of sustaining and extending diversity needs substantial and secure public funding, though there is room for considerable debate about the mechanisms for achieving this.

It is clear that the present flat-rate licence fee is a highly regressive form of taxation which discriminates against poorer households. None of the available solutions is ideal, but the least worst alternative is to fund public broadcasting out of general taxation and to index the annual allocation at a specified level above the Retail Price Index so as to allow for the fact that the costs of producing diverse programming will inevitably run ahead of the general rate of inflation. This would also reduce the extent to which broadcast funding became a political football. Funding public broadcasting through taxation is also the most efficient way to sustain universal access and avoid making it dependent on ability to pay, as in subscription systems. Given the steadily widening gap between the top and bottom income groups since 1979, the effect of pay-as-you-view is to deny the poorest members of society access to the full range of resources they need for effective citizenship and full political participation.

Despite its powerful advocacy of a predominantly 'free' market future for television services, the Peacock Report is by no means fully in line with current government thinking. On the contrary, as Samuel Brittan, one of the Committee's leading figures, has pointed out, its thoroughgoing libertarianism

> exposed many of the contradictions in the Thatcherite espousal of market forces. In principle, Mrs Thatcher and her supporters are all in favour of de-regulation, competition and consumer choice. But they are also distrustful of plans to allow people to listen to and watch what they like, subject only to the law of the land. They espouse the market system but dislike the libertarian value judgements involved in its operation.[14]

During the Thatcher years, the historic split within Conservatism between liberal economics and moral authoritarianism has become more and more evident as proponents of both currents have become more vociferous.[15] The net result is that television's ability to provide adequate resources for citizenship is being comprehensively undermined from both sides of the divide. Not only are programme makers being subjected to an extended apparatus of censorship and political interference, they are also being squeezed by economic policies which reorientate the production system around market dynamics.

THE NEW CENSORSHIP

Although broadcasting is the primary target of the new censorship, its influence extends to the new television industries, and particularly to video. The emerging apparatus of control operates at three main levels: new laws regulating what can be made available for public consumption have been passed or are being considered; existing laws are being applied more forcefully; and a new watchdog body is being established to monitor broadcast output. These moves are underpinned in turn by a more or less constant barrage of public criticism of contentious and innovative programming from senior Conservatives, directed mainly at the BBC and Channel 4.

The most significant new law affecting the moving image industries is the Video Recording Act. This turned the old Board of Film Censors into a statutory body, the British Board of Film Classification, and made it responsible for vetting all video tapes intended for general circulation and either giving them a certificate or banning them. Anyone selling or renting an unclassified tape is liable for a fine of up to £4,000. Since the operation is self-financing film-makers must pay to have their work passed and current rates make it difficult for some community video groups to comply. Unless they show human sexual activity or acts of gross violence however, tapes which inform, educate, or instruct do not need a certificate, although it is up to the Board to define these terms. The Act is a particularly dramatic demonstration of the schism in conservative thinking since, of all the new television technologies, video approximates most closely to the publishing model advocated by neo-liberal economists.

Alongside the imposition of new statutory controls, existing laws are being applied more forcefully, particularly in the area of 'national security' where definitions are being extended to cover almost anything that might embarrass the government. The most important instance of this new rigour is undoubtedly the government's use of the Official Secrets Act to suppress Duncan Campbell's BBC Scotland documentary on the Zircon project. This revealed that behind the public cover of adding an extra satellite to Britain's network of military communications satellites, the government had authorized the development of a signal intelligence satellite to eavesdrop on Soviet radio, telephone, and computer traffic. It went on to claim that the cost of the project, estimated at between £400–500 million, had been concealed from the Parliamentary Public Accounts Committee in breach of a 1982 agreement to inform the Committee of all major defence projects.

The only new piece of information in the programme was the project's code name, Zircon. The other key details were already publicly available in specialist sources. Indeed, when it was first announced that a new satellite was being added to the military communications system, the prime contractor for the project, British Aerospace, issued a statement giving its orbital position as 53 degrees east, placing it over the Soviet Union and Indian Ocean, and making it more or less useless for its stated purpose. Campbell had done what good journalists are supposed to do. He had combed through the expert sources which most people do not have the time to read or the expertise to interpret, obtained corroboration from a highly creditable source, and pieced together a story that the public as citizens needed to know. He had not provided any details of Zircon's capacities or of the precise technologies to be employed that would be of use to an enemy. He had simply revealed its existence and the fact that its cost was being concealed from parliament, and presented the facts in a place and in a style that made them accessible to the public at large. However, it was more than enough to bring the full weight of the Official Secrets Act's apparatus to bear on him.

On 15 January 1987, the BBC's then Director General, Alasdair Milne, announced that following talks with the head of

Britain's signals intelligence centre, GCHQ, the Corporation had decided not to broadcast the programme on 'grounds of national security'. Campbell then decided to publish the substance of the programme's arguments in the 23 January edition of the left-of-centre weekly, the *New Statesman*. The next day, Special Branch Officers entered the *New Statesman* offices with warrants issued under the Official Secrets Act giving them the widest powers to search for and seize documents from the magazine and from the homes of Campbell and his two fellow journalists, in a concerted search for their sources. The following Saturday, Special Branch officers arrived at BBC Scotland in Glasgow where the programme had been put together. To avoid having the offices torn apart by the search, film editors and library staff were summoned from their beds in the middle of the night to locate the material the police required. Although the seized material was later returned, no charges were ever brought against Campbell or anyone else involved in the production.

The unprecedented sight of police demanding entry to broadcasting premises marked a sharp deterioration in the already poor relations between programme makers and government, for some time. Examples include: the castigation of the BBC for putting journalistic independence before support for thinking. This role, which is indispensable to television's ability to function as a resource for citizenship, has been under constant attack from the right, both inside and outside government, for some time. Examples include: the castigation of the BBC for putting journalistic independence before support for the government's position during the Falklands/Malvinas engagement; Leon Brittan's open letter to the BBC Board of Governors urging them not to broadcast the *Real Lives* feature on Republican and hard line Unionist politics in Northern Ireland; Norman Tebbit's intemperate attack on Kate Adie's reporting of the American bombing of Libya for BBC news; and the renewed criticism of broadcasting's presentation of violence, in both news and drama. These attacks have recently been given a more institutionalized focus in the shape of the new Broadcasting Standards Council, which will monitor output and issue reports. Although it has no statutory powers, its existence will almost certainly reinforce the 'chill factor' within broadcast-

ing organizations, which is already making investigative programme making on sensitive political issues more and more
difficult. But increased political pressures are not the only
explanation for the changed climate within which programmes
are now made. The pushes they exert are powerfully reinforced
by the pulls coming from the new economic environment.
Changes in the regulatory regime have been particularly
important.

RE-GEARING REGULATION

These changes are normally described as deregulation. This is a
misnomer. It implies that there are fewer regulations than there
were. This is debatable; not least because 'deregulation' has
been accompanied by an unprecedented growth in the number
of regulatory agencies, with new bodies to oversee telecom-
munications, cable, commercial radio, and video. Much more
important than the number of regulations, however, is their
direction. The really significant shift has been a movement away
from regulation in the 'public interest', however defined, and
towards a regime designed to give maximum scope for entrepreneurs to take maximum advantage of the business opportunities opened up by the new television industries. With the notable
exception of video, the light regulatory touch pioneered by the
Cable Authority is rapidly becoming the norm. Nor is this a
purely British phenomenon. The collapse of confidence in
public enterprise and the rehabilitation of market thinking is
opening up opportunities around the world. The major beneficiaries of this more liberal regime are the leading transnational
communications corporations who have the resources to take
advantage of the new market opportunities. It has allowed the
Maxwells and Murdochs to consolidate their central position by
building up significant stakes in a whole range of communications sectors with the minimum of difficulty. If and when it goes
ahead, the present proposal to allocate the next round of ITV
franchises by open auction will strengthen the hand of the multi-
media conglomerates still further. Although they will have to
promise to uphold diversity before they are allowed to bid, few
other contenders will be able to match the depth of their
pockets. Moreover, once in possession of a franchise it is by no

means sure that the IBA will be able or willing to hold them to their promises. Its recent performance in the relevant areas has been mixed to say the least. It successfully blocked the Rank Organization's bid for Granada but signally failed either to identify the concealed, and illegal, Saudi Arabian stake in TV-am until it was exposed by the *Observer*, or to enforce the original franchise proposals.

The major advertisers have also benefited from the general relaxation of economic controls over the audio-visual industries. The retreat from public regulation has enabled them to enter markets that were previously closed. Murdoch's Skychannel, for example, has introduced advertising via cable into several European countries where it is still banned on the major broadcast channels. Similarly, the Cable Authority in Britain has allowed not only more advertising on cable than on ITV, but more flexible forms, on the grounds that a channel containing long informational advertisements is sufficiently unlike ITV to make the existing rules inapplicable.

In this new environment, television comes to be seen more and more as a marketing operation, selling services to consumers and audiences to advertisers. Programmes are no longer seen as cultural spaces in which experiences can be explored and arguments and explanations debated, but as products to be packaged and sold in as many markets as possible. This is particularly problematic for those programmes that are most central to maintaining diversity, such as investigative documentaries and dramas which engage in depth with contemporary experience, for the simple reason that they are among the most expensive to produce and offer the lowest economic returns in the new television marketplace. In contrast, programmes such as game-shows and action-adventure series, which work firmly within common sense knowledge and established formulas, present a number of possibilities for commercial exploitation, over and above their ability to attract high ratings on their first showing.

FROM PROGRAMMES TO PRODUCT: THE NEW TELEVISION ECONOMICS

One way of generating additional income from a programme is to market spin-off products based on the script, setting, scenario, and stars. The major possibilities are: books based on the scripts or offering a behind-the-scene look at the making of the programme; records of the theme music or soundtrack; computer games based on the format or plot; and rerelease for the home video market. For certain kinds of production, additional opportunities are offered by merchandizing deals where companies are sold the rights to use the characters, settings or programme name as the basis for their own products. These could range from jigsaws, tee-shirts and cosmetics to fashion clothes and wrist watches, although the biggest area of exploitation at the present time remains children's toys. Clearly some programmes are more suited to this kind of marketing than others. A computer game based on a popular action-adventure series or game show is likely to sell rather more than one based on a documentary series on the causes and consequences of inner city poverty or Third World debt. Similarly, most children will be more inclined to play with figures based on *Dempsey and Makepeace* than on the central characters in *My Beautiful Laundrette*. Book publishing offers wider scope, though here again the major markets are for paperback 'novelizations' of popular drama series, and general trade titles linked to series in the areas of cookery, gardening, natural history, and the arts. Investigative documentaries and hard hitting contemporary drama are rather less saleable. As returns from spin-offs and merchandizing become more important to the economics of programming so these kinds of programmes become progressively disadvantaged in the new market environment. We have not reached this situation yet but it may not be too long before we do.

For the moment, though, the major source of additional income remains programme exports, which for English language productions means above all the United States, and in particular, sales to the Public Broadcasting System and to stations that are not owned by or affiliated to one of the three major networks. Although this second market, known as syndication, is expanding rapidly it is only open to programmes that fit the independent station's two main strategies for competing with the networks, counterprogramming and stripping. The first entails running popular entertainment material against the network's news programmes in an effort to build an audience base for the rest of the evening, whilst the second aims to attract audience loyalty by placing shows in the same spot in the schedules every weekday. As a result, syndication requires programming that exists in reasonable quantities and which works with already popular formats. This means action-adventure series like *The Avengers* or *Dempsey and Makepeace* rather than single dramas. Situation comedies also fit the bill, but most British-made shows are too culturally specific to be saleable in their original form. This problem can be circumvented by selling the basic idea or format for the show and allowing an American producer to 'customize' it for the American market. Successful examples include: *Sandford and Son* (based on *Steptoe and Son*), *All in the Family* (derived from Johnny Speight's *Till Death Us do Part*), and *Three's Company* (a version of Thames Television's hit series *Man About the House*). Format deals make good economic sense but there is always the possibility that the requirements of overseas markets will become internalized and that new programme ideas will begin to be evaluated with one eye on their export potential. The result could well be a reduction in the ability of television comedies to engage with the full range of contemporary British experience.

In contrast to the syndication and network markets which only deal in programme forms that have proved their popularity, the Public Broadcasting System is primarily interested in material that fills the most conspicuous gaps in the mainstream broadcast and cable schedules. Since the early success of Sir Kenneth Clark's *Civilization* series in 1970, it has looked to Britain to supply 'cultural' programming with a capital 'C'. This not only fits PBS's version of the public service philosophy, it also suits the major corporations like Mobil who underwrite programme purchases. Their primary motivation is public relations, improving their image by associating themselves with non-contentious 'cultural' productions. To this end they favour historical rather than contemporary drama – the Raj rather than Brixton's Railton Road – and documentaries on relatively safe areas such as the arts and natural history rather than on political controversial issues.

The unequal chances of different programme types in the international market is further reinforced by the growth of satellite distribution systems in Europe. These allow British broadcasters to package and sell entire channels. This is the *raison d'être* behind Superchannel, which is jointly run by the main ITV companies (with the exception of Thames and TV-am) to distribute a mixed schedule of popular programming to cable systems around Europe. Two ITV companies, Granada and Anglia, also have stakes in British Satellite Broadcasting, the consortium which will operate Britain's DBS project. This will provide three channels for direct reception on home dishes. Although aimed primarily at the United Kingdom they will be obtainable in Europe. In addition, LWT is part of a consortium which is aiming to use one of the channels on the new Luxembourg based satellite, Astra, whilst the BBC is currently playing a leading role in moves to set up a pan-European sports channel financed by a mixture of advertising and sponsorship, in partnership with Rupert Murdoch. As these initiatives make clear, far from resisting the advent of international television, broadcasting organizations in Britain are eagerly competing for a central position in the new system. Here again, though, the economic attractions need to be weighed against the costs for citizenship if production becomes too firmly geared to trans-national distribution. The problems this poses for diversity are already evident if we look at the other major way of entering the international television market – through co-production.

Sharing the costs of production with outside investors makes sound economic sense to financially pressed British programme makers. Indeed, for the more expensive forms of production, such as filmed drama, co-production is now the rule rather than the exception. At the same time, it can have significant consequences for diversity as funders seek to ensure that the products they have invested in fit the requirements of their home markets. This often results in what we can call televisual tourism, in which Britain's unique selling points – its heritage, 'culture' and quaintness – are integrated into programme packages in ways that audiences in America and elsewhere will instantly recognize. This puts a premium on historical series rather than contemporary dramas, on Royalty, aristocracy, castles, and stately homes, and on the high arts. As a result, without any conscious intention to do so, the transnationaliza-tion of production reduces broadcasting's ability to explore the full range of experiences, perspectives, arguments, and aspira-tions generated by the dislocations of living in contemporary Britain. We increasingly come to see ourselves through the distorting mirror of the most globally saleable version of 'national culture'.

This is not an argument for pulling up the drawbridge and barricading British broadcasting against foreign influence. In the satellite age this is neither feasible nor desirable. On the contrary, we urgently need to develop international programme exchanges and co-productions that will advance diversity and challenge the island mentality and lingering imperial illusions of British political culture. We need to see more productions that bring outside scrutiny to bear on familiar situations such as Northern Ireland; more that articulate other nation's experiences from their vantage points rather than from ours; and more that penetrate behind the simple dualisms of east/west and north/south to examine the complex web of connections which integrate nation-states into the modern world system. As well as providing additional resources for citizenship these initiatives would make it more difficult for government to massage the public agenda to its advantage. If these hopes are to materialize, even in a modest way, public broadcasting organizations throughout Europe need to recover their nerve and make the extension of diversity their primary goal. As the recent history of the BBC indicates however, the signs are not at all encouraging.

BBC INC.

The Corporation has been quick to adapt itself to the new television marketplace, partly out of the necessity forced on it by a steadily falling real income from the licence fee, but partly also out of opportunism. As a result, its thinking has been increasingly reoriented around a concern with costs, markets, and deals. Despite the assurances of the then Director General, Alasdair Milne, in 1985, that 'we are not in the business of making money',[16] his Assistant Director General, Alan Protheroe, was still moved to complain that: 'We have become too preoccupied with "value for money", with commercial concerns, with "cost-effectiveness", with the exploitation of what we produce – to the extent that we have damned nearly lost sight of what we are supposed to be about.'[17] Two years later, after Milne had been ignominiously sacked by the Board of Governors, the tone of remarks from senior management was rather different. The in-coming Director General, Michael Checkland, who had worked his way up through the ranks of the Corporation's cost accountants, celebrated the BBC's new economic 'realism', arguing that the Corporation must now be seen 'less as an elderly institution and more as a modern £1,000 million company, adapting to competition and change as many other companies have to do in this country, and doing it with enthusiasm'.[18] There is some force to this argument. Programmes cannot be made without money and the careful husbanding of scarce resources coupled with concerted efforts to raise additional income that can be ploughed back into production, could help to increase diversity. This has certainly been the BBC's argument for some time. As one senior executive put it in 1980: 'ventures into profit-making acitivities must be seen as extensions of the public broadcaster's mission. They must be more than self-supporting. They must be profitable enough to finance the development of programme services at all levels.'[19]

Even so, behind the rhetoric of recent statements there are hints of a significant reorientation in the BBC's view of its audiences, away from a conception of them as political actors who need adequate resources for full and effective citizenship, and towards a model of the viewer as consumer and honorary shareholder, who wants a service that provides value for money and caters to their existing demands. This is entirely consonant with the ethos of consumerism which underpins the new television industries. This directs people to solve their problems and satisfy their wants, not by pursuing their rights as citizens, but by purchasing a commodity, whether it is one of the new communications facilities themselves or one of the products and services featured in the advertising they carry.

Although the advertising lobby failed to persuade the Peacock Committee to recommend the introduction of spot advertising on the main BBC channels, the Corporation is by no means entirely removed from the business of company promotion. Sponsors' names already feature very heavily in the coverage of sporting events supported by major corporations and there is a concerted push to allow the sponsor to contribute to programme budgets in return for on-screen credits. At the moment this kind of direct sponsorship is prohibited, but in view of the government's demand that that BBC take 25 per cent of its total programming from independent producers within three years, the present rules are quite likely to be relaxed. Since the Corporation will not be able to finance every project in full, independents will need to top up their production budgets from other sources, and sponsorship money offers an attractive option. Such a move would have clear implications for diversity. At its best it would guarantee 'quality' programming in the first sense we defined earlier. At its worst it would mean that a further slice of public broadcasting time would be commandeered by what Asa Briggs once called 'the propaganda of goods', with a consequent reduction in the space available for other voices.

RETHINKING PUBLIC BROADCASTING

We cannot return to the supposed 'golden age' of public broadcasting in the 1960s, however much some commentators would wish it. Nor should we want to. Despite the dynamism, innovation, and genuine respect for dissent that characterized that era at its best, it was still marked by an unacceptable degree of exclusiveness. New voices were recruited, particularly in drama, but they were overwhelmingly male and white. They spoke for and to a particular range of working-class experience, but their sources were seldom allowed to speak for themselves. Nor were they offered many chances to contest the way they were represented. The major beneficiaries of broadcasting's relative freedom remained the intelligentsia who were licensed by authorship, expertise, or professionalism to speak for England.

A genuinely diverse programme system cannot do without the knowledge and skill that professional journalists and independent experts can bring to investigation and analysis. It must be able to tell people things they didn't know and reveal connections they did not suspect. It also needs to give space to the quirky, passionate, and disturbing visions of established writers and film-makers. At the same time, it must continually look for ways of widening the range of experience and argument that is brought into play, by encouraging new voices to speak in their own way and by opening channels of communication between those who make programmes and those who watch them. This is a far more flexible and effective way of ensuring accountability than establishing new watchdog bodies peopled by the 'great and good'. In these respects, the most promising working model of a public broadcasting system adapted to the new age is not Hugh Greene's BBC but Jeremy Isaacs' Channel 4.

It is tempting to attribute the success of Channel 4 in extending diversity to its policy of commissioning almost all its output from independent producers. Certainly this structure has considerably broadened the range of viewpoints and experiences allowed onto the screen, but only because that is the Channel's stated aim and because it has been able to pursue it at one remove from the direct demands of advertisers. Without these key supports the result is more likely to be American-style programming. The major American networks obtain almost all their output from independent producers but with a few notable exceptions such as MTM Enterprises (makers of *Hill Street Blues*) very few have done much to advance diversity as we have defined it here. They are not required to. American commercial television is about promoting mass consumerism not about providing resources for citizenship.

Independents in Britain already have to operate without firm guarantees of continued support. They are therefore particularly vulnerable to the economic dynamics outlined earlier. These pressures will increase if Channel 4 and the BBC steal too many of the new marketplace's best tunes. This will reduce the range of production that is viable. It will also accelerate the tendency towards concentration in the independent sector itself, as smaller companies fold or are taken over. According to Charles Denton, the chief executive of Zenith Productions, even without such a shift there will inevitably be 'a move towards agglomeration, and to cope with the economic realities there will be some very complex cross holdings. When this industry matures, you will find maybe half a dozen, even fewer, large independents and we intend to be one of them'.[20] He speaks with some authority since Zenith has recently been acquired by Carlton Communications, one of the major independents and a partner, with LWT and Saatchi and Saatchi, in a consortium aiming to run a pan-European channel on the Astra satellite.

The best available counter to these forces is increased public funding for independent production and a resolute defence of a conception of public service which makes the extension of diversity its primary goal and allows the BBC and Channel 4 to pursue it with varying mixes of in-house and outside production, but without direct pressures from advertisers, however expressed, and subject only to the law of the land. Anyone arguing this case in the present economic and political climate is heading into a very strong wind indeed. But if the case is not made, and made forcefully, it will slip from the public agenda altogether and with it any real hope of television being able to provide the resources for citizenship required by a mature democracy rooted in solidarities which recognize and respect difference and dissent and do not seek to liquidate them in the imagined communities of nation and market.

NOTES

1 See *Marketing Week*, 26 June 1987, p. 35.
2 Richard Brooks and David Randall, 'TV engulfed by its own froth', *The Observer*, 1 February 1987, p. 49.
3 *Marketing Week* and David Docherty, David Morrison and Michael Tracey, *The Last Picture Show? Britain's Changing Film Audiences*, British Film Institute, 1987, p. 62.
4 Docherty *et al.*, *The Last Picture Show*, p. 74.
5 John Clemens, 'Satellite dishes to satisfy a real hunger', *The Guardian*, 22 December 1986, p. 9.
6 Home Office/Department of Industry, *The Development of Cable Systems and Services*, London, HMSO, April 1983, Cmnd 8866, para 87.
7 ibid., para 130.
8 Cable Authority, *Annual Report and Accounts 1986*, para 45.
9 Michael Tracey, 'Television – the next decade', *The Listener*, 1 September 1983, p. 9.
10 Alasdair Milne, 'Insight and novelty', *The Listener*, 10 October 1985, p. 7.
11 Tracey, 'Television', p. 9.
12 Home Office, *Report of the Committee on Financing the BBC*, London, HMSO, July 1986, Cmnd 9824.
13 Brian Winston, 'Paying the piper and all that', *The Listener*, 10 March 1988, p. 25.
14 Samuel Brittan, 'The fight for freedom in broadcasting', *Political Quarterly*, 58: 1 (January-March 1987), 4.

15 See Ruth Levitas, *The Ideology of the New Right*, Cambridge: Polity Press, 1986.
16 Milne, 'Insight and novelty', p. 7.
17 Quoted in Denis Barker, 'BBC chief calls for act to keep broadcasting free', *The Guardian*, 23 October 1985, p. 3.
18 Quoted in Peter Fiddick, 'Tricky decisions left to BBC staff', *The Guardian*, 20 March 1987, p. 4.
19 Robin Scott, 'Public broadcasting: the changing media scene', *Intermedia*, 8: 6 (1980), 17.
20 Quoted in Peter Fiddick, 'Risk-risk at the tip-top', *The Guardian*, 15 February 1988, p. 21.

5

Innocence and manipulation
Censorship, consumption, and freedom in 1980s Britain

SEAN CUBITT

It is almost a truism now to say that the United Kingdom of
Great Britain and Ireland is among the most heavily censored of
all the industrial nations. The Prevention of Terrorism Act, the
Official Secrets Act, the various Broadcasting Acts, the laws of
evidence, libel, slander and contempt of court, Local Government Acts covering the exhibition of film and video and
legislation such as the Obscene Publications Act, the Cable and
Broadcasting Act, and the Video Recordings Act – added to the
paranoia of a government in the mid and late 1980s increasingly
embarrassed by leaks from within the civil service, the revelations of retired spies, and the use of parliamentary privilege to
expose scandals and corruption (as in cases involving bank fraud
allegations and the Falklands War, Belgrano affair) – all this, all
these statutes and practices point to an increasing state involvement in the relationship between producers and consumers, in
both news and entertainment media.

The Watergate scandal could never have occurred in the
United Kingdom: D-notices would have been served, official
secrecy and the defence of the realm invoked, and the laws of
contempt applied in the unlikely event of perpetrators being
brought to justice. Likewise, despite the aura of 'permissiveness'
that hovers around legislation of the late fifties and mid-sixties,
homosexual acts between men under the age of twenty-one,
members of the armed forces, and anyone at all in the North of
Ireland, are still illegal, and it is still forbidden to portray a wide
variety of sexual acts pictorially, acts which are standard fare for
overseas sex industries. In addition there are voluntary (but
generally considered binding) house agreements in both the

major broadcasting networks that violent or erotic material should not be broadcast before nine o' clock (the 'kiddies truce') and a particularly English fear of 'bad language' at any time and in any medium: according to statements by the Director General of the BBC at the 1985 Edinburgh International Television Festival, 70 per cent of calls received by duty officers concern the use of language.

I want in this chapter to outline the ways in which recent moves have tied together political and moral issues (particularly in television and video), some of the intellectual and ideological traditions upon which they draw for support, the misunderstandings of viewing practice that they make, and the possible routes forward. Of all the issues associated with leisure activity, broadcast media and related technologies have become the hottest political topics since the early 1980s. The soccer terraces alone have generated as much interest and concern, particularly since television's live coverage of the Liverpool-Juventus European Cup Final, the occasion of the tragedy in the Heysel Stadium in Brussels. Why is it that the electronic media have become such central items on the agenda of politicians? What has the political response been to developments and trends in broadcasting technology and viewing practices? How adequate is the politician's understanding of the production of meaning in the moving-image media?

The United Kingdom has one of the lowest penetrations of telephones in the West, but 90 per cent of households have one or more television sets, and of these over 40 per cent now have a video cassette recorder (VCR). The increasing cheapness of video equipment – new or secondhand, bought or rented – and the rapid expansion of video rental shops have meant that many working-class homes now have a major alternative to broadcast television at the centre of domestic leisure. There has moreover been a sudden and enthusiastic response to video as an access medium, focusing around the amateur/hobby market and the community workshop movement, the latter bolstered substantially by various kinds of support from Channel 4. Video technology makes possible a direct intervention in the production of images, either of events in the domestic scene (weddings, parties, even childbirth) or of community and campaigning issues (*Framed Youth* by the Teenage Lesbian and Gay Video

Collective, *The Miners Campaign Tapes* by a number of workshops for the NUM and *Death Valley Days*, an anti-nukes 'scratch' video by Gorilla Tapes are good examples).

Video technology offers several useful qualities for the consumer. It is compatible with existing leisure equipment. Cameras are cheap to hire and can produce adequate tapes for hobby and family use without further handling. Editing is becoming easier to get access to, at least in metropolitan areas (there are an estimated 200 video groups in the Greater London area alone and *Independent Video*, the sector's magazine, sold, in 1986, 10,000 copies monthly). Simple 'crash' editing can be done using domestic equipment, and though the results are often muddy, some interesting work has been done, for example, by the south London group, Nocturnal Emissions. Time-shifting of broadcast programmes allows for a very different kind of attention as well as an alternative to the structure of television schedules. And finally the circulation of rented videos, whether from the commercial or the community and campaign ends of the market, offers a kind of viewing that does not relate at all to structures of control as they exist in broadcasting.

Here we begin to hit a problem within the capitalist organization of domestic leisure: the problem of copyright. The United Kingdom laws of copyright were drafted first in the age of the printing press, as a way of ensuring an author's right to the profits from his or her work. New technologies have begun to alter the ground on which this law operates, as the manufacturers of hardware have expanded from 'receiving equipment' to 'duplicating equipment', especially since the introduction to the mass market of magnetic recording tape. There is here a conflict between hard and software manufacturers, not helped by the fact that hardware (including blank tape) is largely in the hands of multinationals based in the newly industrialized Far East, while software is distributed on a territorial basis – in the United Kingdom by largely British-based companies like Thorn-EMI and Rank. (It's worth noting in this context that Thorn-EMI have recently sold their Screen Entertainments division, thus dividing one of the few United Kingdom-based companies that straddled this gap before.) When a distributor buys distribution rights to a geographical area, they are exclusive within the media that rights have been bought for. Thus an episode of *Dallas* purchased for network broadcast by an ITV station cannot be broadcast by any other network. Although the station may also purchase the right to use extracts from the episode as a trailer, it would also have to purchase extra rights, for example, in order to re-use a particular scene for a news broadcast on the shooting of J.R. Cinema, broadcast and video rental rights are distinct categories in copyright law, and may be held by different companies. This, incidentally, means that the 'author' of the film or programme, however it might be determined who she/he is, is excluded from taking a direct cut in the profits: all income from distribution goes to the distributor, who may also cut or otherwise alter the product – as frequently happens to films when broadcast, either for moral reasons or for reasons of length. The images and sounds therefore belong in any geographical territory to the local distributor. There is no equivalent in the moving image area to the right to quotation which is available with regard to the printed word. Thus any use of a clip from a broadcast programme, especially if it is for gain, is an infringement of copyright, unless agreed, usually for a fee, with the distributor. It is far from uncommon to find that this right is used to refuse the use of a clip. This can become quite a serious problem when an entire event, such as a banquet for visiting dignitaries, is taped for press release by an agency of government, which retains copyright in the clip and thus indirectly to the event itself, as occurred with some footage used in *Death Valley Days*,[1] the anti-nuke 'scratch' video mentioned earlier. If video cannot be cited, as in the case of printed sources, then the 'scratch' form based on compilation will be a victim of the copyright laws indefinitely.

However, although software producers clearly wish to keep control over their products and the profits associated with them, hardware manufacturers are equally clearly involved in producing the goods that seem purpose-made for rerecording and reconstructing broadcast material. There is here a fundamental conflict in the capitalist organization of leisure between two determinant functions. On the one hand, in order to maintain growth, hardware manufacturers must produce new machinery for the domestic consumption of leisure to replace markets such as those for radios and television sets which have reached saturation. On the other hand, a key function of the state is to facilitate the (re)production of social cohesion so as to provide a stable market and a stable workforce for producers. The inadequacy of copyright laws in the age of domestic electro-mechanical reproduction (to waylay Walter Benjamin's famous phrase)[2] is notorious. The difficulties of rewriting them are equally well known, especially given the push towards trans-national markets for cable and satellite and the need to draw international copyright agreements that will allow for some form of common practice. Clearly a very large proportion of the United Kingdom population has access to VCRs already, and the logic of capital is such that few governments would dare to interfere with such a prosperous market.[3]

The one route that remained open was to intervene in the manufacture of software. Traditionally this has been done voluntarily in the cinema – by local governments agreeing to abide by the standards set by the British Board of Film Censors – and by statute in broadcasting by the BBC and IBA. Both systems allowed for a degree of negotiation, whereby films and programmes might be pre-censored or self-censored at the scripting or any subsequent stage, or banned outright at the final breakdown of compromise. The same remains true of advertising, controlled by the Advertising Standards Authority. The force of recent and proposed legislation is to enforce strict moral guidance on software production on and off-air, and thus effectively regain control over the use of the electronic image lost with the introduction of the VCR. The two key items of legislation were both introduced as Private Members' Bills, showing government reluctance to be seen to be intervening in the issue at all, though both have had clear tail-winds from the Home Office, the government department with responsibility for broadcasting. (Film is, incidentally, part of the brief of the Department of Trade and Industry, as it does not count as an art in United Kingdom law.)

I want first to deal with the Video Recordings Act, introduced in 1984 as a Private Member's Bill by Mr Graham Bright, Conservative MP for Luton, who was released from his duties as a junior minister at the Home Office for the duration of the bill's passage. The Act as passed calls for the certification of *all* videotapes with a selective list of exemptions for tapes of an educational, religious, musical or sporting nature, and for tapes of family events circulated to people who took part or who had some close connection with them. The regulations specified the British Board of Film Censors as the appropriate body (the BBFC, till then a voluntary body, immediately took on the new title of 'Classification', rather than Censors, although they now had for the first time a statutory role). Fees for classification ranged from £4.60 per minute for new features to a discretionary £1.20 for films deemed by the BBFC to be charitable and non-profit-making. Classification labels are to be shown both on the box and on the cassette itself. Thus far there have been few trial cases – the first involved pirate Hindi cassettes – and no use made of the internal appeals procedure since the Act became law in September 1985. However, several tapes of feature films have been given new certificates, in line with the rather ambiguous phrase 'suitable for viewing in the home' used in the Act.[4] New certificates allow for a category '18R' which will only be available in licensed sex shops. Among those threatened are *Last Tango in Paris*, *Empire of Passion*, and *The Evil Dead*. It should be noted that there are no licensed sex shops in the North of Ireland, and in many other areas of the country where such licences are in the gift of local governments. The delays experienced so far and the expense of certificating back catalogues will undoubtedly lead to the loss of several films from catalogues.[5]

Interestingly, there appears to be no defence available under the law that a tape is suitable for viewing in the home, should a renter be prosecuted for circulating an uncertificated tape. The one available defence is that the tape falls into one of the exempted categories. This removes from juries the powers they have under the Obscene Publications Act (OPA) to decide whether a product is 'liable to corrupt and deprave', a necessary feature of items prosecuted under the old law. However, tapes that slip through the net can be prosecuted under the OPA if Video Recordings Act prosecutions are unsuccessful. This particular aspect of the law should be seen in the context of a wider political move to lessen the powers of juries in a range of different kinds of prosecution such as common assault, driving while disqualified and, more significantly, fraud.[6] It also needs to be seen in the context of the extension of police powers under the Police and Criminal Evidence Act which came into force on 1 January 1986, and other public order legislation sparked off by the inner city uprisings of 1981 and 1985 and by the coal dispute of 1985. The current ruling faction of the Conservative Party is strongly committed to stronger policing in public order areas, and the rhetoric deployed around issues of public order bears a strong resemblance to that used in issues of morality.

One final feature in the political genesis of the new legislation needs to be taken into account. Film censorship has been, since the silent era, enforced in law by local authorities. But it is again current Conservative policy to remove as much power as possible from local authorities; and in fact the Greater London Council (GLC) and the Metropolitan Counties, responsible for the government of all the United Kingdom's major cities, ceased to exist on 1 April 1986 – a suitable choice of date for a monumentally ill-conceived action against local democracy. The Video Recordings Act should be understood as an element in the breakdown of local control over local cultural issues, especially in light of the enormously important role played by the GLC and the metropolitan counties in supporting work in grant-aided film and video. Figures from the Independent Film and Video-makers' Association (IFVA) and the British Film Institute (BFI) suggest that the GLC alone was spending nearly £2 million per annum on film and video production, much of which was reliant upon the circulation of tape for its prime use. The BFI was offered, and accepted, a sum of £1 million to replace all spending in these areas for all the abolished councils, a sum which also had to replace expenditure needed for exhibition, distribution, training, and publications.

But although economic and political factors have had a great part to play in the production of the Video Recordings Act, the proposed Obscene Publications Act (Amendment) Bill, and in the deliberations of the two Private Members on the introduction of amendments, what most characterized the setting in motion of the legislature over the period 1983–7 was the use of the press to popularize quasi-scientific discourses around video and television.

The 1987 Conservative Party Manifesto pledged reform of the Obscene Publications Act, in particular by bringing broadcasting within the terms of the Act. At the time of writing the legislative procedure is yet to begin, but quasi-scientific discourses on the effect of television were turned up full volume in the summer of 1987 on the occasion of the tragic deaths of innocent people in the Hungerford massacre in August. This was a revealing instance of the Press interest in curtailing the portrayal of violence in the electronic media. The coverage of Michael Ryan's armed assault on the small town of Hungerford widely attributed such behaviour to a prevailing climate of violence in the visual media. Without any evidence whatsoever that Ryan watched home-movies or violent videos his act was instantly labelled as 'Rambo-style'. All the major political parties have accepted the commonsense but unproven conclusion that moving-image representations of fantasy violence are causative of real social violence.

Such discourse has politicized the uses and relationships developed around the television and the video-recorder, and made them a focus of public debate, moral outrage, and rushed legislation. In short, domestic consumption of moving-image technologies has become a political arena in the current era of dramatic social and economic decline in the United Kingdom. This development must itself be seen in terms of the perceived decline of the family since the 1960s and the arguments of born-again Christian campaigners associated with the Festival of Light and the National Viewers and Listeners Association (NVALA) concerning the natural sanctity of the family and its authority over individuals. Clearly economic, social, and institutional changes have implicated the institution of the family in their shifts, and attacks on social services, education, and health care, especially for the elderly, have placed new demands on the family to 'look after its own' (the over-riding message of the BBC's hugely successful 'social realist' soap opera, *East Enders*). Such factors as the increase in divorce, the diminishing social stigma surrounding relationships unhallowed by church or state, and the legalization of abortion are seen not only as challenges to the role of the welfare state, but as dereliction of moral duty. The media have been singled out as a particularly important 'intrusion' into the natural history of the family, especially by Mrs Mary Whitehouse, the Northamptonshire headmistress who came to prominence in the mid-sixties with her public and acerbic attacks on the 'permissiveness' of the BBC.

At first these attacks were specifically aimed at issues of

promiscuity, and explicitly to the preservation of the family, but violence soon made its appearance in the canon of media ills, notoriously in the case of protests about the British science-fiction series *Dr Who*.[7] This latter case also foreshadowed the concentration, in the eighties, on the effects of television on 'our' children. The concern with the media as destabilizing contributors to a perceived breakdown of social values (as indicated by the breakdown of social institutions) is closely tied to political censorship. Mrs Whitehouse said to me in the summer of 1985 that broadcast footage from Soweto had 'caused' the uprisings in the Handsworth district of Birmingham. Her wealthy backers and advisors frequently suppress the more overtly political elements of her discourse, usually in the interests of securing parliamentary support for 'moral' legislation without having to broach party political issues.

The most recent debates (or as Petley and Newman would have it, controversy)[8] have centred on the two Private Member's Bills introduced by Tory MPs, the Video Recording Act and the Obscene Publications (Protection of Children etc.) Amendment Bill. Much of the acquired common sense of the reactionary view of the media can be read off from the reports of the self-styled 'Parliamentary Group Video Inquiry' and from the proceedings in both Houses and in committee around both bills. The latter in particular has produced such startling grounds for legislation as the following statement by Winston Churchill, MP for Davyhulme:

> There is no evidence that the rising tide of violence and pornography is leaving the youth of our country unscathed or that there is no link between such material and the horrifying increase in violent crime, including violence of a sexual or sadistic nature.[9]

Knowing that there is little proof on the other side of the argument, and that such as there is has been frequently discredited either because the result required was specified from the outset, or because there have been disparities in the data, or because the methods employed, especially in psychological testing, fail to reproduce the terms of domestic viewing, it is possible to argue that only television companies selling space to agency media buyers need absolutely to believe in the power of the medium. In the case of morality campaigners, it is necessary to look beyond conspiracy towards a more genuine misunderstanding of the operation of the media, media policies, and the nature of social life within which viewing takes place.

On the same day as Mr Churchill's intervention quoted above, Willy Hamilton MP noted the disparity between Tory espousal of 'market forces' and the wish to control viewing. Yet is there really such a disparity? The effect of the introduction of new technologies is analysed elsewhere in this book (ch. 4); we should look here at how the 'deregulation' of the market actually helps to standardize the product. The left-wing weekly *News on Sunday* needed start-up capital of about £6 million in 1986. Three years earlier the sum required would have been £30 million. But because the medium is becoming cheaper, will it become more diversified? Papers jockeying for a share of a fixed market will hit smaller audiences, and employ fewer journalists if they are to remain competitive. This will undoubtedly lead to an increase in syndicated news items and the expansion of the role of press agencies – as is already the case with Independent Local Radio news in the United Kingdom. Such a process of standardization through proliferation – such as has happened already in the American newsprint media – is also, in recent experience, a normative process. And it is precisely in this way that the new Obscene Publications (Amendment) Bill is designed to operate: as a normative factor. The homophobic elements of the rhetoric surrounding the new bill have been well-documented, for example the singling out of gay film-maker Derek Jarman for particular slurs.[10]

The drift of Conservative crisis management is not to reinvent a Victorian economy of entrepreneurs, but to consolidate the economics of scale. Whatever the aims of moral legislation, it will fit in well with the cultural effects of this drift. To it may be added an effect of Tory Party management of social services, which have been severely cut on the principle that the family rather than the state should shoulder the role of caring institution. The Whitehouse ideology of the family has been purloined in the interests of managing the public debt and financing election-winning tax cuts. It is probably for this reason that the incidence of child abuse and incest in the family has traditionally been given such a low profile in the rhetoric of the ruling faction in the Conservative Party, and an idealized model substituted.

But we should beware crediting the ruling faction with imposing such new configurations on the population. The shift in popularity from the 'community' soap opera of *Coronation Street* to the 'family' soap of *East Enders* may be read, for example, as a token of the shift in self-perception of the viewing audience towards a model of the family first and the rest of the world after, perhaps brought on by Tory legislation, perhaps by the global crisis of capital, or by the increasingly vast and distant structures of the economy with their apparently arbitrary effects on daily life. In any case, the family has achieved an unprecedented status as the site where crises can be resolved – as, for example, in the rhetoric surrounding the 1981 uprisings, where many prominent figures were quoted as blaming 'the parents' for civil unrest. This new model of the family is also disciplinarian, and parliament has been encouraged to see its role as supportive of the firm but fair, tough 'n' tender, cruel-to-be-kind family of the 1980s.

In this model, the media are seen as intruders (headlines frequently use words like 'plague', 'virus', 'addiction', 'peddlers', 'invasion') with traditional fear of the electronic technology of television recruited to isolate the set as an alien entity, uncontrolled, according to its critics, by any functioning statutory body (BBC and IBA alike have been heavily criticized for a perceived failure to abide by their own guidelines for the portrayal of sexual and/or violent behaviour). This again rests on a simple misunderstanding: that the consumption of television programmes is performed by a single subject, the mass audience. This in turn has two effects: first, consumption is reduced to a mere phase of production,[11] entirely subordinate to it; and second, the media are established, in their role as pollutants of the populace, as an Other, an entity defined by its difference from the 'real' world of society, and which by that effect of difference helps to maintain the 'reality' of its opposite – in this case, the audience as innocent consumers. It is a process familiar, for example, in the casting of black youth as a social Other, whose alleged criminality is the proof of the normality of white rule. This latter quality underlies the former: normally consumption is subsumed under production; abnormally production from elsewhere irrupts into the cohesive society, so that 'right-minded people' have to take a 'principled stand' against the merchants of sex and horror. This not only simplifies the complex production of televisual meaning, it effectively annihilates any attempt to come to terms with the micro-cultures of television viewing.

The right-wing model of cultural production is one of internal and external coherence. There are no battles within broadcasting institutions, their discourses are held to a norm by market forces, their audience is undifferentiated. The dialectics of race, class, gender, age, and all the rest are simply excised from the monodirectional history of the message, formulated at the core, received at the periphery, with an utterly transparent distribution process that cannot inflect reception.

A more critical and socialist analysis should, I believe, begin with analysis of the struggles over meaning that go on in the living rooms, pubs, and clubs of the United Kingdom, and that raddle the television industry and its products. This is to argue that the many influences on the multiple overdeterminations of individual practice – of which the media constitute just one – have to be seen as in conflict over both the individual and the social meanings which can be gleaned from a given evening's viewing. Despite the lip-service given to competition by the Tory right, theirs is not a conflict model of society. Although the declared object of their media policy is to increase choice, clearly the choices are for those who can afford to pay for them (thus, for example, the cultural priorities of the Greater London Council, aimed at serving disprivileged communities such as gays and black people, have been a constant target of right-wing ridicule). What is left is the development of oppositional cultures based in wilful reading against the grain of what might be seen as broadcasters' intentions. Thus, for example, the reading of a breakfast television aerobics instructor as object for an heterosexual male voyeurism, incidentally colluded with by the tabloid press. Thus, also, the now traditional left parlour game of 'Spot the ideology' in any media product.

Media control is simply impossible. Not only is there no body capable of monitoring every transmission. Media texts themselves – apart from the difficulty of identifying the text: an item? a programme? an evening's flow? a season? – are polysemic, offering an excess of meaning that viewers sample and inflect according to their own needs and desires, their own social and cultural formation. The causal model of the media shared by such unlikely bedfellows as Mrs Whitehouse, Tony Benn, and Women Against Violence Against Women is attractive because of its simplicity and obviousness.[12] But a harder analysis is needed, not simply because such a model leads to censorship (maybe this is an essential factor in democratic societies) but because any democratic development must respect the existence of the individual, and attempt to understand even what it will go on to condemn. Thus the problem is not 'What are we to do about pornography?' – which begs the important question for political control, 'who are *we*' – but 'Why is there a market for violent and sexist images?' Most of all, anyone who wants to see society change has to be able to escape from the cultural pessimism of the view that 'the media control consciousness'. Were such a view valid we could not hope for change – the media would simply rule supreme, its/their powers entrenched, all-embracing, and unchallengeable.

Clearly, two factors need to be taken into account: societies do change, and viewers do watch in different ways, drawing different kinds of pleasures/displeasures and meanings from comparable experiences. It seems straightforward to argue on this basis that media are not the sole determining factor in the exchange between screen and viewer. Ergo: viewing is an activity, undertaken in conjunction or in conflict with other activities, over-determined by other discourses, engaged in with different degrees of attention and involvement. Beyond this, there are further differences which need to be explored and accounted for; these are notable otherwise by their absence – the question of the specificity of relations between image and viewer in the different media.

Working-class women interviewed by Ann Gray for her research into women, domestic labour and the VCR said that they felt quite guilty about watching a time-shifted programme, that it was not the same as watching whatever happens to be on as scheduled by the broadcasters.[13] Clearly video, with its capacity for playing back at any time, is a mode of selection which goes far beyond 'channel zapping' on broadcast, denoting a specific kind of attention based on that choice. As John McGrath, a leading television dramatist, noted recently, 'drama has lost that quintessential quality of television – that of being an event brought to us simultaneously as a nation. . . . This was the quality that made it different from film, and linked it to the heroic unrepeatability of the experience of theatre.'[14] McGrath writes from the standpoint of regret for a lost medium, that of live television drama, but his observation is correct: the VCR introduces a quite different mode of viewing, as different from viewing broadcast television as broadcasting was from cinema. Much broadcast television is produced in short segments – the length of a song, an item in a magazine programme, a continuity announcement, or a sequence in a soap opera: deliberately, so that the distracted mode of viewing in the domestic living room can be allowed for. Video viewing is more concentrated – although also subject to interruption, you can always start again where you left off. And it is much less possible to view tape as 'live', to watch for company, as one might turn on the television simply for the contact rather than the content. Much of the experimental research carried out in laboratories applies theories derived from the very different viewing situation of film, and in conditions far removed from the disruptive and distracting family. Live television thrives on the representation of uncertainty and alteration: video is always already recorded, and has therefore a different status, a different address, a different presence. Yet technically what both share is a radical incompletion. The electronic apparatus of the television screen, the scanning of lines to build up the whole picture, is never complete, and can only appear so to a sluggish human eye. Even at this bare photo-mechanical level, the electronic image media demand an active viewer. Confusing different types of media allows the introduction of legislation such as the current Obscene Publications (Amendment) Bill which draws invalidly upon the same body of research.

Beyond this it is virtually a truism to say that television and video are both media of representation, that is, that their presence and the presence of the images they show, rest on the absence of the 'real' which they represent. The condition of existence of a picture of a space shuttle is that it is absolutely and completely different from a 'real' space shuttle, and that the presence of the real thing would preempt the existence of the image. We have a troubled relation with the absent object of representation, complex and fluctuating. John Berger uses the example of a snapshot of a young boy. For his mass readership, the photo signifies a presence; for the boy's father, a migrant worker, it signifies an absence.[15] To this dialectic we must add the determinants on opinions, values and beliefs of class, gender, age, race, education, sexual choice, and a host of other factors which together go to make up our individual intellectual and emotional biographies, determinants that will come into prominence – or crisis – at different times, affecting the ways we relate to the screen.

The act of consumption is not a one-way process of cause and effect. I would prefer the Hegelian model of consumption, whereby the consumer effectively and totally alters the content and form of the thing consumed. To eat an apple is to destroy its 'appleness' and change it into something (or things) else: food, nutrition, taste, even symbol, moral or political (Eve's apple, South African boycotts). To watch as complex an entity as a feature film on tape or an evening of television is surely even more of an activity of changing and altering. The programme ceases to be for us a pattern of light and sound, or a package of intentions and designs or messages from the producer. It has to enter into our world, be translated into a meaningful thing, it must speak to real people with real emotions, intellects, and failings. It must rely on our competences in language, music, and in deciphering the codes of television – distinguishing between genres, following the ellipses of narration in flashbacks or cross-cuts, competences acquired and themselves subject to shifts of ground. Nor are children the unutterable naïfs that right-wing ideologies paint them as. Childhood is a period when all sorts of anxieties must be experienced and negotiated, and the mass media now play a large part in that process. Children will be bored – excluded by programmes that do not address them and their interests, but these interests range far beyond the agenda set for them by adults, who produce an ideology of childhood innocence for their own purposes, without significant recourse to children themselves. So children too, those great consumers of fictions of every kind, have these competences and skills in abundance – something the work of my colleagues in the media education movement constantly unearths. Such skills and their contributions to what is perceived as pleasurable, worth-while, or whatever, should not be underestimated or dismissed.

Simply to conceptualize children as *tabulae rasae* on which the bad guys and good guys fight their fight is to show less respect for children (and ultimately for all viewers) than they deserve.

Reading is part and parcel of the production of texts. Without the reader there is nothing. With one, there is a field of possibilities, circumscribed to some extent by the nature of the text, but by no means determined by it. In fact the constitution of a period of broadcasting as a programme – for example, mentally deleting the programme breaks, adverts, announcements, station identification – is itself the act of an active viewer. If the viewer or reader is marginalized, and the concept of reading abandoned, then the acceptance of the model of the passive viewer will preserve old values and block any possibilities of change. But if we want a more accurate picture of a real process, rather than any crude causal one-way model of the media's effects upon consciousness, we must look closely at the various stages in the viewing process. We must learn why men, particularly, want to watch violent and obscene works, what they do with them, how they feel about them, if we are to alter the state of play. Nor should we allow the naked power of the state to perform our censorship for us: the push should be towards local control over local media, not centralized governance by ukase.

NOTES

1 Jon Dovey, 'Copyright as censorship – notes on *Death Valley Days*', *Screen*, 27: 2 (March–April 1986), 52–5.
2 Walter Benjamin, 'The work of art in the age of mechanical reproduction', in *Illuminations* (edited and with an introduction by Hannah Arendt), London: Fontana/Collins, 1973, pp. 219–53.
3 The French experience is unusual. Imports of VCRs were directed via a customs clearing house in Poitou, and with no domestic production this effectively held back the mass marketing of the product for some time. Eventually Monsieur Mitterand's government was forced to raise the ban. It is significant that television has traditionally had the role of *state* broadcasting in France since de Gaulle's time.
4 In the view of at least one prominent lawyer, Geoffrey Robertson, author of several books on the laws of obscenity, this phrase 'in the home' was introduced to make up for the fact that

United Kingdom lawyers had had removed their monopoly on conveyancing: the ambiguity of the new law would give them ample scope for creative pleas (talk given at the Institute for Contemporary Arts, London 1985).

5 Peter Dean, 'Classic cuts of the video censors', *Stills* (December 1985/January 1986), 7. However, the W. H. Smith newsagent chain, followed by other chain stores and a particular drive from the very large record retail outlets, has begun marketing a low-price sale-only catalogue of classic movies that, should it prove successful, may well alter this gloomy prognosis for at least some minority interest feature films.

6 George Jones, 'Plan to end jury trials for fraud', *Sunday Times*, 29 December 1985.

7 See John Tulloch and Manuel Alvorado, *'Doctor Who': The Unfolding Text*, London: Macmillan, 1983, p. 158.

8 Julian Petley and Kim Newman, 'More controversy than debate', *Monthly Film Bulletin*, 51: 610 (November 1984).

9 See *Hansard*, 90: 43 (24 January 1986).

10 See Joan Smith, 'Mrs Mary Whitehouse's Private Members', *New Statesman*, 13 December 1985. This needs to be linked with the effective censorship operated by Her Majesty's Customs and Excise against imports of homosexual literature by the London bookshop Gay's the Word. See debates in *City Limits* throughout the Winter of 1985/6. Not only were Derek Jarman's homo-erotic films *Sebastiane* and *Jubilee* specific targets for Obscene Publications Act reformers – Winston S. Churchill was especially vociferous on this – but the Local Government Bill (due to become law in 1988) explicitly forbids the 'promotion of homosexuality'.

11 See Marx's critique of the 'inane' Jean-Baptiste Say in the Introduction to *Grundisse: Foundations of the Critique of Political Economy*, Harmondsworth: Penguin, 1973, p. 94.

12 See Ian Connell's excellent essay 'Fabulous powers: blaming the media', in Len Masterman (ed.), *Television Mythologies*, London: Comedia, 1984, pp. 88–93.

13 My thanks for ideas used in the following paragraphs to my colleagues who met in December 1985 to discuss their research on the use of VCRs: Ann Gray, Ben Keen, Leslie Haddon, Steve Brockbank and Dave Morley.

14 John McGrath, 'Strike and the fiction factories', *Edinburgh International Television Festival Magazine*, no. 10, 1985.

15 John Berger, *The Seventh Man*, Harmondsworth: Penguin, 1975.

Part three

Consumer culture(s) and the market – some case studies

6

What's next?

Fashion, foodies and the illusion of freedom

DIANA SIMMONDS

Has fashion been democratized? Yes or no? We think we think about what we wear, how we live and how we live our lives? But do we? Perhaps we should think again – maybe for the first time.

Mass production has made fashion available to anyone who can get to their high street chain store or who can get hold of the latest mail order catalogue.[1] Yet it has not democratized fashion. Rather, over the past twenty years it has created discrete areas of fashion which do not automatically seek to emulate or follow one another.

For years the fashion press regularly promoted 'the look' for the year – or the season. Once upon a time that was just 'Paris' which, in dilute form, finally filtered down to the local ladies' modes. Then came the mythic sixties when young people suddenly acquired their own cash and really got into looking different from old(er) people and when social class momentarily took a back seat. A 'look' was as promotable to the Mary Quant/Biba/Bus Stop/Tuffin and Foale customers as the upper echelons were sold on Coco Chanel. There was high fashion, which like *haute cuisine* was largely indigestible to the majority, and there was swinging youth where, according to the breathless new pop mag pundits, fashion was at. Everyone else tended to wear clothes and look respectable (Her Majesty the Queen, your mum and her friends, for instance).

Outside London (did *anyone* live outside London?) the picture was not quite so simple: getting hold of the latest fab gear in 1966 Swindon was akin to finding mange-touts in Caithness in 1985. *Honey* magazine recognized this and acted on it in an extraordinary way with the launch of the 'Honey boutiques' in

121

the major conurbations, so that the groovy styles portrayed in the magazine could be had by hitherto deprived readers in whatever part of the sticks they had the misfortune to live, with no more trouble than a Saturday day return fare.

During that time the main emphasis was on the female as fashionable: hemlines rose inexorably with the soaring British economy. Social commentators noted that this phenomenon was not new: bright colours and rising skirts apparently went with good times whilst body concealment and drab tones accompanied depression. David Bailey, the photographer whose lens pinned the swinging sixties forever to the wall, noted in 1985 that the mini-skirt was directly attributable to Jean Shrimpton's legs, more of which he exposed with each successive photo session despite Vogue's initial efforts to airbrush in what he'd hiked up. Nevertheless, Bailey's personal vision of 'the Shrimp' – her wide-eyed-long-legged form – became synonymous with the times.

The male of the species, displaying peacockery unprecedented for a century or more, was despite paisley, ruffles, velvet and all, secondary. This position as 'also attending' in the daily panoply of style was not for want of effort: 'the Dedicated Follower of Fashion' was no sartorial doormat; but it was acceptable and expected that the female, complete with which ever secondary sexual characteristic was currently 'in', should be the object of absolute scrutiny. According to the legend, the sixties were awash with new social freedoms and sexual liberation; thus, the mini-skirt inched its way ever further from the Plimsoll line of modern respectability – the knee – and in doing so subliminally exposed with the ostensibly gamine, but essentially coy, knock-kneed fashion poses, the easy availability of the female genitalia.

'The pill' made such vulnerability permissible: if a girl could no longer be 'got into trouble' then obviously she would want to participate enthusiastically in the newly fashionable and possible 'free love'. No accident that the preceding round of fashion for women had emphasized the breasts (which virtually disappeared as a fashion accessory in the sixties). After all, if a fellow was not allowed below waist level – and the all-in-one pantie girdle was impregnable without traitorous and lustful help from the inside – then what else was there but hours of despairing mauling of the mammaries, offered up as they were with the aid of uplift-under-wired-half-cup-sponge-rubber-lace-nylon and steel display cases.

The male meanwhile suffered no such exposure of his obvious masculinity: he was not the object of 'the look' – that which is sexual and voyeuristic. Although his trousers might acquire or lose turnups and more or less leg width; his shirt evolve from plain white to a variety of colours and patterns, along with minor (but crucial) alterations to collar cut; and his ties perform similar minuets together with the length of his hair, he did not ever, unless actually appearing on stage in *Swan Lake*, have to make a big thing of – his big thing. Of all the fashions of the past that have been dredged up, dusted off, and revamped, only in poor Shirley Conran's imaginatively malnourished Lace-trimmed sexual fantasies has the codpiece ever even looked like making a reappearance; which is curious.

There are only two varieties of western male who routinely and deliberately display what they may or may not have been born with (rumours of radiator hoses and sockfuls of sand abound) and they are the matador and the heavy rock 'n' roller. The former dons the flamboyantly explicit costume of the fifteenth century to perform the most clear-cut display of male bravado ever devised. He slowly and deliberately offers his most vulnerable, visible, and precious possession to A Big Black Bull; placing the actual in direct conflict with the symbolic, time after time; tempting the forces of the primeval with the swirling deep pink petals and folds of the gaping and potentially enveloping cape. No wonder men and women alike roar and wet themselves with fright and delight as the horns scrape past the boldly offered (and artifically enhanced) *raison d'être*. No amount of posturing, thrusting, self-fellating, and general guitar heroics by the pre-synthesizer rock stars can disguise the deep insecurity and essential artificiality of cock rock.

So far, only gay men, who for long have had to think and make choices about maleness, have had the nerve to make a meal of male sexuality.

Women, on the other hand, have a different set of problems. Their femaleness (sexual availability) is never in doubt. For decades women have agonized over their breasts – either too big or too small; their overall body shape – no waist, bum too big, legs too short; and the various component parts of face and hair, all of which have to be altered, enhanced or de-emphasized at regular intervals.[2]

After the whambamthankyouma'am of the sixties, the seventies barely existed in their own right, but were more a kind of dream time when no one wanted to admit the good times had gone, or indeed had never really been. It was also the rising time of the women's liberation movement (mid-century phase) and with it an outspoken refusal of conventional fashion. Instead the women's movement devised its own strict code of appearance which served to speed up the fragmentation of the fashion scene. Immortalized wrongly but concretely by the call to burn bras, the women's movement actually advised a policy of refusal of crippling stiletto heeled shoes, distorting and uncomfortable underpinnings and garments as mere titillation. In a million bathrooms, pores breathed sighs of relief as the trowelled-on layers of moisturiser, foundation, blusher, shaper, powder, eye liner, eye shadow, mascara, lashes, and lipstick were scraped off for the first time in decades.

For the majority, an increasing casualness caused a crisis in the tie industry as young men discarded the item worn by their fathers even for digging the garden or carving the Sunday roast; the latter simultaneously appearing on the endangered species list too, but as victim of inflation rather than fashion. Young women meanwhile ran the gamut of possibilities from the Third World's untapped richness of natural fabrics and ethnic styles, with varied but usually voluminous results. All in all, fashion in the seventies, along with just about every other aspect of life in the west, was, by and large, a mess. Not yet a terrible mess, but a vaguely irritating, vaguely disquieting, formless mess. And that was rather less than the effect these fashion fancies had on Third World local economies. A village-based fabric weaving and dyeing business was quite unused to the sudden whims and vagaries of the capitalist fashion industry. Styles, patterns, colours, decoration, these were perpetual, scarcely changing decade upon decade, until the intervention of the trendsetter, that is; one snap of whose fingers – those sensitive tips continually monitoring the pulse of What's Next – and a community half the world away would be plunged into chaos, ruin, and confusion with bales and bales of unsaleable indigo, mirrored, bell-sleeved embroidered-yoke blouses to show for their efforts. Even now, in the golden age of Live Aid, Band Aid and copycat conscience jerkers such as Comic Relief, a form of this piracy continues, as will be discussed later.

The final realization of the New Depression, brought quietly into the world in May 1979, with the unsuspecting British electorate as midwife and the Thatcher government as proud foster-parent (the natural parents are holed up even now in the boardrooms of the multi-national corporations), coincided with rumblings of some significance from the separate continental plates of the fashion world: after a decade in the doldrums 'fashion' was born again and became a word once more in general use. At one pole, self-identified as the upper echelon, the top people basked in a golden glow revisited by Brideshead and enshrined as 'Sloane'. These were creatures above fashion – or so they liked to think – their look characterized by exquisite dullness and a certain cock-eyed practicality, epitomized by the much favoured Barbour jacket. This tough, all-weather garment, actually designed for field sports wear, features capacious pockets suitable for the stowing of dead birds whilst in Wiltshire, or, more often than not, a hanky, purse and cheque book in town. All this in a subtle and mandatory shade of duck-pooh green with stormproof waxing *de rigueur*. They are also to be seen in neat pleated skirts of the kind to be found at Jaeger and Country Casuals. Pastel striped shirts worn with a clashing regimental or old school tie are most popular with the men, who also lean towards an extremely good and essentially well-worn tweed jacket when not in City duds, the whole accompanied by much 'yahing' in Knightsbridge watering holes.[3]

Their 'look' changes almost imperceptibly; between 1975 and 1985 for instance, a major style point can be seen in the daywear of the young (24-year-old) yah female: in 1975 her swanlike neck might have risen from the neat collar of a Jaeger shirt with single strand of pearls and a scarf tied as cravat in attendance. By 1985 this businesslike severity has given way to a white pie-frill collared blouse from Laura Ashley. The cravat has gone but the pearls are still there. This subtle shift has a great deal to do with the current fashion accessory of an eligible husband rather than an eligible boss. It is also an echo of early Princess of Wales, although she herself – having a much more down-market nose for fashion – moved on long ago. Her patronage of Bruce Oldfield notwithstanding, the Princess' instinct for clothes, once freed from the stultifying dullness of her ultra-yah family, has proved to be more High Street than *haute couture*; witness the acres of Di-wear replication in major chain stores and at weddings and company dances the length and width of the land (and in Australia and the United States too where she is a considerable star). Diana is the only Royal to contend with fashion seriously, however, and even her forays, and subsequent influence on the clothes-buying public, are muted in the end by the perceived conventions of regal dress – a curious amalgam of upper-class conservatism and middle-class respectability.

No such inhibitions stunt the growth of the rag trade at the polar opposite point from the basking Sloanes. The 'look' in this stratum is as considered and serious a matter as it is for any Sloane, and just as rigid. It involves sharply cut three-piece suits, or carefully pressed Italian pastel casuals for the male, and a whole range of feminine clobber in similar icecream pastels for women, including the down-market fashion accent of summer 1984: totally impractical white fabric ankle boots. Gold jewellery for men and women is important at neck and wrist; supplemented by a fine gold chain around the female ankle to complement the Ambre tan achieved in the Canaries in January or one of the Costas in July or August.

Kevin Keegan, the Liverpool soccer-player, was one of the foremost proponents of this look, and footballers' wives were equally glitzy consorts. It is a 'dressed' look; old jeans and misshapen tee-shirts have absolutely no place here; neither, anymore, does the archetypal Keegan perm and glam-rock hairstyle of the seventies, which has now given way to the smoothly sculpted cut with every hair in its layered place. It is a harder look that denies unemployment, actual or probable; it refuses the fact of recession and industrial decrepitude; it stares the social lie of mid-eighties Britain right in the eye and lies right back. The trouble is, for the millions of aspiring *nouveau* nobodies, the fabric and cut of the smart clothes are most often poor. The look is dazzling but transient; in three wearings and a press the stiffness has gone from the material and the cool pastels are greyed. In the sixties, fashion was such that a girl or a fella could afford a new Biba dress or John Stephen shirt every other week, they cost 35s 9d and who cared if they fell apart at the launderette. Now, few can afford to discard the eighties equivalent of disposable fashion, the market stall tat from East End sweat shops, but for those with the readies to spend on real flash (these are the ones who know that LV means Louis Vuitton as well as Luncheon Voucher) never has it been more important to make a clear and expensive statement about the level of personal well-being and survival.

For the chinless chap in his chalk-stripe blue suit, strolling to wherever he performs the daily ritual of being 'something in the City', or the geezer negotiating the early morning traffic in from Romford in his late model Ford and Italian sweatshirt, their individual style says clearly: I am here and this is where I want to be, you can tell exactly what and where that is from looking at me. I'm alright Jack. So be it.

Not so in the seething maelstrom of the middle class which separates the upper and lower. This is where the action is and where social mobility is the norm rather than the exception. The industrial revolution spawned the rise and expansion of the middle class to the point where it was cordially loathed from above and despised or aspired to from beneath. It seemed unstoppable, spreading like green fly and just as blind to the disapproval of fellow citizens. Indeed, the middle class actually came to believe it had inherited the leafy suburban earth. Then came the crunch. When a population gets out of balance with its environment disaster occurs: starvation, ecological collapse, and ultimately, the population falls upon itself for a bit of frantic nibbling and other distressed rat-type behaviour.

By the late seventies the middle class had expanded beyond the point of safety and disaster did strike. At no time in history has there been more opportunity for a middle-class person to rise, yet, at the same time, the possibility of falling to great depths has similarly increased. Each week, as another dodgy expenses claim or redundancy/bankruptcy threat has been weathered, the middle-class person breathes a sigh of relief. However, what many fail to realize is that they are already falling; just because they've passed the nineteenth floor without mishap doesn't mean all will be well when ground zero is reached. Those who have recognized the cool clear rush of air for what it may presage have already taken steps to ensure the accurate placement of a safety net. They too are alright Jack.

Thatcherism has made it compulsory not to care. The rise and rise of the young conservatives and the 'new Right' are proof positive of that. On the other side of the gender fence, 'post-feminism' is the equivalent movement and is having its fifteen minutes in the spotlight. In all of this – in matters appertaining to 'taste', that is – there is a new kind of predatory cruelty in the air, which is now as much a part of the successful survivor (also known as the yuppie) as Paul Smith togs, a Betty Jackson outfit and extruded plastic or brushed aluminium accessories. This cruelty is all to do with looks and style. Not necessarily one's own physical good looks – some of the battalions of the style fascists look as if their mothers should have considered smothering at birth – but the look of others who do not look right (a subtle but fundamental difference).

Michael Foot was one of the earliest victims of this phenomenon. When he attended the Armistice Day service in his donkey jacket, walking stick, and gammy leg, he provoked not only the predictable snorts from the Respectably Dressed camp, but also a less coherent and actually much nastier howling from stylocracy – he looked so *awful*.[4] They said he looked so old, so out of it with his old-fashioned long white locks, pathetic specs, stupid limp, and that cringe-making old coat. Ye gods, no wonder there was a visible shuffle to the right. No matter that Foot was easily the most honourable and sane person to occupy the post of leader of a major political party since who knew when – he just *looked* so gruesome. Funny that no one has ever noticed Mrs Thatcher's knock knees and pigeon toes, but then, the ever considerate television news cameras always film her from the knees up, so who's to know. Then again, it's worth noting the heart throbs of the British parliamentary throng: the Davids (Owen and Steel), and Michael Heseltine, Cecil Parkinson; power is one answer to George Michael (once of Wham!) it seems.

Cecil and Michael are a good point at which to resume a discussion of the new cruelty (if only because there's nothing chic or otherwise important to be said about either). This cruelty, coupled with spinelessness in the case of Cecil Parkinson, is manifest in the privatization of care, the abdication of social responsibility, and the continuing failure of an effective opposition to that thrust. The reason for that failure can be summed up in one word: 'Next'. 'Next' and its ilk – the new wave of bright, white, high-tech clothing emporia – are where the shoppers are in a generation which has suddenly realized it has arrived. This generation was the heart and soul of the caring years: they marched for the National Abortion Campaign (NAC) against White and Corrie; they got their picket line bruises at Grunwick, their degrees from Cambridge, Keele or Warwick. Their collections of fading lapel badges are as much a history of bloody and defiant campaigns as those of any old soldier. Their uniforms were the practical donkey jacket, the denims, and the comfortably sturdy boots in red, yellow, bright blue or green. By vociferous and Herculean effort they shifted society – it seemed – towards a more humane and liberal stance, for a brief, golden moment, then Blat. One morning they woke up to find the Blessed Margaret in charge whilst their own leaders resembled very recently decapitated chickens. More than that, the caring *crème de la crème* were also confronted by the result of what had put them at the forefront of that generation in the first place: they were very good at what they did (teaching, lecturing, theorizing, media of all kinds, creativity of all stripes), and they were becoming, perish the thought, Successful. Which is where 'Next' came in. A 35-year-old high-powered media person might well still be radical after all these years but – denims, a donkey jacket – the collective shudder was almost tangible. 'Next' was the answer, emerging as a tasteful, well-designed phoenix from the grey chalk-striped corpse of the executive look. It provided a subtle bridge to the promised land of successful survival: not overtly trumpeting the triumphant rebirth of conspicuous consumption, but nevertheless easing in an almost unconscious separation from raging youth. A decade earlier the process might have been dubbed distanciation, instead it passed with the merest ribbing and rueful acknowledgement of the new plumage.

And all those who had silently wished with all their might that they might dare challenge the hegemony of dowdiness took to 'Next' like ducks to water.

'Next' is not exactly fashion, not what *The Face* or *Vogue* would recognize as such anyway, but then successful survivors have far more important things to think about than fashion; it is more a statement of lifestyle. It indicates that the wearer understands the notion and the pleasure of quality without being grossly into hedonism; thus the emphasis on fine knits, delicate cottons, good cut and subtle colours. But it is not about a pair of pure silk knickers at a cost that would keep a Sudanese village in staple meals for a month, rather it is sporting cotton, and giving the rest of the money to Oxfam.

Piquantly, for the caring generation, the desire for natural quality materials has also caused a boom in the leather trade: it is an extremely committed and unusual member of the new elite who can resist the high style leather goods that now abound. Once upon a time leather was rugged black cowhide; utilitarian, fetishistically zippered and oozing macho anti-social symbolism. To wear such a garment was an act of aggression in itself. The significance of the new styling is plain to see: the softest, most delicate skins are lavished on the anti-utility, anti-macho blouson. The low cut, dropped shoulder – reminiscent of the courtly fop of other centuries – and the sumptuous colours refuse any connection with the tough twentieth of Brando or the Jets. It is a bold colonization by a group that knows it is – and shows itself to be – in the ascendant.

But in the ascendant from where? Fashion areas are discrete and not democratized, by and large, but where it counts – in the discerning eye of the beholder – it has become an increasingly troublesome factor in determining who's who. So how do you underline who and what you are without actually . . . underlining who you are? If the exclusive is now commonplace (it isn't really, but unfortunately some people don't know that), and if exclusivity can mean so many different things simultaneously, it has now become necessary to look beyond just fashion in apparel to explore what the class-cultural dynamics now are. And that brings us to Foodies – which is where the plebs and the klutzes really fall head first into their shortcrust. To be a Foodie, to be recognized by other Foodies as such – that is the most succulent form of bliss. To be in the ranks of the Foodie Fascists is, quite frankly, the living end.

Foodie-ism is the logical conclusion of the new Me generation, the I'm-alright-Jacks, the professional ex-carers and the trendy new right. To be a Foodie requires self-absorption, self-love, self-delusion, self-confidence; in other words selfishness to a

degree unsurpassed in modern times. Food as a fashion accessory, and a clear statement of social position, began as part of the
original Habitat lifestyle of the early seventies. French (Proven-
cal) and Italian (Tuscany) country cooking came back from villa
holidays along with strings of rapidly moulding garlic, terracotta
floor tiles and peasant-style crocks; all made possible by Elizabeth David and Terence Conran.[5] In recent years, however, the
impassioned and intelligent dinner conversations held over
hearty cassoulets, with rapidly emptying bottles of Beauj' or
Burgundy, have become the subject of satire (primarily and
most successfully by *The Guardian*'s cartoonist Posy Simmonds).
There has also been a growing and restless desire for something
new – and a fresh way of making that vital statement. It led,
tentatively at first, to High Tech with its borrowings from
industrial functionalism; continued with forays into Revived
Deco, the fifties and a nod towards Japan, all eventually
combining in an apparently homogeneous contemporaneity.
Yet, because of its magpie genesis, the new Look was vulnerable
to the sharp-eyed but short of cash. A further dimension –
exclusivity – was required and developed around food. 'Good
taste', ingenuity, intelligence, and energy – the sharply honed
attributes of the would-be successful survivor – all were as
nought in the absence of one other ingredient: hard cash, and
lots of it.

This modern gluttony phase, as distinct from Henry VIII's
fourteen courses of boiled, stewed, roasted, or stuffed beasts,
has simply inverted excess. It began when the long-time hegemony of French cuisine (*cuisine ancienne*) was threatened by the
growing me-consciousness of cholesterol. Jane Fonda led from
the front, to a disco beat, and suddenly Hollandaise was a dirty
word. Nevertheless, the French performed a volte-face worthy
of their government's foreign policy habits, and gave the cardiac
arrest generation *nouvelle cuisine*, or *cuisine minceur* and then
cuisine naturelle, as it quickly became when the first fanatical
asceticism mellowed. Design (colour, shape, and form) and
minimalism of ingredients were the identifying marks of the
new fashion, epitomized by the archetypal and exquisite composition of three pink slices of duck breast laid on a discreet puddle
of clear burgundy coloured sauce, fanned by four mange-touts:
and one thimbleful of puréed carrot placed thoughtfully beside

a similar amount of finely diced kohlrabi; all on a highly polished hexagonal plate (preferably black). The latter was the final authenticating stamp of genuine, no-shit, Foodie-ism.

Piquantly enough, Foodie-ism is as prone to the whims and shifts of favour as the fashion industry itself. The first casualty was the poor Kiwi fruit. At first it was the darling of the dinner table, its cool green flesh with speckled black centre adorning anything and everything, appropriate or otherwise. Its forgiving nature and subsequent popularity proved to be the Kiwi's downfall however: ordinary palates quickly developed a taste for it too and, from being a deli or specialist greengrocery item, requiring hours to track down (note the vital equation: time to spare + money to spare = status) it quickly became a supermarket staple in the expanding section of exotics. So speedily did this reversal occur that *A la Carte* magazine, the glossy guide to fashionable guzzling, was neatly caught twixt correct positions in just one issue. They carried an authoritative piece on how Nobody but Nobody was even thinking Kiwi any more, let alone giving them fridge room. Then, some way further on, in a feature of self-congratulation and vicarious identification, the svelte couple whose lifestyle and dinner party habits were being extolled in full double page (low cholesterol) spread colour for emulation by fellow believers, were clearly seen in full frontal and blatant use of the Kiwi – *plus ça change*, as Clarence Birdseye might have said. Nevertheless, the unfashionable explosion of popularity was just as well for the Kiwi growers of the world, unlike those previously mentioned victims of a passing fad, the madras cotton producers of India.

It is in the area of food, its fashions, and the politics of the industry, that the question of the democratization of fashion – has it happened, yes or no? – can be most sharply seen and answered. And the answer is: no, it has not been democratized, and much more important, the question is irrelevant. While fashion, be it in clothing, home environment, or food, remains the domain of capital and thus primarily the old world, any movement or change within it is meaningless when considered only in relation to itself. The faddish demands of consumers in the moneyed classes wreaks havoc in communities thousands of miles from those modish dinner tables and wardrobes.

Tender green beans grow in soil which could be better

employed providing food for Kenya's peasants. Instead their ill-paid labour means that the beans can be air-freighted at considerable cost to arrive at supermarkets with flavour and crispness intact. Multiply those beans by the fruits and vegetables that we now expect to find on supermarket shelves twelve months of the year at affordable (cheap) prices, and the dilemma of a million malnourished and improverished producers of luxury foods is reflected in every casual purchase.

It is currently fashionable to forswear flesh eating in the interests of animal rights or a lower cholesterol level. Yet the popularity of vegetarianism owes much to the great variety of vegetables and fruits and lower costs achieved by the expanding exploitation of the Third World as a market garden. Questions of health or the rights of animals must be regarded sceptically – unless of course the health and human rights of the labourer in the rice paddy or soybean field count for less – which is probably closer to the truth. It is all very well to point out how much food is munched by an animal in order for it to develop a nice juicy back leg or plump shoulder, but what is rarely taken into consideration is the amount of fertile soil and poorly paid labour required to produce the well-fleshed *habitués* of vegetarian eateries. Plato said, *inter alia*, 'There is no such thing as a free lunch'. And if that is so, then we must consider the question: who pays for our cheap food? And our cheap clothes for that matter. Fashion garments may and do cost a great deal, but break down the component parts of that price and the sum paid for the natural fibre fabrics begins to look a little odd. Nowhere was this cock-eyed way of running a world more poignantly overlooked than in the Band Aid, Live Aid efforts to help the hungry.

It isn't that famine in Africa is actually anything new; the emaciated, wide-eyed child of a decade of Oxfam advertisements is far too familiar to allow that. But the scale of the tragedy exposed by Michael Buerk and his BBC camera crew, and the response it provoked in the no-bullshit, energetic, passionately caring rock musician Bob Geldof meant that old-world attitudes towards the plight of helpless peoples have been given the biggest jolt since the anti-slavery campaigns of the nineteenth century.

Bob Geldof's initiative resulted in the biggest ever sum of

money being wrung out of the haves on behalf of the have-nots; in itself and in isolation an admirable achievement. But Live Aid *et al* cannot be seen in isolation, and that is where it is revealed as less than world-shifting. Geldof insisted, time and again, that Live Aid was not political. By that he sought to avoid alienating the apolitical majority. In that act of letting the congenital non-participants off the hook, a once-in-a-generation chance of politicizing those millions was lost. In turn it meant that governments were let off the hook, because the potentially irresistible pressure of millions of outraged citizens demanding meaningful action and the changes of policy necessary to effect permanent change, was never harnessed and never applied. Instead, governments were able to get away with lending fleets of military transport planes and the real benefactors were the armed forces for whom it was a giant PR exercise and useful practice.

At the same time Common Market food surpluses moulder away all over Europe, and Geldof rounding upon and ranting rudely at those responsible – on the floor of the European parliament – didn't even provoke a blush from those portly and clarety gents. Unwanted sugar is purchased from the Caribbean islands and stockpiled by the United States, who would rather spend billions of dollars annually in this way (to keep the region 'stable') than help those nations develop an alternative and more useful crop – food, for instance. Meanwhile, for one glorious day, millions were able to 'take action' and assuage a whole year's guilt in one go, by writing a cheque, phoning in a credit card number, or trotting along to the local collection point with cash. In return, the nasty pictures of miserable walking skeletons were taken away. (And when they reappeared on screen, another wave of the plastic wands did the trick again.) What no one had to do in all this was think. It didn't occur to the purchaser of the pure cotton Live Aid souvenir tee-shirt to ponder the fact that the Sudan provides a huge amount of the raw cotton demanded by the cheap tee-shirt industry, yet millions of Sudanese citizens have never had a square meal in their lives. It is this attitude of institutionalized and traditional myopia that could lead to an annual monster Aid event, and the continuance, in slightly altered guise, of the Third World as helpless victim that we know and understand.

Not thinking – the energetic refusal to consider anything – is, perhaps, the final and most fundamental characteristic of the successful survivor. The resurgence of 'fashion' as a topic high on the agenda, the preoccupation with food and clothing as matters of status and importance, provides as big and as successful a distraction now as it ever did. It cancels out thought, and in consequence, any possibility of examining the root selfishness. There is a direct parallel between the enormously exaggerated zoot suit of the thirties and forties and the similar styles of the mid-eighties: extravagant quantities of fabric displayed in great draped jackets with huge, padded shoulders.[6] Both fashions occurred in an era of desperate shortage and hardship for millions; zoot-suited dandies were beaten by angry mobs on the streets of New York and the style was finally banned. But although it could be seen as the fashion of protest – what could be more defiant at a time of recession and social decay than seemingly lavish, luxurious clothes? So the argument goes, and it certainly looks more radical than the tired old tat of punk, yet it seems just as likely that there is an unconscious impulse to flaunt having in the faces of those who do not. (And even the most deprived European is rich in the eyes of a citizen of rural Africa, India or South America.) It means that fashion and 'style' will continue to be taken ridiculously seriously. It also means that any kind of thought not in tune with these imperatives is, by definition, unfashionable and will not prosper; which just happens to suit our masters and mistresses very well indeed.

Monetarist economics requires that peoples be dependent. The more a government squawks about 'individual freedoms', 'non-intervention by the state', 'private enterprise', and the other great rallying calls of capital, the more certain one can be of the total control by that state of its citizens. Self-sufficiency is anathema to capitalism and, despite the already mentioned exhortations, is not what is required. A self-sufficient community is a thrombosis, a deadly block to the essential free flow of profits. Before the intervention of the pale-skinned colonists from the north, such social systems were common in the Third World. They had to be: their needs were tailored to the environment and their capabilities for life within it, rather than an acquisition target that related to profitability and plain old materialism. It meant that colonial administrations had an extremely difficult time controlling these peoples. Crucially, they found it almost impossible to make them work for a wage. Unfortunately, the savage wretches had no use for paper money, nor for the apparatus and infrastructure of a moneyed society. Nevertheless, it was not long before control was achieved, and the method used was that which had already and long ago done for the peoples of the old world.

If a person does not want something, the quickest way to instil the necessary desire is to create urgent and inescapable need. One by one, colonial powers imposed taxes that were only payable in hard cash, and the way of life of the gatherer-hunter, the nomad, and the pastoralist was immediately and fatally unbalanced. Dependence was imposed and the rest is history – and green beans, cotton tee-shirts, patronage, and serfdom.

In the old world continual distraction has become the major weapon of control – bread and circuses – or the modern equivalent: football, royalty, and fashion. And fashion is, perhaps unexpectedly, the most powerful of these devices, as it permeates every aspect of daily life via advertising and the media. Is it Martinique or the Seychelles this year? Does your kitchen look like an operating theatre, or are you still cooking in a replica Sienese farmhouse? And how could you buy your kid New Balance trainers when everyone is wearing Reeboks right now?

This self-obsession, the looking inwards and away from the real world, represents a full circle turned in approximately twenty years, and this time it has official sanction and encouragement. In post-industrial Britain both the self-satisfied and the desperate are able to feel justified in clinging on to what they have, or grabbing what they haven't; at no time – even in the middle of the Live Aid telethon – is there a suggestion that there might be more to life than such behaviour. And those in power (or waiting for power) are not about to suggest alternatives. Their power rests on the continuing ability of the old world to refuse to think, see or care about the Third World. And what better way than to render all of those things unfashionable.

The mere existence of fashion as an industry and integral part of capitalism means it is, by definition, undemocratic; and so further underlines the impossibility and futility of the question. 'Sitaki mafi zako bwana' (Don't give me your shit mister –

Swahili slang), as my ayah once said to a door-stepping American missionary.

NOTES

This chapter was written in 1985.

1 Elizabeth Wilson alleges that 'feminism has been as simplistic – and as moralistic – as most other theories in its denigration of fashion', *Adorned in Dreams: Fashion and Modernity*, London: Virago, 1985, p. 13. She goes on to argue that the popular aesthetics of fashion created space for individual expression, but that fashion remains, like capitalism itself, double-edged. We remain, in her final words, 'drawn to it, yet repelled by a fear of what we might find hidden within, its purposes masked by the enigma of its Mona Lisa smile' (p. 247).

2 On some of these alterations in fashion images – producing ideal-image women as boys: 'lean, tall, flat-tummied . . . leggy, tight-bummed, curveless' see 'It's different for girls', in Judith Williamson, *Consuming Passions: The Dynamics of Popular Culture*, London: Marion Boyars, 1986, pp. 47–54.

3 On the Barbour jacket, green wellington boots, the visual style of the 'Range Rover and horsebox crowd', see Deyan Sudjic, *Cult Objects: The Complete Guide to Having it All*, London: Paladin Books, 1985, pp. 84–9.

4 Michael Foot's appearance at the Cenotaph Remembrance Day ceremony in 1981 was given massive press exposure. In his green (not black, but colour daily journalism was not yet with us then) duffle-coat or donkey-jacket, Foot conveyed an ordinary, casual, popular persona, unsuited to the occasion. Walter Johnson, Labour MP for Derby, likened Foot to an out-of work navvy on the way to a demo. The *Daily Telegraph* said that he was like an old man looking for a dog-end. Foot, himself, said later that 'respect for the dead isn't a matter of the clothes you wear'. Ironically, given the hostility generated by his attire, it has been pointed out that 'in his green coat, brown shoes and plaid tie Michael Foot . . . presented a spectacle of peaceful solidarity'. See Patrick Wright, 'A blue plague for the Labour movement? Some political meanings of the national past', in *Living in an Old Country: The National Past in Contemporary Britain*, London: Verso Press, 1985, p. 136.

5 Sir Terence Conran's impact on retailing in Britain has been immense, with fashion conscious facelifts transforming the British High Street and shopping plaza and metamorphosing the old departmental store into a maze of thematized lifestyle choices. Conran's first Habitat store opened in London's Tottenham Court road in 1964. In 1980 the Habitat flotation was valued at £25 million. Mothercare, Richard Shops, and British Home

Stores have since been transformed by Conran's brand of designer-led retailing. See Peter York, 'NW1's first family', in *Modern Times*, London: Heinemann, 1984.

6 On the politics of the zoot-suit in postwar America see Stuart Cosgrove 'The zoot-suit and style warfare', *History Workshop*, 18, (Autumn 1984), 77–91. Zoot-suit riots in 1943 were, Cosgrove suggests, 'An emblem of ethnicity and a way of negotiating an identity. The zoot-suit was a refusal: a subcultural gesture that refused to concede to the manners of subservience' (p. 78); not explicitly or strictly political, the zoot-suit was nevertheless, for many, 'an entry into the language of politics, an inarticulate rejection of the "straight world" and its organisation' (p. 89). For a short account and discussion see Elizabeth Wilson, 'Oppositional dress' in *Adorned in Dreams*, ch. 3, pp. 198–9.

7

Mills and Boon
The marketing of moonshine

DEBORAH PHILIPS

Mills and Boon has become a generic term for a mass popular fiction for women, and with that metonym has defined an area of study of popular cultural forms. Over the past few years, that area has rightly moved from a marginalized position in cultural theory to become a focus for discussions around language, female desire and popular narratives. Early studies of the contemporary romance form tended to offer somewhat disbelieving accounts of the readership figures for a fiction in which marriage was invariably offered as the solution for female anxiety; as in David Margolies' attempts to do this in his application of the tools of literary criticism to the most consistently successful publishing concern in the world.[1] Recent feminist analysis has been more sophisticated, concentrating on the nature of the texts themselves, and on readership surveys; most notably in Rosalind Coward's[2] psychoanalytic account of the pleasure of the text and in Tania Modleski's[3] sophisticated reading of the Harlequin Romance, the Canadian branch of Mills and Boon.

All these studies acknowledge that Mills and Boon is a 'phenomenon in publishing'[4] but little work has been done on the marketing and production side of a phenomenon which claimed a readership of 250 million worldwide during 1984. Studies of the book trade and of the commerce of publishing are of little help here, referring to the romantic paperback variously as 'non-books', 'formula fiction', and 'products manufactured on an assembly line' by 'fiction factories'.[5] While Mills and Boon themselves rigorously deny that they produce 'formula fiction', they remain unique as a publishing house. The only publishing company to sell on the basis solely of their imprint,[6] their sales figures alone are enough to make them a publishing phenomenon. In 1984 the Mills and Boon/Harlequin imprint sold 20 million 'units' (as they refer to their books) to 8.5 million readers in the United Kingdom and Ireland, a figure which is inevitably an underestimation of the actual readership. Any second-hand bookseller or charity shop can testify to a roaring trade in the once read and discarded romance volume. Mills and Boon titles are distributed to and translated by thirteen local language paperback companies; particularly successful export markets are those in the Middle East, North Africa, South Africa, Australia and Europe. With figures like these, analyses of textual pleasures are not enough; some attention to the context in which the texts are produced, reproduced and circulated is necessary.

Mills and Boon is but one of perhaps a dozen companies in what their company profile describes as 'the competitive and fast-growing world of romantic fiction'. The distribution between these various companies, and their international markets is not, however, straightforward. Mills and Boon is the world's largest publisher of romantic paperback fiction, claiming a 65 per cent share of the United Kingdom market. It is also the longest established.

Founded in 1908 by Mr Gerald Mills and Mr Charles Boon, Mills and Boon began life as a general fiction publishing house, with such luminaries on its list as Jack London, P.G.Wodehouse and Horace Walpole. The success of *Secrets* in 1910 (author now generally forgotten) shifted their emphasis, however, to the marketing of popular fiction, and launched a cultural phenomenon. This story, of Mary, in love with a lowly clerk (tall, dark, handsome and actually an aristocrat in disguise) owed a great deal to the sagas of class confusion and frustrated passions to be found in contemporary fiction magazines and the 'penny dreadful novelette', both in its packaging and plot. *Secrets* went on to lend its name to a women's fiction weekly, and for Mills and Boon it laid the basis for a house style.

A recent exhibition of Mills and Boon front covers over seventy-five years of publishing demonstrates that the packaging of their company image, 'the rose of romance', has not varied very much since.[7] The front cover of *Secrets* depicts Mary in dishevelled crinoline anxiously awaiting, while Gothic script informs the reader that 'for too long – for too long they had savoured those anxious moments. . .' Most of the titles have continued to work on a similar principle, whereby the title and image work towards a paradoxical suggestive propriety. While the one may hint at sensuality, the other is conventionally chaste. Thus, the 1932 title *Wife to Christopher* is coupled with an image of a rumpled and pyjamed *ingénue* confronting a stern male profile, while the suggestiveness of *Savage Love* (1982) is tempered by a cover depicting a squeaky clean couple keeping their distance in a daisy field.

From 1910 to 1984, the basic structuring of the iconography has remained remarkably consistent, despite Mills and Boon's own assurance that 'tastes in romantic fiction have altered considerably'. The look of the covers is central to the consistency of the brand name, ensuring that each volume conforms to expectations and that it is concocted to the same recipe. Almost invariably, the cover imagery depicts the male figure in a state of total preoccupation with the woman, while she gazes beyond the frame, engaging the viewer (you, the reader) in a complicit acknowledgement of her sexual power over him. Within this structure, details of dress and hairstyle may vary. The illustrations draw on the imagery of contemporary popular culture and the titles refer to current popular fictions, popular song for example, as in the 1940s reference to the Andrews Sisters' song 'I'll be With You'. The heroine of the forties is likely to look like Rita Hayworth; by the sixties she is close to Audrey Hepburn; and in the seventies, Julie Christie.

The narratives too have a consistent patterning, as the many textual analyses of the genre have demonstrated; from Richard Hoggart's 1957 account of 'Sex in Shiny Packets'[8] to Modleski's[9] Barthesian reading of the codes of the contemporary romance. Modleski offers a useful précis of the plot structure:[10]

the formula rarely varies: a young inexperienced, poor to moderately well-to-do woman encounters and becomes involved with a handsome, strong, experienced wealthy man, older than herself by ten to fifteen years. The heroine is confused by the hero's behaviour, since, though he is obviously interested in her, he is mocking, cynical, contemptuous, often hostile, and even somewhat brutal. By the end however, all misunderstandings are cleared away and the hero reveals his love of the heroine.

In this construction, gleaned from a close reading over a range of texts, Modleski comes close to the guidelines offered by Mills and Boon themselves:[11]

> a simple tale introducing only a few characters besides the hero and heroine is often very successful. . ..If the hero is meant to be a man of authority used to being obeyed, he should be shown as such and the other characters should react to him accordingly. . .

Mills and Boon, however, rigorously deny any charge of producing 'formula fiction'; their instructions to potential authors, as they insist, and as some critics have noted with surprise,[12] add up to little more than an encouragement to 'freshness and originality of approach'. 'Some people' the editorial department writes reproachfully, 'have even tried to reduce [the success of Mills and Boon] to a formula'. Nonetheless, the recommendation to a standard length (about 190 printed pages, between 50,000 and 55,000 words) belies the claim that 'originality, imagination and individuality are the most important qualities in a romance writer'. The tipsheet clearly expects that the aspiring author of romantic fiction is also a reader of the genre, and thus is familiar with its conventions: 'Think of what you as a reader would like to read.' The PR department endorses this: 'You cannot develop a love of writing them if you have not loved reading them'; the conventions of the form are internalized to such an extent by both authors and editors that they are no longer acknowledged as such; they are simply assumed.

The handbook, however, that is recommended for potential writers, *You Can Write a Romance and Get it Published*,[13] breezily enjoins its readers to 'Remember that these are formula books – tried and proved to be successful' and proceeds to outline the characterizations and plotting that are expected of the successful romance. Nonetheless, Mills and Boon are perfectly right in declaring that there is no explicit formula for their texts, for there is no need for one. With an annual rate of 5,000 unsolicited manuscripts, 90 per cent of which are turned down for publication, the editors are in a good position to choose exactly what is required for 'the rose of romance' brand-name. Editorial decisions are backed by extensive market research, and manuscripts selected and edited according to 'whether the story lives up to the high standards that Mills and Boon readers have set for us. . .we can't please every one of our readers all the time, but it isn't for want of trying!'[14] A 'Mills and Boon Romance' is defined in editorial terms more by virtue of what it is not, than by its own narrative conventions, which are unstated; 'we reject anything that is obviously not a romance', the PR office states, but when pressed on what constitutes 'romance', their response is 'no murder, blood, guts or gore, and nothing pornographic either; there's nothing romantic about pornography'.[15]

For the critic concerned to identify the narrative structures of the contemporary romance form, there is actually no need to apply a semiological analysis to the twelve volumes of a Mills and Boon monthly output, or to draw upon the morphology of the folk-tale, as some theorists have undertaken. What either of these methods might produce would not be far removed from the Silhouette 'tipsheet' for authors. Silhouette is an American company, producing the transatlantic version of the Mills and Boon romance, and not unrelated to the British company, or to the Canadian equivalent, Harlequin. They are, however, rather more explicit in their demands of the romantic novel.

The heroine of the romance novel is presented at a moment of transition in her life, an isolated figure; the romance narrative depicts *young* women at a point of defining themselves as adult women, a definition that must come from the heroine in the absence of any supportive network:

> The Silhouette heroine is young (18–24). . . . She is basically an ingenue . . . . Though she wants to work and often plans to after marriage . . . her home and children always come first. She is almost always a virgin . . . . She is usually without parents or a 'protective' relationship . . . . She is starting a career, leaving college, unhappy with her present job or too caught up with her work – anyway, she's open to change and accepts adventure, though often not by choice.[16]

Other women in the narrative may not be friends, but are always constructed as rivals for male attention: 'She does not consider herself a beauty and this element is used to play off against the beauty of the other woman (women) . . . .' *The Other Woman* has a category to herself in Silhouette's construction of the necessary elements of the romance novel, an indication of the extent to which she is considered to be an essential ingredient: 'The Other Woman Usually means over sophisticated, well groomed. She NEVER gets our hero.'[17] 'Our hero' (possessed by the reader?) has the single defining characteristic that he is financially viable, and therefore a desirable proposition in the heroine's search for professional, personal and economic status:[18]

> *The Hero* Older, arrogant, self-assured, masterful, hot tempered, he is capable of violence, passion and tenderness . . . . He is always older than the heroine, usually in his early or mid-30s, rich, successful in the vocation of his own choice . . . he is above all virile.

Whether stated or unstated, these conventions remain true for all Mills and Boon, Silhouette, and Harlequin romances. The conventions are so rigorous that any break with them would require a new genre; the editorial leaflet makes this clear enough:

> Sex and romance are the key ingredients to these books and these elements cannot be stressed too strongly. Nothing in these romances should be vulgar or explicit . . . . It is all right for the hero and heroine to go to bed together, although if they actually make love before they are married, a wedding should follow immediately. Bringing them to the brink of consummation and then forcing them to retreat either because of an interruption or because one or both of the lovers suffer from doubt or shame is an appropriate Silhouette device.

Clearly, one of the invincible conventions of the 'Romance' label is that desire should not be consummated before at the very least a proposal of marriage has been secured by the heroine – 'the only pain permitted is the sweet pain of unfulfilled desire'. . .

The consummation of that desire, and the admittance of 'erotic sensations' on the part of the heroine represents such a break with the romance genre that it requires a new form, the development of a sub-genre. Silhouette also provides this with their new 'Desire' label, which was developed in response to 'consumer demands for a new series'. The 'Desire' volume is distinguished from the 'Romance' with a different packaging and series brand-name. Like the 'Romance' format, it issues twelve volumes monthly. The 'Desire' heroine is constructed as older, more assured of her status, and, therefore, more open to sexual advances:[19]

> a mature, capable woman in her twenties who has a strong sense of her own individuality . . . . Desire intends to mirror real lives of modern women . . . . Sexual encounters – which may include nudity and lovemaking even when the protagonists are not married – should concentrate on highly erotic sensations . . .

The existence of the 'Desire' category in the publishing of romantic fiction acts as a filter and displacement for those elements that could challenge the conventions of the romance, thus leaving the romantic formula unchanged. The resources which go to make such a development possible are bound up with the processes of the marketing and the production of the romance volume. Any cultural practice involving consumer goods is based on a commodity relation. For Marx, a commodity is:[20] an object outside us, a thing that by its properties satisfies human wants of some sort or another. The nature of such wants, whether, for instance, they spring from the stomach or from fancy, makes no difference. The use-value of 'fancy' is clearly there for the Mills and Boon novel, which further satisfies Marx's criteria for the 'commodity' in completely obliterating the actual process of production. The writer of the novel is an absent category. Mills and Boon are bought and sold on the basis of a brand-name, not an individual author. However it may be constructed, the romance formula can ensure such a consistency of product that the texts are marketed through a standing order principle through retail outlets, ranging from supermarket checkouts to station bookstalls. The language of the marketing echoes exactly that of any supermarket brand-name: 'our readers perceive us as a brand of books with a special flavour and image'. Like Cadbury's chocolate, the recipe and packaging of the Mills and Boon volume may not have altered much since its inception, but the methods of marketing and distribution have changed dramatically since the early days of the twopenny library.

The publishing history of Mills and Boon emulates precisely that of the developments in mass market publishing in Europe and America; it may be an extreme but the dating of shifts in their ownership and distribution structure conforms to the major historical changes in the publishing industry. From the small private London company of 1908, Mills and Boon have become part of a million-dollar industry.

What made this possible was the 'paperback revolution', usually dated from the Allen Lane publication of the Penguin titles in 1935. The 'revolution' refers not only to the paper binding of volumes (which had already occurred in the nineteenth century) but much more to a shift in distribution methods, away from specialist outlets for books. The postwar expansion in the book market allowed for a wider distribution (with paper covers, at lower prices) and books became a commodity to which the newly developed sales techniques and marketing methods could be applied. Those small owner publishers who could not cope with the new financial pressures were forced to expand, to merge with other larger companies, or go bust. It was in the thirties, with the expansion of the commercial library (Boots lending library, for example) that Mills and Boon concentrated their attention on the production of romance fiction, published in cheap brown bindings.

As the lending library market began to subside under an increasing onslaught of cheap paperback titles, Mills and Boon themselves moved into paperback production. And it was with this development that the company expanded internationally; it prompted Harlequin, a Canadian based publishing house to approach Mills and Boon for the North American rights to some of their titles. This proved to be so commercially successful that it became a reciprocal arrangement, with Mills and Boon importing Harlequin titles. This arrangement still stands, although a clear distinction between the two companies can no longer be made; in 1972 Harlequin and Mills and Boon merged, and with that merger, the mass market for paperback romance really took off; between 1972 and 1974, sales of Mills and Boon titles rose from 27 million to 40 million.

The merger of Mills and Boon and the Harlequin imprint acts as a paradigm for the sequences of company mergers and takeovers that took place in the sixties and seventies in publishing in Britain and America, a period in which the ownership structures of publishing underwent a profound shift away from specialist producers and distributors of books, towards groups of publishing houses owned largely by corporate organizations whose primary interests were not in publishing. Between 1958 and 1970, there were 307 publishing mergers in America alone, of which 224 were ultimately to be owned by communications groups. By the mid-seventies, almost all hardback and paperback publishers were owned by conglomerates, and by 1976 there was no independent paperback publisher. In 1976, 81 per cent of total American paperback sales were controlled from eight large houses. Companies involved in the takeover of paperback houses in America between 1970–7 included: the Hearst Corporation, RCA, CBS, Warner Communications and Gulf and Western; all mass communications conglomerates, with interests in film, television and newspapers. This trend towards the concentration of publishing into corporate organizations meant a centralization and Americanization for most European publishers too. In Britain, the early 1970s had marked a crisis in publishing with rising print and production costs. With cutbacks in library purchases of books, no publisher could afford to withstand the commercial potentials that the mergers represented, nor the opportunities for synchronizing publicity that the video, television, press and film links of the communications corporations could provide.

For Harlequin, this shift in the production and distribution of books was marked by the Torstar Corporation taking over a 52 per cent share of their company stock in 1975. The Torstar Corporation, a Canadian based communications organization, was itself an amalgamation; in 1967, the Toronto Star Ltd and Charth Investment and Publishing Company Ltd had merged to form the largest communications conglomerate in Canada. It is, according to the Torstar 1983 business profile:[21]

a broadly based information and entertainment communications company. Its operations include The Toronto Star, Canada's leading metropolitan daily newspaper, Harlequin

Enterprises, publisher of romantic fiction; Metroland Printing and Publishing, commercial printers and publishers of community newspapers and consumer advertising supplements; the Miles Kimball Company, direct mail marketers of gift items; Comac Communications, publisher of controlled circulation magazines; and Infomart, pioneers in developing two-way electronic data-based communications.

Property: Owns real estate for parking, storage, garage etc. . .

By 1981 Torstar had acquired the whole of Harlequin Enterprises Ltd, and as part of the Harlequin Overseas subsidiary, Mills and Boon was included in the deal. Or, as the Mills and Boon press office prefers to put it, the company 'came under the wing of the Canadian-based Torstar group'.

In 1984, Torstar's net income was £5,337,000 Canadian dollars, more than Spar Aerospace (Canada), or Slater Steel Industries, making Torstar one of the largest Canadian profit making enterprises. And in the same year, Silhouette became part of the group. The technology that Torstar could bring to the romance form, through its various subsidiaries, allowed for an international distribution and advertising network. With their commercial interests across the media, coverage for the romance media in women's magazines, television stations, and newspapers was assured. So, too, were film and video links. Authors belonging to either Silhouette, Harlequin or Mills and Boon could now be serialized in popular women's fiction magazines, and Anne Mather's Mills and Boon title *Leopard in the Snow* became a 'major motion picture', distributed throughout the United Kingdom and North America as an 'Anglo-Canadian Co-production'.

It was simultaneous with the involvement of Torstar that romance took off as a 'publishing phenomenon', with a confidence that could ensure print runs of several million for each title. In the two years between 1972 and 1974, the sales of Mills and Boon titles rose by 13 million. By 1981, a Harlequin trade advertisement could boast that 'In eight years, sales have increased by 800% and research shows that the romance category can easily double.' Sales of the Harlequin group worldwide now total over 200 million volumes. Advertisements for a video series entitled 'Images of Love' began to appear in women's magazines and in trade journals in 1984. Their description of the titles is reminiscent of the brief for Mills and Boon, Harlequin and Silhouette novels: 'Soft-centre, not soft-core, these beautifully made films combine strong plots with a good dash of unabashed romance . . . . Stock Images of Love and we promise you'll be crying. All the way to the bank.'[22]

If it is true that 'Bestsellers are not born, they are made. And they are made largely through promotion . . . successful promotion through movies, television and various tie-ins in turn, guarantee the sale of books to the public',[23] then the Torstar corporation has the resources for that promotion. The company that owns the rights to *Leopard in the Snow* also owns and controls the newspaper, magazine, television video and film networks appropriate to promotion needs. For a romance title there is no necessity for 'a long pitch to convince outsiders from book-clubs to print houses and the movies',[24] those networks are part of the same corporation.

No Mills and Boon title has less than a print run of almost 100,000, a figure that makes most bestseller lists look like chickenfeed. Every romance title is a best seller, most are assured of sales of 'several million books worldwide through the Harlequin network'. Each title may have a short life-span, but its sales are assured. In America, it is estimated that 25 per cent of paperback sales are through supermarkets; the romance title is rigorously marketed like any other brand-name; like chocolate bars, the newest variety is given prominence on the sales stands. In a strict order of preferential treatment, the newest titles are placed on the top rack, and moved down weekly, until the volumes on the bottom rack are superseded and returned to the publisher for pulping. This method of retail distribution operates throughout Britain and America; titles are sold to news-agents, drugstores and other outlets on a sale or return basis.

It is not true of the romance form that 'once you've read one you've read them all'. Mills and Boon are sufficiently confident of the compulsion of the romance formula to offer six free novels as an introduction to their 'Rose of Romance Book Club'. The contemporary romance novel is a self-perpetuating genre, both textually and in its modes of marketing, offering in its texts a perpetually unfulfilled 'Desire' that can only be answered through the purchase of a new volume. And the brand name acts as a reassurance to the reader that the terms of that salacious propriety, Romance, will not vary. Like the detective novel, the romance abides by a hermeneutic code, in which the outcome is always assured. For the thriller, the solution to the narrative's enigma is the unveiling of the criminal; for the romance, it is what Germaine Greer described as the 'Almighty kiss'.[25] As Yvonne McManus, in her advice to aspiring writers explains:[26] 'the thing that keeps your reader turning pages is to find out what happens to make them realise they're meant for each other. . .you've got to keep the reader wondering how it'll all come to pass'. The advertisement for the video equivalent of the Mills and Boon novel declares: 'Because they're a branded series, your customers will see one and keep coming back for more (it may be a new concept in video, but publishers like IPC and Mills and Boon have been doing very nicely on it for years';[27] thus heralding a new departure for the form.

The pleasures of the romance novel are not dissimilar from those of the chocolate bar; naughty but nice. The Mills and Boon, Harlequin or Silhouette brand name assures a consistent recipe and packaging, which, like Cadbury's, has remained fundamentally unchanged since the product was first conceived and marketed. Mills and Boon is a paradigm for understanding the marketing of literature as a commodity, and that market must be accounted for in any understanding of the 'pleasures of the text'. Analyses of the texts themselves are insufficient to account for the phenomenal sales figures of the romance genre. With 250 million volumes sold annually, Mills and Boon is the source of a construction and perpetuation of a particular concept of female desire and sexuality that can always be assuaged through the consummation of a heterosexual romance.

The romance novel is unique in popular culture, as a narrative form that is produced and marketed exclusively for a female audience. These narratives consistently address material conditions and contradictions in women's lives; and the international sales figures indicate that those contradictions are not restricted to women in the western cultures of Britain and America. The negotiation of reputation; how not to be defined as either a 'slag' or a 'drag' by men; the juggling of male expectation with the pursuance of a career: these are all questions that the romantic novel consistently deals with in its narratives. 'We offer the literature of reassurance' states the press office for Mills and Boon: a reassurance that has been marketed with resounding success, a success that would not have been possible for Mills and Boon or for Harlequin without the intervention and resources of the Torstar Corporation. The material conditions of production and distribution have been crucial for the perpetuation of the romance form, and the romance form continues to thrive because it so well answers the commercial demands of a mass-market paperback and communications industry.

NOTES

1 David Margolies, 'Mills & Boon : guilt without sex', *Red Letters*, 14, (1982), 5–13.
2 Rosalind Coward, *Female Desire: Women's Sexuality Today*, London: Paladin, 1984.
3 Tania Modleski, *Loving With a Vengeance: Mass-Produced Fantasies for Women*, New York: Methuen, 1982.
4 Margolies, 'Mills & Boon: guilt without sex', p. 5.
5 See, for example, L.A. Coser, C. Kadushin, and W.W. Powell, *Books – the Culture and Commerce of Publishing*, New York: Basic Books Inc., 1982; Michael Lane, *Books and Publishers*, London: Lexington Books, 1980; Thomas Whiteside, *The Blockbuster Complex – Conglomerates, Show Business and Book Publishing*, Connecticut: Wesleyan University Press, 1980.
6 It is interesting to note that the same may be becoming true for texts published by Virago and the Women's Press, also publishing companies which cater to a female readership, and which produce texts written almost exclusively by women.
7 'The changing face of romance', Mills and Boon sponsored exhibition at the Barbican Centre, London, 1984.
8 Richard Hoggart, *The Uses of Literacy*, London: Chatto & Windus, 1957.
9 Modleski, *Loving with a Vengeance*.
10 ibid., p. 36.
11 Mills and Boon, editorial leaflet, 1985.
12 See, for example, Margolies, 'Mills & Boon: guilt without sex'; Hoggart, *The Uses of Literacy*; Ann Snitow, 'Mass market romance: pornography for women is different', in *Desire: The Politics of Sexuality*, London: Virago, 1984, pp. 258–76.
13 Yvonne McManus, *You Can Write a Romance and Get It Published*, London: Coronet Books, 1984.
14 Mills and Boon, editorial leaflet.
15 Mills and Boon press office, 1985.

16 Silhouette, editorial leaflet, 1985.
17 ibid.
18 ibid.
19 Silhouette 'Desire', editorial leaflet, 1985.
20 Karl Marx, *Capital*, London: Lawrence & Wishart, 1977, vol. 1, p. 43.
21 Moody's International 1983.
22 Images of Love, trade advertisement, 1984.
23 Coser, Kadushin, Powell, *Books*, p. 221.
24 ibid.
25 Germaine Greer, *The Female Eunuch*, London: Paladin, 1971.
26 McManus, *You Can Write a Romance*, p. 232.
27 Images of Love, trade advertisement, 1984.

8

Tainted love

The influence of male homosexuality and sexual divergence on pop music and culture since the war

JON SAVAGE

In a then notorious homosexual novel of 1953, *The Heart in Exile* – whose pink spine was a crucial signifier in those treasonable times – Rodney Garland's hero visits the Lord Barrymore and falls, as one will, into reverie:

> The young were living mostly in exile, but exile gave them possibilities of which they had seldom dreamed before. Everything around them became slightly abnormal, the new occupation, the environment, the dress they wore, the physical and emotional climate. The concrete things of the past, like postal-addresses, time-tables, road-signs, became less probable and friendships became all-important because it was unlikely that they would last. Nearly all of them, willingly or unwillingly, became creatures of the moment, living in an everlasting present; the past had vanished, the future was uncertain.[1]

In 1953, such a territory was alien, almost invisible, a schizo-world of as yet unimagined pleasure; yet today it is disturbingly familiar, this condition described by Jameson as living 'in a perpetual present and in a perpetual change that obliterates traditions of the kind which all earlier social formations have had in one way or another to preserve'.[2] Although couched in the typically occult language of the time, Garland's prescient account catches society at a crossroads: those young homosexuals adrift in a postwar landscape without signs may now be seen as harbingers of a new way of life and a new economic order – variously described as pop culture, youth culture or the Teen age – which stand at the heart of 'late, consumer or multinational capitalism'.[3]

Sexuality lies emblazoned across the surface of pop culture in the careless whispers of countless love songs, yet this apparent confirmation of dominant sex codes – heterosexual, same-age, monogamous relationships – cloaks a far more ambiguous relationship to sex and gender that illustrates well the ambiguous standing that pop culture has within our society. In England pop culture has a simultaneous function – inextricably intertwined to a degree unmatched anywhere else in the world – of exploitation and expression: exploitation as the product of an industry at the sharp end of the new conditions of capitalism, expression by virtue of its position – which has occurred by default – as the main area of activity in our society which freely admits voices of both youth and change. The tension between these two contradictory functions has provided the space within which new signs and new attitudes can break through; it also, depending on which function is in the ascendant, explains pop culture's vacillation to date between empty reaction and charged visions of possible futures.

These complexities are totally lost to the dominant culture. In this world pop music is isolated and exploited as a younger, sexier version of traditional showbiz, where culture tycoons like Maxwell of the *Mirror* or Murdoch of the *Sun* fight for the services of a man, John Blake, whose gossip columns reinforce pop music's most banal surfaces. Alternatively the pop industry is seen as an amoral instigator – so unlike Fleet Street! – of whichever moral panic is being associated with youth this week: 'Never mind morals or standards . . . the only notes that matter come in wads'[4] ran an emblematic headline after the public's 'discovery' of Punk Rock in December 1976. From this current perspective, pop is either Light Entertainment – taking its place as a cheeky yet responsible apprentice in the adult world of showbiz – or tawdry trash that is beneath contempt. It isn't important; pop is thus marginalized, and whatever it has to say of greater import is ignored.

Yet this you would expect; it is one of the hallmarks of the dominant culture, after all, that it is about thirty to fifty years behind what is actually occurring in the world in the present time. The way in which popular culture communicates – when it does – is as important as what it communicates. At worst this means a culture of style over content, with which we are engaged at present; at best a visionary flash, the secular equivalent of a miracle, which can transform people's lives. Pop culture thus works through an amalgam of attitude, inspiration, intuition and detail (for nobody is as obsessive as the true pop fan, whose obsession is rarely given the respect it deserves); crucially, it works best not in public, where the terms of discourse are set by the dominant culture, but in private space. Hence the failure of most issue-based, formally political pop, hence the way in which popular music and culture as 'modern leisure, is transformed into the very fabric of personal life, the most significant context in which we have the chance to affirm ourselves'.[5]

What is then ignored in most accounts of consumer capitalism is the way in which consuming can be an active as well as a passive choice, or in this context how people can *use* pop music. It is thus fitting that nowhere has pop been so active as in that area so firmly delineated as 'private' by the dominant culture – and woe betide those who, like politicians in sex scandals, mix the public and the private, or otherwise transgress the narrow boundaries – namely those of sexuality and gender. It is above all the body, enveloped in sound, in dance, that stands at the cross-roads of popular music and leisure time;[6] here the word 'Love' that is omnipresent in the pop lexicon reads not so much as a romantic cliché but as a coded entry into the world of the private, into the world of pleasure and self-discovery.[7]

This is patently not an area that has been officially acknowledged. Even in its inchoate beginnings, pop culture was forced to turn to the sexually divergent or avant-garde, for it was only in the spaces that they inhabited that this new world could be recognized and could develop. Pop's relationship to different ideas of sexuality and gender is thus deep and intricate: although it frequently denies it, it is from the milieux and sensibilities of the sexually divergent that pop culture draws much of its sustenance. And occasionally, when the market or those subterranean voices demand, they will get their due accord before dropping back out of sight. For that instant, for many people, the world will have been redefined.

In the perpetual 'Dunkirk of the spirit'[8] of the immediate postwar period, 'dressiness was confined largely to homosexuals. Since they were cut off from the mainstream anyway, both sexually and socially, they had nothing to lose by outrageousness in their clothes'.[9] By 1953, the refusal that such dressiness displayed had spread to a hitherto unexpected and unexplained location: the working-class boys and girls who, congregating around various London centres, had assumed what had been up until a couple of years previously a homosexual style, the Edwardian Look. This had been floated in 1948 by the clothing establishment as a discreet gentleman's fashion harking back to the golden days before 'socialism and formica',[10] but had been quickly coopted and camped up by the gay underground; the more exaggerated aspects of this style caught the first Edwardians' eye and, together with the Western Look that pervaded their favourite culture, American cowboy films, it formed the first youth style proper.

If homosexuals had sartorially predicted the first Teds, then both they and these first teenagers inhabited the same psychic and social space. Both were lying – as Garland's novel makes clear – beneath the surface of an England where 'the same mood of an old upper and upper-middle class order safely restored dominated almost every area of national life'.[11] Under the patriarchy of Winston Churchill, homosexuals and teenagers were not marginal but invisible, except when they surfaced as victims of the latest moral panic, of which there were many in those days. Both states were regarded as not only undesirable but criminal: after the Burgess/Maclean scandal in 1951, police prosecutions against homosexuals reached a peak in 1953/4, while the scare headlines accorded by the press to the Clapham Common murder in the summer of 1953 lodged in the public's heads the equation that people who wore Edwardian clothes would knife you at the drop of a hat. Such was the penalty of divergence.

It is worth emphasizing quite how serious a refusal this finery of the first Edwardians represented. Andy Medhurst locates as 'the central visual themes of the 1950s male pin-up in Britain – what one could call the hegemony of the tweed jacket or the ideology of gentrification'.[12] The dominant male of the period, like Kenneth More or Michael Dennison, was sexless, full of 'common sense',[13] above all, decent: the exaggerated nature of the Edwardians' dress, its appropriation from middle-class roots, and the obsessional nature with which they pursued it, all spoke of people who did not *know their place*. Having transgressed these invisible, but powerful, boundaries, the Teds were fair game for anything that could be thrown at them. 'A similar interpretation of a sexual twist (homosexuality) in the make up of Teddy Boys could be ascribed to their excessive interest in their own and each other's clothes and hair-styles, such as the habit of the early Teddy Boys of having their hair waved.'[14] To contemporary commentators like Fyvel, the only other section of the population who behaved in such a way were the homosexuals; what he didn't know was that this pursuit of pleasure, and concentration on self, were exactly those traits that would become desirable, and eventually, socially acceptable, with the extraordinary success of Elvis Presley and the Teen age that followed.

'The dam had burst';[15] the contemporaneous impact of Elvis Presley and Suez in 1956 washed away the vestiges of pre-war England. The new Prime Minister, Harold Macmillan, combined old-style Tory patriarchy with a definitely new-style endorsement – in the famous (and misquoted) 'You've never had it so good' speech of July 1957 – of the developing consumer culture that was being imported from America, of which the Teen age was an important spearhead. This new consumer culture sold televisions, washing machines, fridges; the new popular music – whose pulling power Elvis Presley had demonstrated so devastatingly – sold sex. Public sexuality now belonged to the young, and where they led, the rest of society was to be trained to follow.

But this commercial peg: 'All industry knows that to please the teenagers is the golden way to big dividends',[16] contained all manner of occluded and contradictory messages. It's quite clear, as Little Richard hitches his pants and ecstatically rolls his eyes in 'Don't Knock The Rock', that rock 'n' roll represented an explosion of black consciousness into mainstream white American culture. Loaded as it was with connotations of the body and pleasure – analogous to homosexuals in the United Kingdom, cast as out-groups, as bogeymen by the dominant culture, but attempting to fashion their own necessarily coded, meanings – rock 'n' roll was at first tolerated, because of its economic attractiveness, and then actively suppressed. But by then the damage was done; the demons had escaped Pandora's box and, not for the first time, the demands of *laissez-faire* capitalism had subverted traditional moralities. These nuances were lost in the

United Kingdom, where rock 'n' roll was seen as another exotic American import like chewing-gum or cowboy films; its explosive sexuality was seen as the key selling point of this product – like the X-tail-fin on a new Ford – rather than as a process, and was thus isolated and marketed accordingly.

The selling of this new product was accommodated within the existing structures of an industry used to selling the pale imitations of American pop. This resulted in farce: 'I have never forgotten seeing footage of a British manager which began on his moccasined feet, wafted over his monogrammed door mat, and ended up opposite the sofa on which lounged five of his charges, scowling greasily'.[17] Early English pop was riddled with homosexuality and that sensibility which we would now call camp: partly this was due to homosexual familiarity with those areas of human activity which were now being exploited, and partly to the early music industry's seedy beginnings on the fringes of established showbusiness. This marginality is well described in Peter Wildblood's chapter on 'Perry and Bella' in *A Way of Life*: 'the strange world of people who for one reason or another are out of step with the times',[18] or by Colin MacInnes:

'I heard one of your arias on the steam, last evening', I told him, '"Separate Separates", if I remember. Very nice'. 'Which of the boy slaves was it sung it? Strides Vandal? Limply Leslie? Rape Hunger?' 'No, no . . . Soft-Sox Granite, I think it was. . . .' 'Oh, that one. A Dagenham kiddy. He's very new'.[19]

This sensibility, which MacInnes, as a homosexual outsider, was perfectly suited to capture, underlay the kind of sexuality that English pop was selling. The music industry packaged rock 'n roll – noting the charged effect that Elvis Presley had on his fans – as pop for a new generation of economically enfranchised young women, grafting extreme youth and a generic look – greasy hairstyle, sideburns, a sallow pout – onto the 'romantic' stylings of earlier idols. Yet the milieu within which British pop operated undercut then dominant modes of masculinity: 'Images of men must disavow this element of passivity (caused by putting the body on display) if they are to be kept in line with dominant ideas of masculinity-as-activity'.[20] As befits the objects of homosexual desire at that time, this new generation of teeny-bop pop stars were 'boy slaves' – more Limply Leslie than Rape

Hunger – and failed to emerge from the pin-up process with their masculinity intact. Instead they took on the passivity of the adored object in an equation – homosexual desire translated into female adoration – that has haunted English pop ever since from the Beatles through the Bay City Rollers to Wham!; as one of Wham's managers, Simon Napier-Bell, makes explicit in his memoir of the sixties:

> It was surprising that an industry generating so many millions of pounds was prepared to use little more than the manager's sexual tastes as its yardstick of talent. Most of the managers were men and most of them liked boys. A few of the managers were women and one or two of them liked girls[21]

But this 'feminization' only went so far: 'Still only boys for singers? No signs of any breasted thrushes?' 'We've tried one or two of them, but the kids just don't want to know. No, for the minors, it's still males'.[22]

It is now possible to see the desperate farce of late fifties pop as a first tremulous step towards the liberalization to come: the publication of the Wolfenden Report in September 1957 recommended the limited legalization of homosexuality, while a newer generation of pop stars, like Adam Faith or the female icon, Helen Shapiro, pushed in from the margins towards society's centre. The emergence of the satire movement in the early sixties 'marked a new stage in the social revolution': 'Like the pop artists (and the pop singers yet to come) the satirists formed part of a new generation coming to the surface in English life, one young enough to have been moulded by the garish, anarchic and youth-conscious atmosphere of the late fifties . . .'[23] It was fitting, granted pop's liberation of the private, that the sexuality that had lain for so long as 'private' under the dominant culture now became public with shocking force: 'I noticed that several of the men and women present had weals across their back and buttocks. Others had shocking bruises.'[24] Mandy Rice-Davies and Christine Keeler's revelations about the seamy underbelly of England's public life rocked the government and effectively ended the Tory Party patriarchy: 'The upper-class. . .image of Mr Macmillan himself had acted as a catalyst for all the aggression that was to unleash the New England of Mr Wilson and the Beatles.'[25]

Youth and pop music now occupied centre stage in society – to a degree that is now inconceivable. The Beatles were courted by leaders of both parties: Harold Wilson won, corralling them at the Variety Club luncheon of 1964, and ensuring their MBEs – for export services – in late 1965. For a while, the most successful pop groups had the power to shift mass consciousness to an unprecedented degree and this confidence expressed itself in a plethora of new sexualities brought into the public eye, offered up for public consumption and then put into practice in people's lives. The variety of sexual identities then possible took control of the 'private' out of the hands of the dominant culture; it is this fact, just as much as the actual physical acts, that made the 'permissive' society (as it was called by the right) a phenomenon to be at first feared, and finally to be held up as what was wrong with Britain.

Androgyny – of an explicit and active kind – was the key sexuality of the mid-sixties. It began as fashion – signified by the growth of long hair for men – and ended up as politics. The explicit blurring of the male and female into a different, 'third' sexuality represented a quantum leap from fifties timidities yet it originated from a similarly homosexual milieu and sensibility: the difference was in scale and in sophistication. This was epitomized by the youth style that underpinned this stage of the sixties: Mod:

> The only other person we saw was a tall, well-dressed young negro who bought a pair of the coloured denim hipster trousers. The negro was obviously homosexual and I realized that homosexuals had been buying that stuff for years. They were the only people with the nerve to wear it, but in the early sixties the climate of opinion was changing, the Mods were wearing the more effeminate and colourful clothes of Carnaby Street.[26]

Like the Edwardians, the Mods assumed what had been an exclusively and outrageously homosexual style and used it as a key to cross into the 'private' space of the body and of self-discovery; unlike their forebears, they were far more intimately involved with black culture, from the new black music of the Tamla and Sue labels, to the 'bluebeat' clubs that were opening, as an index of Britain's more visible black community. Most Mods weren't gay – although Peter Burton writes well of the cross-over between the two sub-cultures[27] – but to any person unfamiliar with their ideas about pleasure and self, they certainly looked it: 'Mods were more interested in themselves and each other than in girls. . .there was a time when Mod boys used make-up and mascara'.[28] Although carefully coded, the Mods' narcissistic flamboyance eventually transgressed the norms of the dominant culture and they became the objects of their very own custom-made moral panics. The first, the 'Mods And Rockers' violence, wasn't new, but the second one, a whole new form of self-discovery, was: drugs.

Parallel with this style ran the cultural and financial activities of Britain's new pop aristocracy. Starting from the twin poles of the Beatles and the Rolling Stones, the new, more articulate, and assertive, breed of pop musicians used androgyny as their 'private' device to achieve their 'public' ambitions: financial, sexual and social freedom. The Beatles began in the showbiz style of a previous generation – homosexual manager, 'variety' type packaging, 'romantic' lyrics – but quickly expressed a fresh sexuality that supplemented their huge class impact: 'neither boys-together aggression nor boy-next-door pathos,'[29] they challenged pop's previous masculine division between Stud and passive Boy Slave. Similarly, after passing through, in Keith Richard's words, 'a heavily camp phase', the Rolling Stones quickly widened out the Beatles' androgyny into something at once more perverse and disturbing. From the macho stereotyping of their earlier material, coded rhythm 'n' blues threats taken out of context, their polymorphous presence – Jagger's rubber lips, Keith Richard's aggressive stance, Brian Jones' perfect page-boy cut – soon signified a deep and fundamental challenge to the dominant culture.

What had begun as a process – the Mods' narcissism and the Beatles' androgyny illustrating new ways of regarding gender and the self – quickly became a sales device (Beatles' wigs, etc); yet as this public exploration of sexuality met no barriers and the blurring effect of drugs took hold, it turned back, in 1966/7, into an ever deeper examination of more 'private' layers of sexual divergence, of which homosexuality had always been the most easily codified. The Who's 'I'm A Boy' turned mod narcissism and profound identity confusion into an almost psychoanalytic parable: as they leered 'Put this frock on, little boy', they confronted you with how rigidly constructed society's ideas of gender were. Pink Floyd, in the vanguard of the drug evangelists, matched distorted, bending music to a simple, child-like tale of a transvestite, 'Arnold Layne'; as Syd Barrett's deadpan vocals offered no judgement, the record was quickly banned. And in late 1966, the Rolling Stones wound themselves up into a pitch of fury with 'Have You Seen Your Mother, Baby, Standing In The Shadow?', one of the most nihilistic records ever made. Peter Whitehead's film for the song intercut footage of a riot at the Albert Hall in September 1966 with blinding, strobe-like cuts of the Rolling Stones dressing up in drag. As Brian Jones dissolved into an amoral Pan-hysterics at the end of this incantatory footage, the equation was made clear: sexual equals social revolution and something must break.

'The year 1967 was something of an *annus mirabilis* as far as liberal legislation in the sphere of sexual mores was concerned.'[30] Three Acts passed that year put into implicit political terms the principle underlying the mid-sixties statements of 'public' androgyny: 'Excessively polarised personality types thrive in a culture that demands the repression of certain natural tendencies while people are developing the so-called "masculine" and so-called "feminine" traits which society considers to be appropriate for each sex.'[31] The Abortion and National Health Service (Family Planning) Acts made conditions significantly easier for women to take advantage of increased social freedoms and to take control over their own sexuality, while the Sexual Offences Act ended a ten-year battle to decriminalize homosexual acts between men. (As if to attest to their virtual invisibility, homosexual acts between women had never even been covered by the law that was being repealed.) Within two years, the Divorce Reform and the Equal Pay Acts had been passed, banishing further remnants of Victorian morality and putting the 'private' at the cutting edge of reform.

Yet despite the (partly chemically induced) euphoria of pop music in the summer of 1967 – as the youth utopia seemed to be within grasp – that year also represents the highwater mark of the Teen age, of the love affair between the dominant culture and youth. No longer would youth and its culture have such a power to affect society as it had had for those brief few years from 1963 to 1967: although the sharp end of youth culture was confusing purchasing power with political power and demanding change, many of its constituents were caught by the freeze that, introduced the previous year, signified the end of the ten-year boom that had thrust youth into prominence. The youth market, which had been held together in a fragile unity, fragmented: on the one hand into Teenybop, on the other into the Underground. Revolution was now the buzzword, as pop allied itself with the youth riots that occurred throughout Europe and America in 1968 and 1969; although overtly concerned with inner space, pop went public with a confusing mixture of ideology and rhetoric, to which private concerns like self and sexuality were subordinated. Indeed the lasting effect of this period is seen better in the political pressure groups – the Gay and Women's Liberation movements – which it spawned than in the actual pop music of the time.

This public libertarianism, whose very real sense of possibility has remained at the heart of every subsequent 'utopian' movement (like the early days of Punk Rock), foundered against the worsening economic climate and the 'tough' mood of the new Conservative government under the 'abrasive' Ted Heath. This mood found its youth cult expression in the aggressively proletarian and puritanical skinheads, who turned the body into a walking instrument of violence – the ultimate expression of 'traditional' masculine qualities. 'The survival of Rock has depended on its position as the core of *Male* Teen Culture. But the bovver boys have rejected Rock's traditional status which explains the lack of vitality in British Rock in the early seventies.'[32] Yet it was through the derided Teenybop that the next pop generation came, as young women quickly moved from varieties of Osmond to something a bit meatier – men who instead of masking the femininity of the adored object, flaunted it and made it part of the package.

Glam Rock simultaneously celebrated the new sexual freedoms and, through the very refusal to look outwards from its reflection in the mirror, reflected the harsher social climate within which it operated. The most important Glam figure, David Bowie, announced his career in January 1972 with a public statement of his homosexuality, but, characteristically, hedged his bets as a 'bisexual'. Homosexuality was plundered partly for its shock value but more importantly the sensibility, which quickly permeated Glam Rock, with which it had long been associated: camp. 'It is one way of seeing the world as an aesthetic phenomenon. That way, the way of Camp, is not in terms of beauty but in terms of the degree of artifice, of stylisation.'[33]

> David Bowie came out properly in a blaze of obvious self-recreation – from Terry Nelhams through Andy Warhol – and it touched every suburban heart. You don't need to be you: you can change your clothes and your name and your hair and be an entirely new person![34]

Glam's translation of this high art idea of camp into pop (seen at its most powerful in Roxy Music's 'In Every Dream Home A Heartache'),[35] resulted both in a primitive post-modernism – turning yourself and your body into an Art Object with all the irony and the distancing that that implied – and a mocking entry into a 'public' private fantasy, as it offered a cultural space for a mass white audience to play with hitherto repressed ideas about self, consumption, and masculinity.

Typically, its social effect was highly ambiguous: this placing of the private at centre stage was in part a flight from harsher social conditions, in part a coded opposition to them: 'glam rock revelled in a display that was intent on demonstrating that the assumed "privacy" of sexual matters then being so fervently insisted upon by Mrs Whitehouse, was an illusion'.[36] Yet, in retrospect, Glam dovetailed exactly with developments in consumer capitalism. From the early 1970s the idea of revivalism in consumption and aesthetic theory had become rampant, as people started to buy things for their 'kitsch' value or their references – note the Deco dream world of Biba's store in Kensington High Street as the high water mark of this style in the United Kingdom. In its total concentration on self, Glam presaged the invasion by capitalism into the hitherto most private areas of people's psyches, in the Me-Decade. In the United States, homosexuals became an important market and – a process which spread over here – a political movement slowly mutated into a consumerist, self-sufficient ghetto: politics replaced by pleasure.

As the style passed, Glam left a couple of stings in its tail. Two albums by David Bowie suggested possible options for this concentration on self: 'Diamond Dogs' (1974) made explicit the equation that the Velvet Underground had hinted at in the mid-sixties, namely that divergent sexuality of every type was only an inevitable consequence of a civilization at the brink of apocalypse. The world is ending, so anything goes. And, as importantly, 'Young Americans' (1975) reintroduced black music, with all its connotations of forbidden pleasure, in the form of disco back into the mainstream white audience.

In the fading days of the postwar consensus, under the Labour patriarchy of that civil servants' union boss Jim Callaghan, Apocalypse seemed more viable than pleasure. Surrounded by the commercial tat of a failed sexual 'revolution', Punk Rock threw sex back into the face of society in an apocalyptic vision; as the name Sex Pistols made clear, sex here was not a means to pleasure, or self-discovery but a weapon: ' "It's the only way to smash the wretched civilisation." I said. "Yes. Sex is the only way to infuriate them. Much more fucking and they'll be screaming hysterics in next to no time." '[37] Despite the myriad perversions emblazoned across Vivienne Westwood's clothes for 'Sex', Punk Rock's concerns were not private but public: the Self here was amplified, in songs like 'I Wanna Be Me', into a desperate assertion of individuality in a Burroughsian world of collapsing values and dehumanized sex, and the body was not something to be celebrated but – in songs like 'Bodies', with its excoriation, 'I'm not an animal!' – objectified through fear. Indeed Punk Rock's attitude to the sex act itself was not libertarian but puritan:

I don't believe in sexuality at all. People are very unsexy. I don't enjoy that side of life. Being sexy is just a fat arse and tits that will do anything you want. I personally look on myself as one of the most sexless monsters ever.[38]

This puritan streak in punk caught the political and cultural shift into 'hard' styles only too well: 'It'll be English (fascism): ratty, mean, pinched, hand in glove with Thatcher as mother sadist over all her whimpering little public schoolboys, the seventies Unity (Mitford) to finally consummate the fascist union.'[39] As Punk Rock codified from a post-modern art movement – very similar, in late 1976, to a United Kingdom version of Andy Warhol's Factory – into a 'public' movement with a crudely 'tough' style, it nevertheless delivered a disturbingly accurate political polemic. Slogans like No Future! accurately presaged the twin dominant political forces of the late seventies and early eighties: Thatcherism and unemployment.

Yet its most sophisticated effect was cultural. Buried beneath the sensationalism – for Punk Rock's public face was nothing if not lurid – was a considered critique – derived in part from libertarian theories like Situationism, a big influence in the sixties and since – of pop music and youth culture's place at the cutting edge of consumer capitalism. Pop was no longer a community of youth as it had been in the sixties, nor a means of changing society, but a meaningless marketing exercise which deserved to be exposed for the charade that it was. Yet Punk was betrayed by its libertarian roots: despite the rhetoric and the packaging, the Sex Pistols were utopian, and their obvious pleasure in and mastery of the pop form inspired countless others to take up instruments and make meaning through music. Yet it changed pop's possible meanings irrevocably: if pop was about marketing, then it would include the marketing in the actual product (namely – McLaren's 'Ten Lessons' in 'The Great Rock 'n' Roll Swindle'). Pop would forever carry about an awareness of its commercial process.

And, too, its past: 'Behind punk's favoured "cut-ups" lay hints of disorder, of breakdown and category confusion: a desire not only to erode racial and gender boundaries but also to confuse chronological sequence by mixing up details from different periods.'[40] Early Punk clothing mixed up every youth style since the war and joined them together with safety pins; as its radical content faded, this was to supply a rich compost for new styles to grow, as each constituent part – Mod, Ted, skinhead – was unravelled in a series of revivals. There was no time common to all popular music, as myriad fragments of past, present, and future whirled in a mad dance. Thus, despite the threat that it had posed to the music industry, for six months from December 1976 to June 1977, Punk Rock was quickly recuperated into a new kind of pop music that accurately reproduced the latest conditions of consumer capitalism.

In the early 1980s, pop as private pleasure as a flight from harsh external reality into self, or as a celebration of the 'new leisure' became fashionable again. One crucial element in this was the resumption of centre stage by a type of music that had been in the dominant culture throughout Punk rock – black disco music. 'The Afro-American tendency to extend the body in musical terms signifies in the case of soul and disco an important marriage of pop's romanticism to the contradictory material possibilities of daily life in the contemporary world'.[41] From a mass popularity in 1975–8, disco had moved beneath the surface to take root in the self-contained homosexual ghetto, which had been quietly developing newer definitions of self and pleasure. Slowly, homosexuality and the (male) deviant sex it introduced became yet again a metaphor for ideas of the 'private', or the hidden – as pop, once more, concentrated on ever more fragmented ideas about private possibilities – introduced, by way of example, 'case histories' that could serve as models for this new round of pleasure and fantasy.

What did it feel like, this popular music, as every kind of male sexuality was wheeled out of the closet and onto the marketplace with a febrile flourish?

> Constant shift of movement, of interest suddenly taken up and dropped. Pillars, dance floor; rectangular, well lit area at street side of disco. Back bar smelling of amyl and sex. Side pool bar with those who wait on their chairs. Man in red shirt, jeans, sits leg cocked up, waiting, waiting. Pair standing up by central pillars begin to argue – older man about 40, haggard looking – younger man on defensive. Businessman in suit white hair bites his nails nervously. . .[42]

This description of Heaven, London's biggest gay disco, omits the sense of camaraderie (and occasionally, solidarity) that can exist in gay venues, yet it captures a state akin to that of Jameson's second basic feature of modernism, which he terms 'schizophrenia':

> the schizophrenic will clearly have a far more intense experience of any given present of the world than we do, since our own present is always part of some larger set of projects which force us selectively to focus our perceptions.[43]

From Frankie Goes to Hollywood – who presented the image of two leather queens – through Marc Almond – in the image of a northern gay boy – through Bronski Beat – presented as 'out' political gays – to the rash of transvestite and transexual 'gender bender' stylists like Marilyn and Boy George, sexual divergence has crossed over into the mainstream in a psychological paradigm that services perfectly pop's current industrial situation.

> Culture turned completely into commodity must also turn into the star commodity of the spectacular society. Colin Kerr. . .predicts that in the second half of this century culture will hold the key role in the development of the economy, a role played by the automobile in the first half (of this century).[44]

The current form in which pop reproduces itself, the music video, is the perfect post-modern form, standing as it does at the vector of the leisure industries' new situation. With music video, the industrial interdependence of previously separate businesses is enmeshed in a new multi-media agglomerate, as the film, music and television industries combine to develop and exploit this new form. The music video is an advert turned into product: pop is now culture in the situationist sense, with its own past, its own references, even its own marketing, as part of a seamless package. With its industrial importance, it can't afford not to be.

Popular music has thus dissolved from a specifically youth-oriented product at the margins of society into a new type of industry which effectively draws areas that were previously considered private and 'hidden' in our society into the centre of consumption and governmental strategy. The dominant culture has caught up! 'If Britain's economic future too depends on the expansion of the electronic leisure goods industries, on the exploitation of new communications technology, then leisure will continue to be a material as well as an ideological problem'.[45] As the leisure industries move towards the heart of consumer capitalism's new conditions, then pop's sexuality is increasingly as controlled as it is exploited. It is thus eminently possible for the homosexual sub-culture to inform and, on occasion, dominate virtually every pop style since the 1950s – and none more so than in mid-1980s – but still to find itself politically disenfranchised, socially marginal, and vulnerable to attacks from the New Morality. So while music video, bar a few exceptions, reinforces the most obvious aspects of the 'dominant' sexuality, in the tired arrogance of advertising techniques,

an explicitly 'out-gay' and highly successful pop group like
Bronski Beat will split up because their politics can't cope with
current pop practices. The spectre of the homosexual as
Bogeyman too (just like in the 1950s) returns with the moral
panic over the disease AIDS and the sensational press coverage
of the Cyprus 'Spy' trial. In these conditions, the type of
homosexuality that is mediated through pop music can only go
just so far: in a perfect paradigm, Frankie Goes to Hollywood exploited the gay image of lead singers Paul Rutherford and Holly
Johnson – for 'Relax' – and then dropped it like a hot potato as
soon as another marketing device – this time, nuclear war –
became available for 'Two Tribes'. Divergent sexuality, it is
clear even now, is only permissible as long as it allows itself to be
stolen, as long as it conforms to existing industry patterns and
dominant sexual stereotypes.

While male homosexuality has been the main subject of this
chapter, it is worth noting that 'male beauty and narcissism,
playing with "self" and sexual ambiguities, still indicates a male
privilege in public life. Pop culture acknowledges the sign of
"gayness", but there is not yet a whisper of female sexual
autonomy, of lesbianism.'[46] This opens the door still further.
Despite pop's current cutting adrift of male homosexual signs, it
is still possible for sexual analyses and critiques of consumer
capitalism, such as can originate in the experience of gay men
and women, to emerge from pop's cultural discourse in order to
point to the future:

> a new consciousness (that) is arising out of a morass of a
> declining society that has bent too far towards rationalism,
> towards technology, and toward the acquisition of power
> through unbridled competition. The new consciousness takes
> note that our society has become over-balanced in favour of
> the so-called masculine qualities of character.[47]

To begin with, it is a question of making sure such messages get
through and are acted upon.

NOTES

This is very much an exploratory attempt to pull together a
different perspective on sexuality and pop music; I can't therefore
claim to be all-inclusive. Even within the scope of male

homosexuality – as an index of sexual divergence – I've left out several crucial figures, of which Tom Robinson and the Velvet Underground spring to mind as the most obvious: another account may wish to give them their due place.

The copious notes that follow, therefore, are not to display how well-read I might be but to offer material from which such an account might be drawn.

1 Rodney Garland, *The Heart in Exile*, London: W.H. Allen, 1953, p. 58.
2 Fredric Jameson, 'Postmodernism and consumer society', in Hal Foster (ed.), *Postmodern Culture*, London: Pluto, 1985, p. 125.
3 ibid.
4 Shaun Usher, in the *Daily Mail*, 3 December 1976.
5 Iain Chambers, *Urban Rhythms*, London: Macmillan, 1985, p. 17.
6 ibid.
7 Note the 'alternative' readings of 'Tainted Love', understood by many in Soft Cell's interpretation as a 'gay' love song rather than a melodramatic account of a heterosexual affair gone badly wrong (as in Gloria Jones' original). This raises the whole can of worms of 'camp' interpretations of pop songs.
8 Nik Cohn, *Today There Are No Gentlemen*, London: Weidenfeld & Nicolson, 1970, p. 25.
9 ibid., pp. 24–5.
10 Peter York, script for *Teenage*, Granada TV, 1982.
11 Christopher Booker, *The Neophiliacs*, London: Collins, 1969, p. 90.
12 Andy Medhurst, 'Can chaps be pin-ups?', *Ten 8*, 17 (1984), 6.
13 ibid.
14 T.R. Fyvel, *The Insecure Offenders*, Harmondsworth: Pelican Books, 1963, p. 50.
15 Booker, *The Neophiliacs*, p. 117.
16 Voice Over, *The Teenage Consumer*, Pathé News, 1958.
17 Jon Savage, 'Return to Gender', in *The Virgin Year Book*, 5 (1984), 117–19.
18 Dust jacket, Peter Wildblood, *A Way of Life*, London: Weidenfeld & Nicolson, 1956.
19 Colin MacInnes, *Absolute Beginners*, London: MacGibbon & Kee, 1959, p. 112.
20 Richard Dyer, 'Don't look now – the male pin-up', *Screen*, 23: 3–4 (October 1982), quoted in *Ten 8*, no. 17.
21 Simon Napier-Bell, *You Don't Have To Say You Love Me*, London: Nomis Books, 1983, p. 8. Another variant on this theme is Kenneth Pitt, *Bowie: The Pitt Report*, London: Omnibus Press, 1985.
22 MacInnes, *Absolute Beginners*, p. 113.
23 Booker, *The Neophiliacs*, p. 165.
24 The Mandy Report, London: Confidentials Publications, 1963.
25 Booker, *The Neophiliacs*, p. 292.

26 Richard Barnes, *Mods!*, London: Eel Pie, 1979, p. 10.

27 In *Parallel Lives*, London: GMP, 1985.

28 Barnes, *Mods!*, p. 15.

29 Simon Frith and Angela McRobbie, 'Rock and sexuality', *Screen Education*, 24 (Winter 1978/9), quoted in Jon Wiener, *Come Together – John Lennon in his Time*, London: Faber & Faber, 1985, p. 48.

30 Arthur Marwick, *British Society Since 1945*, Harmondsworth: Pelican, 1984.

31 June Singer, *Androgyny*, London: Routledge & Kegan Paul, 1977, quoted in Jon Savage, 'Androgyny', *The Face*, 38 (June 1983).

32 Pete Fowler, 'Skins rule', in Charlie Gillett (ed.), *Rock File*, London: NEL, 1972, p. 24.

33 Susan Sontag, 'Notes on camp' (1964), published in *A Susan Sontag Reader*, Harmondsworth: Penguin, 1983, p. 106.

34 Jon Savage, 'The gender bender', *The Face*, 7 (November 1970). Terry Nelhams is better known to some people as Adam Faith.

35 And at its tackiest in Sweet's 'Ballroom blitz'.

36 Chambers, *Urban Rhythms*, p. 135.

37 Joe Orton, Diary, 26 March 1967, quoted in John Lahr, *Prick Up Your Ears*, Harmondsworth: Penguin, 1980, pp. 135–6.

38 Sid Vicious, quoted in John Ingham, '(?) Rock special', *Sounds*, 9 October 1976.

39 Jon Savage, 'London's outrage', November 1976. There was a vogue that year for a biography of Unity Mitford by David Pryce-Jones. The big talking (and selling) point in that latest account of that over-exposed family was Unity Mitford's close connections with Adolf Hitler and the Nazi Party, whose rallies she would frequently attend.

40 Dick Hebdige, *Subculture: The Meaning of Style*, London: Methuen, 1979, p. 123.

41 Chambers, *Urban Rhythms*, p. 149.

42 Jon Savage, notes, 21 November 1980.

43 Jameson, 'Postmodernism', p. 119.

44 Guy Debord, *Society of the Spectacle*, Black and Red, 1970, paragraph 193.

45 Simon Frith, 'Who'll get pleasure from leisure?', *Marxism Today*, 29: 6 (June 1985).

46 Chambers, *Urban Rhythms*, p. 252.

47 Singer, *Androgyny* – not entirely accurate, note Patti Smith, 'Redondo Beach', 1975. On Patti Smith, Chambers has this to say: 'Her LP *Horses* [Arista] . . . is an important musical statement, setting pop's multi-voiced tradition in a new, assertive female mould . . . the record really worth searching out is the first record she made: "Hey Joe"/"Piss Factory"' (*Urban Rhythms*, p. 228).

9

Frankie said
But what did they mean?

SIMON FRITH

In Britain 1984 turned out to be the year of the coalminers' strike and Frankie Goes to Hollywood. Repeating images – the miners' stolid anger, Frankie's smirking leatherware; juxtaposed stereotypes – pickets as hooligans, gays lounging promiscuously in the night. If pop is a sign of its times, then Frankie's social message during the key political struggle of the 1980s was decidedly oblique.

Frankie were a pop phenomenon just for their sales figures. Their first two releases were million sellers, 'Two Tribes' went straight into the charts at number 1 and was the inescapable sound of the summer; 'Relax' (in all its remixed varieties) was a permanent hit, the most successful twelve-inch ever. *Welcome to the Pleasure Dome*, Frankie's end-of-year double LP claimed record advance orders (though its real sales figures were never made clear), and the group took over the message tee-shirt, using the large print originally designed by Katherine Hamnett for better causes to promote 'Relax' and spawning a cacophony of 'Frankie Says' and 'Who Gives A Fuck What Frankie Says' slogans. Walking down Oxford Street in August, watching the tourists snap up the pirate editions of 'Frankie Says Arm The Unemployed' I decided this was the final triumph of the 'new pop', the eclipse of content by form.

By then Frankie had reached the stage of being famous for being famous.[1] Their success gave them a power that everyone wanted to share; their commercial momentum carried the whole pop world along. And theirs was a comforting rags-to-riches story. Frankie themselves were typical graduates of the 1970s post-punk provincial scene (five lads from Liverpool) in

172

which Bowie boys became punks and skins, dyed their hair repeatedly, hung out in the gay clubs with the furtiveness that marks everyone on provincial streets in the small hours. In Holly Johnson's words:

> My social security number was written on the side of my head. Then I had a mini-mohican. Just a square of blond hair and a beard . . . . The worst was when I shaved my head and used to paint it red and green. You used to get people writing into the Liverpool Echo saying, 'Who's this Martian walking round town.' I used to get battered . . . . Decadence was the key word then . . .[2]

This was the scene – musicians and dance floor posers drawn from the same pool, sex as a slippery transaction – that produced Marc Almond and Soft Cell in Leeds, Boy George, and the early, sleazy Duran Duran in Birmingham. Frankie had nothing much more to offer till they signed to Zang Tumb Tuum (ZTT) the label (named after a First World War futurist magazine) formed by *New Musical Express (NME)* theorist, Paul Morley, and Dollar/ABC/Malcolm McLaren producer, Trevor Horn. Morley had the concept; in Paul Rutherford's words, 'Morley had his strategy all worked out, he wanted it to be like the Sex Pistols – all the outrage, controversy – but this time with all the sex',[3] and it was rumoured that he was first interested in Bronski Beat for the Frankie role – they turned him down. But Horn had the sound, the remarkable ability to create epic spaces in ordinary songs. Frankie's records made best sense in a cheap British disco, where the elementary chorus chants, the beat machines' seedy grandeur, and the stodgy vocals had distinct echoes of Gary Glitter.

As an *NME* writer Paul Morley was the most influential theorist of 'new pop', combining a traditional reading of music's emotional power with a modernist celebration of that power's fleeting ambiguity. His problem was to translate theory into practice and so Frankie's success was, for him, a triumph of rock journalism. But the question remains – was Frankie's undoubted popularity subversive?

I don't think Frankie's radical intentions are in doubt. 'Relax' may only have become a scandal when the BBC in belated confusion (and in response to teasing video clips) banned it, but singers Holly Johnson and Paul Rutherford promote an explicitly gay image, and 'Two Tribes' was a pointed response to nuclear defence policy. It was the smoothness of Frankie's success that was unnerving; it was hard to find anyone (other than ZTT) who even at the height of the sales buzz thought that Frankie, or their records, had changed the way they understood their lives. They were a best-selling group without real fans, more like the Archies than the Sex Pistols, and they lost significance as rapidly as they gained it.[4] The week after their LP, *Pleasure Dome*, entered the charts at number one it was displaced by Wham's *Make It Big* and the Frankie moment was over. By the time they toured for the first time, in 1985, they seemed silly – nothing dates as fast as an advertisement.

Frankie's fall reflected the way they made it in the first place, through marketing rather than live performance. Their energy was the energy of pop's sales teams rather than its consumers. There were, by 1984, more television pop shows than ever before, more knowing pop people in record company control, more competitors for the leisure pound. Frankie was *their* triumph and so the final point of their story wasn't its 'outrage' but its cosiness. Frankie's very success made them part of the pop family, by the end of the year Mike Reid, the deejay who had initiated the BBC ban on 'Relax', was the voice over their television commercials. Frankie, a pleasure-chasing group led by out-front gay men had become family entertainers. What did it mean?

Frankie were interesting not musically but ideologically. The story of commercial co-option is familiar in pop history but the terms in which the story is told change, and Paul Morley's words about Frankie were thus more important than Frankie themselves. The practice of pop involves, by its nature, the practice of theorizing; people need to make sense of the continuing processes of musical evaluation, choice and commitment whether they are musicians, entrepreneurs or fans. The results may be low theory – confused, inconsistent, full of hyperbole and silence, but still theory, and theory which is compelled by necessity to draw key terms and assumptions from high theory, from the more systematic accounts of art, commerce, pleasure and class that are available.

To understand the Frankie story, then, it is necessary to

understand the low theory that informed it, and to place this theory historically. To put it very generally, from the mid-1950s (the rock 'n' roll moment) to the end of the 1960s the dominant sensibility in pop was a rock sensibility which had, at its cutting edge, an account of itself which drew on the Marxist critique of mass culture.[5] From the mid-1970s (the punk moment) to 1984 the dominant sensibility was a pop sensibility which had, at its cutting edge, an account of itself which drew on an avant-garde critique of mass culture; this was the account developed by Paul Morley and the other theorists of the 'new pop'.

Different sensibilities produce different aesthetics, different criteria of subversion and co-option. Rock arguments in the late 1960s thus focused on commercial 'sell-outs', on the transformation of culture into commodity, on rock's relations to community and community action. The term which fused aesthetic and political values was 'authenticity'. The new pop sensibility, by contrast, took artifice for granted, celebrated cult not community, defined its subversions in self-consciously formalist terms.

I have not got space here to go into the sources of new pop theory – they include avant-garde art music, the new technological and computer processes of mixing and recording sound, art school flirtation with structuralist and post-structuralist theories of representation, punk flirtation with situationist theories of the spectacle – but their combined impact was to focus attention on popular music as a *construction* of sound and image.[6] The authority of musicians as such was undermined; political interest moved from the reorganization of production to the disruption of consumption.

Trevor Horn's most interesting project before ZTT was, therefore, Malcolm McLaren's *Duck Rock* LP. This was, from a rock perspective, an obvious 'rip off' (McLaren mixed together African field recordings, New York street and radio noise, studio tricks, and claimed the results as his own) but, from his own pop art position (pioneered by the Sex Pistols), it was a political gesture, exposing the cultural assumptions of our usual sound standards, raising questions about what music, if any, is 'natural'.

Horn had, in a different way, addressed similar issues in his work with ABC, using the 1980s routine of issuing singles in a variety of mixes not just to exploit the fans but also to expose the studio processes and calculations kept hidden when records are presented as 'finished' goods. And ABC's Martin Fry – who did write his own music – was no less subversive than McLaren in accounting for his own authority. Fry drew mocking attention to the fact that what is involved in pop is not simply music, but music as articulated through a performer or, rather, through an image of a performer – and if musical meaning is conventional, not natural, so is our sense of pop personality. We read qualities like sincerity, anger, sexuality and warmth into performers because of the way they organize the signs of their personality. The basis of pop performance is not spontaneity (which binds rock to nature) but calculation (which binds pop to culture). And Fry and the other new pop stars (Human League, Kid Creole, Soft Cell, Culture Club) also realized that pop works not through any old combination of sound, image and personality, but through their combination as a commercial package. Artistic interest in the making of meaning does not end when the music is made, the record released, the performance over, but is equally invested in the way in which it takes on its public meanings, via the media of television, radio, advertisement, the star system, Fleet Street gossip columns, poster magazines and so forth.

The rise of the video-clip encouraged this blurring of the traditional rock distinction between making music and marketing a commodity. The new pop groups were expected by their record companies to construct their music as its own advertisement, as a video spot on MTV, Sky Channel, TV-am. The effect of video-pop was to shift the balance between pop's aural and visual elements (and to favour genres, like teeny bop, in which visuals have always been crucial – hence the 'second British invasion' of the American charts and the success of groups like Duran Duran and Wham!); and to raise questions about the construction of pop sexuality.

Pop videos themselves are consistently reactionary in their sexual imagery (and this is an aspect of the cooption of new pop to which I will return) if only because they draw on visual conventions of masculinity and femininity (taken from cinema history and television commercials) that are much more coherent than pop's adolescent ambiguities. What was more important for new pop sexuality, then, was the rock-despised 'artificial' 1970s genre, disco, which, in its very use of formulas, raised questions about the pop construction, via dance, of the body. Disco offered an alternative to rock's boy-meets-girl party conventions and Britain's dance-floor poseurs, Bowie boys, and girls initially, became the New Romantics, a movement spawning such ambiguous and even asexual stars as Boy George and Marilyn.

Such dressing-up was, like glam rock before it, a boys' affair. Male homosexuality, bisexuality and transexuality have been coded into pop imagery in ways in which lesbianism and female bisexuality have not. Female sexuality, it seems, is still defined as 'natural'; women remain 'the sex'. This is obvious in Frankie's videos. Holly Johnson's and Paul Rutherford's games with masculinity and male pleasure are set in remarkably old-fashioned contexts, in sixties-style 'liberated' party settings, women as available, threatening receptacles of desire. If Frankie, like David Bowie before them, suggest that the most 'natural' of rock's meanings, its 'raunchiness', is just another (and rather dreary) pose – a pose in which the other boys in the band are, ironically, trapped – women are still excluded from the fun.

As an *NME* writer at the beginning of the 1980s Paul Morley was the most pretentious and most entertaining of the new pop theorists. While his colleague Ian Penman explicitly linked his critical judgements to high theory figures like Derrida, Foucault and Barthes, Morley remained true to rock's low theory concern with music's emotional effects; his analyses of the pleasures of the text were subordinated to rhapsodies on the pleasures of the (listening) subject. The Morley/Penman project had a negative thrust – 'rockist' duly became a term of abuse as casually applied by pop fans as 'selling out' had been by 1960s rock fans – but its tone was relentlessly optimistic and Morley was duly rewarded for his faith in market forces (and in Dollar in particular) by being invited into Trevor Horn's record label plans. It is important to stress, though, that a pop critic's power is limited. Writers do not influence consumers' tastes, they respond to them; they do not create trends but explain them. The importance of music press writers like Paul Morley, and of disc jockeys like Peter Powell (or John Peel), is to make available a public language in which private musical judgements can be legitimated.

Writers are important for their interpretation of pop as a theoretical practice, but, almost inevitably, after the event. Frankie Goes To Hollywood did not become successful because of Morley's sales campaign; rather, his sales campaign became significant because Frankie were successful (and Morley's hubris in thinking otherwise fed into Frankie's fall – new pop was easily co-opted because its radical intentions were of no consequence for its commercial practices). The important question is not how popular cultural sensibilities shift but why they do. Ideologies change in response to material circumstances and needs and the 1970 rock/pop shift was not just the result of some random play of stars and influences. It reflected changing means and relations of cultural production and consumption.

This is not the place to outline these in detail but, to put it simply, in the late 1970s the record industry faced a 'crisis' (a stagnation in record sales after twenty years of expansion) brought on by two simultaneous developments: on the one hand, an economic recession which hit particularly hard the most important sector of the record buying market, working-class youth; on the other hand, technological developments in the leisure industry which meant either new sorts of competition for people's leisure resources (home computers and video recorders become as significant in young people's lives as record players, for instance) or disrupted record companies' profit-making routines (home taping thus became the industry's chief bogey).

The record industry's response to this situation was not particularly systematic but by now some trends are obvious: the average age of the pop market (and especially the pop single-buying market) is younger than it was; record companies devote more attention to building big mainstream stars than to servicing a variety of musical tastes; stars are now conceived and sold as multi-media performers; there has been a steady decline in the significance of live music making except as a promotional device.[7]

This was the context in which the rock sensibility began to falter (a faltering marked by the 'crisis' of punk). What collapsed was the idea – which emerged in the 1950s and gave cultural shape to the 1960s – that 'youth' is a community. The rock sensibility always included a strand of folk ideology – folk musicians and folk ways, particularly the celebration of 'live' performance, were central to the development of rock in both Britain and the United States. The sociological fantasy that pop musicians could be some sort of organic intellectuals was remarkably stubborn; it dominated initial left-wing responses to punk, and it was only when the material basis of the fantasy – youth as class – broke down in the late 1970s recession, that different ways of conceiving pop politics began to be attractive.[8]

Youth unemployment, and particularly its denial of school leavers' 'independence', also raised new problems of pleasure. When work can no longer be taken for granted nor can leisure, and this, in turn, calls into question the hedonistic routine on which rock had been based. Thus, though a record like Wham's 'Wham Rap!' (a disco-based assertion of the right not to work, to have a good time *all* the time, 'You've got soul on the dole!') was a big hit, it worked as fantasy rather than as any sort of explicit political comment.

The old cliché has it that in hard times pop culture goes soft, entertainment becomes more trivial, more 'escapist'. But this is not just a matter of cultural manipulation – rulers laying on circuses when there is no bread. 'Escape' from hard times is a cultural necessity and the harder the times the more fantastic and precarious and desperate a business it becomes. The 1980s working-class youth sub-culture is thus the 'casuals' who, at first glance, epitomize the employed half of Thatcher's two nations, neatly dressed in their designer-label sports goods, clutching walkmen and video-tapes. In truth, though, like the punks and skins, the casuals emerged from the dole queues and football terraces, from the 'delinquent' world of drugs and brawls and menace. The visible affluence of these supposed state dependants implies, in itself, illicit goods, and their flaunting of their 'free time' is a reminder that a leisure society creates its own forms of disorder. The conventional sociological reading of youth sub-cultures as resisting bourgeois cultural hegemony makes no sense of the casuals – they're involved in a stylistic refusal to be *excluded* from dominant images of the good life.[9]

The casuals realized, quicker than most commentators, that the radical aspect of the Thatcher government's response to the recession is its rejection of the Protestant Ethic. Leisure is no longer defined as something earned by work; work, rather, is to

179

be made available by leisure. For the Tories the long-term solution to the recession lies in the expansion of the leisure goods industries, the development of communication technologies.

This is a fantasy, but a fantasy with immediate ideological consequences; relations of consumption have become as important an aspect of class struggle as relations of production, as important an issue, that is, for state regulation (or lack of regulation), corporate investment and social control. From the perspective of youth culture and pop music two aspects of this are significant.

The 'leisure economy' describes, of course, a situation in which the affluent are serviced by the non-affluent, the 'new' workers will work directly on other people's pleasures. What is really new about this vision, though (the non-affluent have always serviced the affluent) is that hedonism becomes the moral dynamo of the economy: pleasures are justified by the work they provide, having fun becomes a moral duty. This is to reverse the conventional relationship between youth and age. Youth has always been the ideological sign of pleasure because it is a time of irresponsibility, possibility, change; young people are envied and feared and so feature in the organization of consumption as a recurring adult fantasy. But in the leisure economy projected for the 1990s young people will be the workers – low paid, low skilled, subservient. Pleasure will be an adult privilege, a mark of economic power, class status and moral superiority. Consumption will be organized around fantasies of grown-up success; hence the Yuppie phenomenon in the United States, and hence the casuals, accepting this ideology of leisure, defying their subordinate place in it.

The second point about the leisure economy is that it places people's use of their 'free' time at the centre of capitalists' (and governments') concern. The continued power and prosperity of multi-media entrepreneurs like Rupert Murdoch and Robert Maxwell depends on their goods being 'entertaining', and 'giving the people what they want'/'making sure people want what they're given' is not as straightforward a business in this context as it is often presented.[10] In particular, the more people's leisure choices are 'privatized' – pushed into the home, made a matter of individual taste – the more they become a matter of public interest. A Tory economic strategy which rests on Sunday shopping, cable television and fun parks rests on people behaving in ways in which they have no need to at all. People would not die without computer games, the latest Sylvester Stallone movie or a bank holiday trip to Alton Towers, and 'the leisure economy' is thus dependent on essentially unstable, individual, market needs and choices.

From the capitalists' point of view the sensible long-term strategy is to control the means of transmission and distribution (which are necessary, whatever people's tastes) and to leave the risks of cultural production to small, more competitive businesses. This has certainly been the record industry strategy: in the last ten years the major companies have consolidated their control of the manufacture and distribution of records, tapes and videos while leaving more and more of the musical enterprise to the 'independents'.[11] But even in this framework, consumption must be orderly – people can indulge themselves, make free with their time, form their own tastes, but only within limits. The choices involved must be market choices, and this is the whole thrust of the developing Tory strategy on leisure licences and regulation.

This is the context in which the new pop concern to disrupt consumption can be seen as a valid political project. The problem (and this brings us back to the Frankie story) is what the disruption of consumption means. The new pop retained its radical credibility as long as the music business was on the defensive; and in the late 1970s context of falling sales and punk politics there was, indeed, a sense that pop's usual gatekeepers (Artists and Repertoire departments, radio programmers, music press editors) were not in control of what was happening. But once record companies went back on the sales offensive the new pop was easily coopted. By the time ZTT was formed the new pop sensibility had been subtly transformed into a commercial sensibility – the way to make sense of the pop process was in terms of market competition and success. As noted earlier (p. 178), the commercial practices prevailed over any radical intentions. A good record, by definition, was one which sold; good times were guaranteed by joining in the fun of buying it too. Peter Powell became the voice of Radio 1; *Smash Hits* the dominant music magazine; EMI's Duran Duran Britain's biggest group.

But perhaps the easiest way to follow the new pop story is in the pages of *The Face*, a magazine founded in 1980 at the conjuncture of music, fashion, art and design. Its early juxtapositions of discourse were wonderfully exciting; more clearly even than Morley and his colleagues, *The Face* showed how pop style works – as a production, as a phantasm, as a source of skewed discontent and momentary carelessness. And then, slowly, the tone changed, grew more consistent, more self-congratulatory. By the time of the special fifth anniversary issue success was claimed as 'the credo of the decade': *The Face*'s own success (a circulation of 80,000 and rising; an incomparable influence on other consumer magazines), success as an intangible personal quality.[12] The deconstruction of the pop sales process had become a breathy celebration of sales people. Authority and art are mythical terms again but applied now not to musicians but the designers, copy-writers, businessmen. Paul Morley, Trevor Horn, and Jill Sinclair were the 'stars' of Frankie.

The 1980s pop story is full of ironies. The new pop stars – self-conscious frauds, tackily glamorous like Boy George – fed a revival of old-fashioned pop gossip, a staple now of the *Sun* and the *Mirror*. *The Face*, once a cool, mocking style catalogue, now reads like a house journal, a *Tatler* for the design and fashion scene. The rise of the video-clip meant not some startling dissolution of media boundaries, but, rather, the incorporation of pop into the aesthetics of advertising. As already mentioned (pp. 176–7), this had particularly reactionary consequences for sexual representation. Whatever the sexual ambiguities of the 1980s pop voice, the video-maker's work with the clear gender divisions of their semi-pornographic film models: men at the narrative centre of their three-minute stories, women as the trivialized, undressed, humiliated object of the male gaze.[13] As the ways in which pop was written about swayed and shifted in the winds of hand-me-down art school theory, the ways in which it was produced seemed more and more familiar. Cultural theorists fell on pop video with squeals of delight (there is already more high theory of video around than there has ever been of music); pop fans watching the *Whistle Test*'s weekly video vote just groaned.

As Jon Savage has pointed out, pop video is, in fact, a good example of 'post-modern culture', the product, in the words of

Fredric Jameson, of 'a new type of social life and a new economic order – what is often euphemistically called. . . postindustrial or consumer society, the society of the media or the spectacle, or multinational capitalism'.[14] New pop was a post-modern form generally – in its cut-up of styles and media, its genre cross-references, its use of pastiche and parody, its dressing up of mass cultural forms with high cultural claims and *vice versa*. And the pleasure of the best texts, from ABC to Wham!, from 'Don't You Want Me' to 'Strike', did lie in their combination of sensual and intellectual intrigue, in fragmentation and distance as well as melody and beat. But these were surface pleasures and, in the end, the very smoothness of new pop consumption, its implication that all cultural goods, all cultural consumers, are equal, undermined any claims to subversion. Style offers only an illusion of democracy, an illusion, indeed, that in a capitalist society is a necessary part of the leisure process. What are concealed are the material inequalities of leisure power, the unequal distributions of cultural capital.[15] Look carefully at the casuals and see their threads beginning to unravel. The celebration of youth styles has always meant distant views or excessive close-ups – live on the surfaces and the make-up is soon smudged.

The strength of the rock and roll tradition lay in its fantasy of the streets (and in the development of that fantasy by the suburban youth who dominate pop history). The new pop music was, by contrast, mall music, shiny but confined. It is not surprising that the counter-sounds got louder and louder, that new myths developed of roots and region, history, authenticity.[16] There is a limit to how long people can look as though they're having fun. 'Relax!' sang Frankie and there was a strange, desperate tightness to their voice.

NOTES

1 In the sense in which the celebrity is said to have a status which is self-generating once established. The classic account is Daniel Boorstin's *The Image*, London: Weidenfeld & Nicolson, 1962, but the process has, of course, expanded wildly since then with the rise of 'People' journalism and television chat shows.
2 Quoted in one of the numerous 1984 Frankie poster-magazines, this one published by Lionbond Ltd.

3 ibid.
4 Frankie sold records but they never had the cult following of bands like Joy Division – Frankie bootlegs do not turn up in touring Record Fairs (partly, of course, because of their lack of live shows). And even as a pin-up group Frankie did not seem to have the obsessional devoted following of groups like Wham! or Duran Duran. I have not got hard evidence for this, though; the research for Fred and Judy Vermorel's pioneering fan study, *Starlust*, London: Comet, 1985, was done before Frankie's rise to the top.
5 The most influential Marxist analysis of mass culture was developed in the 1930s by the Frankfurt School. For summaries of the issues involved see Ernst Bloch *et al.*, *Aesthetics and Politics*, London: New Left Books, 1979, and, with special reference to rock, Simon Frith, *Sound Effects*, London: Constable, 1983, pp. 43–8. The Frankfurt approach influenced rock culture directly via Herbert Marcuse's *One Dimensional Man*, London: Routledge & Kegan Paul, 1964.
6 This argument is developed in more detail in Simon Frith, 'Art ideology and pop practice', in Cary Nelson and Lawrence Grossberg (eds.), *Marxism and the Interpretation of Culture*, Urbana-Champaign: University of Illinois Press, 1986.
7 The best summary documentation of changes in the record industry is the British Phonographic Industry Limited's annual Year Book, a statistical description. The 1985 edition, which covers the points mentioned here, reveals, for example, 1984 sales of 77 million singles (compared with the 1979 peak of 89.1) and 54.1 million LPs (compared to the 1975 peak of 91.6). Overall, the real value of record industry output was 26 per cent lower in 1984 than in 1978 and record company employment 24 per cent lower in 1984 than in 1980.
8 For application of Gramscian notions to postwar British youth culture see Tony Jefferson *et al.*, *Resistance Through Rituals*, London: Hutchinson, 1975. For the developing problems of the youth-as-class-as-community approach see Dick Hebdige, *Subculture: The Meaning of Style*, London: Methuen, 1979, and, with reference to punk, Dave Laing, *One Chord Wonders*, Milton Keynes: Open University Press, 1985.
9 In 1975, *Resistance Through Rituals* was a radical approach to youth: by 1985 the sub-cultural approach had become the orthodoxy of sociology teaching; check O-Level and A-Level syllabuses, for example, and see Simon Frith, *The Sociology of Youth*, Ormskirk: Causeway Press, 1984.
10 The success of papers like Murdoch's *Sun* (and *Sunday Times*) and Maxwell's *Mirror* depends not simply on huge advertising budgets and bingo prizes, but also on offering readers an image of themselves which they recognize and find flattering. The mass media should be called the popular media if only to focus

analysts' minds on the pleasures they provide. Without understanding such pleasures media critics can only, in the end, fall back on the assumption that the popular audience is stupid.

11 See Phil Hardy, *The British Record Industry*, IASPM-UK Working Paper 3, 1984.

12 Success as a personal quality is intangible precisely because of *The Face*'s indiscrimination. Anyone who has constructed themself as *a* face can be seen to have all it takes to appear in *The Face*. In the fifth anniversary issue we were offered Frankie, Mickey Rourke (the 'new Brando') and snooker impresario, Barry Hearn (see *The Face*, no.61, May 1985). Where these faces came from didn't matter; what was important was that they had arrived.

13 See Mark Hustwitt, *Sure Feels Like Heaven To Me. Considerations on Promotional Video*, IASPM-UK Working Paper 6, 1985.

14 See Jon Savage, 'Pop video', in *The Rock Yearbook*, vol 6, London: Virgin Books, 1985. The Jameson quote is from 'Postmodernism and consumer society', in Hal Foster (ed.), *Postmodern Culture*, London: Pluto Press, 1985, p. 113.

15 The concept of cultural capital is taken from Bourdieu. See, for example, Pierre Bourdieu and Jean-Claude Passeron, *Reproduction in Education, Society and Culture*, London: Sage, 1977, pp. 71–106.

16 The New Authenticity movement was symbolized in Britain by the sudden emergence of Bruce Springsteen from cult figure to popular icon. His sound (undoctored rock and roll), image (working clothes), politics (concern for the survival of working-class communities, from United States steel towns to Durham mining villages) and even sexuality (his stage stories revolve around male heterosexual anxieties and pride) can all be seen in sharp contrast to Frankie's over-productions.

10

Making popular music
The consumer as producer

DAVE LAING

It is a commonplace that production and consumption are interdependent. Without production of material or cultural goods, there can be no consumption. Without a demand for, and consumption of, the use-values embodied in those goods, there is no impetus for continuing production. In certain areas of popular culture, the relation between production and consumption has another aspect. There, the producers of today are frequently the consumers of yesterday. Through the experience of consuming music as a listener, many individuals are drawn into producing music of their own. Folk culture provides the clearest example of this process, since it involves informal but deliberate procedures for the oral transmission of an expanding folksong repertoire from one generation to the next.

In popular music what matters is not the precise transmission of the existing repertoire. There are important instances of the leap from consumer to producer being motivated by a desire to emulate admired sounds as in the rhythm and blues movement among young white Britons during the early 1960s which involved the Rolling Stones and The Kinks. But the motivation can equally be one of dissatisfaction with the music presented to consumers. In this case what results is a revolt of consumers who turn to production of iconoclastic, avant-garde or radical production. This chapter is concerned with one such burst of production powered by dissatisfaction: the independent recording movement which grew out of the explosion of punk music in Britain in 1976–7.

Like a number of other cultural forms, popular music in the west is dominated by a commercial market system, which itself is dominated by a handful of transnational companies. But the most important fact about contemporary popular music is not an effect of that dominance, even though the structure of the music industry is shaped by this fact. It is the centrality of recordings within popular music today.

For most people, popular music equals recorded music, which they hear at home, in the street, at discos and so on. The percentage of the population which attends live performances of music more than very occasionally is very small.

Musicians, critics and cultural commentators often compare recorded music unfavourably with live performance. The arguments are both economic and aesthetic. The economic position has been put most forcefully by organizations representing professional musicians. In Britain, the Musicians Union has mounted a campaign under the slogan 'Keep Music Live'. It points to the way in which the cheaper discotheque has ousted live bands from many venues where in the mid and late 70s young musicians were able to gain experience and learn their trade.

It has been effectively argued that live performance before an audience can be the most crucial part of a popular musician's growth as an artist. Unlike classical performers, the education of a jazz or rock musician has very little of the formal teaching situation about it; these players learn 'on the job', through the act of performance itself.

But to this assertion of the erosion of the traditional 'apprenticeship' system for musicians and of the economic harm done to some younger performers is often added a third reason for denigrating recorded music. This aesthetic argument claims, quite simply, that recorded music is intrinsically inferior to the 'real thing', live performance.

To a large degree, this view is based on a misconception of the relationship between the two types of music. The anti-recording position assumes that a sound recording is literally a *record* of a live event, a momento of it, as a snapshot might be of a holiday or a family event. Its only value (according to this argument), is to call to mind the initial event. Such is the case with some folk or jazz records, but the vast majority of rock music performers see recording as equal to, if not more important than, live playing and regard it as a different cultural form demanding different approaches.

Recorded music has now become a separate expressive form,

thanks to a range of studio technologies deriving fundamentally from the ability to edit and amalgamate sounds, made possible by the use of magnetic tape. The result is that today a recording is seldom the transcription of a single musical event. Instead of being akin to a photograph, it is more comparable to a photomontage. Arguably, too, the listener to recorded music is in a position to take a more active part in the music, by deciding how and when to listen by being able to 'edit' recordings to make up his or her own programmes on cassette tape.

However, until quite recently, the possibility of making recordings in Britain was dominated by a few large companies involved in manufacturing and distributing records as well as originating them. During the 1960s, there were effectively only four companies in the British record industry, led by EMI and Decca. During the 1970s, the major American companies, whose music had previously been licensed to the British firms, set up their own branch companies in Europe. In the 1980s, the economic recession has produced a trend towards takeovers and mergers in the international record industry. EMI has been absorbed by Thorn, Decca by PolyGram and a merger has been agreed between RCA and the German-owned Ariola. A proposed merger between PolyGram and WEA was abandoned in late 1984 because of opposition from the anti-monopoly bodies of the American and German governments.

The percentage share of record sales in Britain accounted for by the large international companies is shown in Table 10.1.

Table 10.1 Percentage share of record sales in Britain by large international companies

Company	Singles				Albums			
	1984	*1982*	*1980*	*1972*	*1984*	*1982*	*1980*	*1972*
CBS	16.0	11.8	13.1	7.6	17.2	14.2	13.9	11.8
EMI	9.1	12.1	19.5	17.0	12.9	12.5	19.0	18.1
PolyGram	16.3	20.2	13.8	20.2	12.3	18.9	12.7	16.7
RCA	9.1	8.8	6.4	9.5	8.4	6.9	5.4	6.4
WEA	11.1	9.6	13.6	6.8	9.8	9.6	12.7	9.8
TOTAL	61.6	62.5	66.4	61.1	60.6	62.1	63.7	62.8

Sources: Phil Hardy, 'The British Record Industry', IASPM Working Paper 3, Exeter, 1984; *Music Week*, 23 February 1985.

While the figures for individual firms fluctuate from year to year (reflecting to some extent the ownership of the biggest hits in each year), the aggregate market share of the five biggest companies has remained remarkably constant over twelve years, at just under two-thirds. This supports the view that, despite their competitive attitude towards one another, the big companies play similar roles at both artistic and economic levels. They offer to the consumer the same broad range of musical production and use a similar range of criteria in choosing which specific recordings to make and distribute. Incidentally, this evidence also tends to undermine arguments that the music industry is in the grip of an increasing momentum towards outright monopoly. There is no reason to assume that the present static situation will not continue.

Because of their heavy running costs, the big companies have a built-in disposition towards the type of popular music which is capable of the widest-possible appeal. This usually means a 'transnational' appeal, unhampered by a particular orientation towards a single national culture. The result is often a skilful music which is also somewhat bland. The most successful example of the last decade has been Abba.

It is also important to add that most large companies also issue recordings of lesser appeal, notably in the classical field. The initial costs of the latter are generally held to be underwritten by the large surplus generated by any big hit record. Nicholas Garnham has argued that this provision of a wide-ranging repertoire also has an economic logic. Discussing the 'use-values' of cultural commodities he has written:

> These have proved difficult if not impossible to pin down in any precise terms and demand for them appears to be similarly volatile . . . . Thus the Cultural Industries, if they are to establish a stable market, are forced to create a relationship with an audience or public to whom they offer not a simple cultural good, but a cultural repertoire across which risks can be spread.[1]

Nevertheless, within the large number of recordings issued, decisions are made as to which will be most energetically promoted. Here, a criterion of 'commercial appeal' frequently comes into play, and this is largely conservative in character.

The only guide available to what may be very popular in the future is felt to be what has been very popular in the past. The result can be an indifference to most innovatory musical work.

During the 1970s, however, countervailing tendencies developed within British popular music culture. There was a growing availability of low-cost technology for recording. Previously, an important part of the major companies' dominance had been the sheer cost of making recordings of the 'professional' standard deemed to be essential to achieve radio play and hence large sales. The average cost of recording a pop single was in thousands rather than hundreds of pounds. Only large record companies had access to sufficient finance to make that kind of investment.

In contrast to the costly and sophisticated technology employed by the major companies were simple but effective 'home studios' costing under £1,000 by 1985, the average price of four-track recording machines had come down to £500 and over 20,000 had been sold in Britain. However, for musicians to take advantage of such technology, they needed to detach themselves from the conviction that high-cost studio technology and expertise was essential for the production of successful and valuable recordings.

Ironically, it was not the record companies who had created the situation in which high-cost technology enjoyed such prestige but the musicians themselves. The Beatles (not EMI) chose to lavish time and money on the making of the Sgt. Pepper LP, while the Beach Boys' 1966 single 'Good Vibrations' was reputed to have been made in four different studios over six months and to have cost £5,000.

These artists, and the 'progressive rock' bands who came after them, were captivated by the potentiality of the studio as a place for creating new sounds. They were also convinced that rock music should be capable of more complex modes of expression. At its best, this genre produced some of the extended song-cycles of Pink Floyd but at the other extreme were dozens of overblown 'concept albums' dealing with elves or spaceships and played on synthesizers and other electronic equipment.

The history of punk as a musical genre is complex and contradictory[2] but its attitude to the prevailing orthodoxies of the record industry and of progressive rock was extremely simple. It was one of unremitting hostility. This meant a reversal of the industry's production values of professionalism and commercial appeal, and of the artistic and ideological preoccupations of progressive rock. Many punk bands extended this antagonism to all established rock musicians over the age of twenty-five.

Punk prided itself on making recordings with all the rough edges showing. The effect was to suggest that what mattered most was the urgent need to communicate a message rather than the need to construct a polished work of musical art.

The musicians involved in punk were also intensely wary of what they saw as the control exercised over popular music by the major record companies. The new music brought with it an ethic of self-reliance, of do-it-yourself. The notion that the involvement of an established record company was necessary in making a record was firmly rejected. Some bands who made their own recordings took the opportunity to encourage others to follow their example. The Desperate Bicycles sang about 'Xerox rock', while Scritti Politti printed details of recording and manufacturing costs on the sleeve of their first single. The studio costs were a mere £138.

The do-it-yourself approach was extended to the sphere of distribution. This part of the record business, getting the records to the consumers, had been even more strongly dominated by the major companies than had the origin of recordings. Established smaller labels, such as Chrysalis, Virgin and A & M had been forced to use the distribution networks of major companies. But the arrival of punk and the flood of self-produced records led to the setting up of new distribution networks which enabled the new labels to keep their distance from the bigger companies. One estimate is that the new independent labels and distributors accounted, by the mid-1980s for nearly 10 per cent of British record sales.

Those sales have shown a considerable overall decline since the late 1970s, with a fall of some 30 per cent in value following 1979. Although the value of United Kingdom record sales began to rise again in 1983–5, the overall position still indicates a drop since the 1970s. Various reasons have been offered for this decline, but the most likely explanation is that the general conditions of recession in Britain have been exacerbated by other factors peculiar to the recording industry. These include competition from the new entertainment media of video and computer games and the widespread practice of private copying or home taping. This involves using cassette players to re-record commercially produced recordings onto tape. After so-far fruitless attempts to create a 'scrambler' signal which could be inserted onto a disc or tape to prevent copying, the record industry has lobbied for a royalty to be placed on blank tapes and tape recording hardware. The income would then be distributed to performers, composers and record companies.

In February 1985, a government Green Paper [3] accepted the basic proposition that a royalty should be levied on blank tape, but the amount was limited to a maximum of 10 per cent on the retail price of the tape.

The fall in record sales during the 1980s has damaged the newer sector of the industry more than the major companies. The latter are all part of large conglomerates with large reserves which can be employed to see the industry through the recession. No such option is available to the more fragile independent sector. A recognition of the need to maintain that sector and through it the full diversity of recorded music in Britain is one reason why the last few years has seen a new interest in the record industry from public bodies concerned with culture and with employment.

Popular music has received very little assistance from the various Arts Councils whose job is to disburse monies from the state and local authorities. These bodies regarded the cultural form as part of a commercialized industry and were unwilling to provide grants for activities designed to make a profit. Another difficulty has been that such councils are attuned to providing finance for the creation of specific works, while the need for support in popular music is not at the point of creation, but for help in reaching audiences. This was one of the main findings of a report to the Gulbenkian Foundation on research in the mid-1980s by the present author together with Tony Haynes and Julie Eaglen.[4]

More recently, certain local authority organizations have begun to take a direct interest in popular music. Their motives are various and include concern about employment in general and youth unemployment in particular, and an awareness of the potential effects of new media, such as cable television, on the quality of life in the locality.

Sheffield City Council and the Greater London Council jointly commissioned a report on cable and community programming, which included wide-ranging discussion of the possible use of these new technologies to aid locally based music as well as the 'transnational' kind. It was published as an Appendix to Hardy,[5] which was itself the result of an inquiry by the Greater London Enterprise Board (GLEB) into the music industry. This GLEB report focused mainly on the manufacturing aspect of the independent sector and recommended the setting up of a modern plant to make records for the smaller companies. Elsewhere both Sheffield and Leeds City Councils have actively considered schemes to set up local recording studios, while one London Borough Council is looking at the needs of its local black music scene.

It is important that those involved in these initiatives and others which may follow understand the priorities for assistance to popular music. What is not required is the traditional form of arts subsidy: the direct grant to an individual or a group. The most important requirement is to improve for all musicians what might be called the infrastructure of opportunity. The issue is one of *access*, particularly for young musicians and for innovators. The study for the Gulbenkian Foundation found a need for a greater availability of electronic and amplification equipment, of rehearsal space, of cheap recording facilities with expert advice and instruction on how to use them and finally for more places to perform in.

Assistance in all these areas would provide the chance for musicians to develop their own potential and to discover whether there is an audience for their music. In achieving that assistance, the two parts of the record industry can also contribute. The independent sector provides some models and much experience for any new initiatives at grassroots level. And the success of the established record industry's campaign for a royalty on blank tape could also contribute. In those countries where the royalty has already been introduced one option chosen by some governments has been to use part of the income from the levy to set up a fund to give special help to the national music scene. In Sweden this is done by a subsidy for recording projects involving Swedish music, while Finland aims to help new music in general. In France, the music industry will be required to devote 25 per cent of the tape levy to the 'encouragement of creativity', under a law which came into force in January 1986.

Britain currently possesses a large pool of popular music talent, thanks primarily to the ease with which the independent sector has enabled consumers to become producers. To ensure that this channel of transformation remains open and available, deliberate intervention by public bodies may well be required. Any radical policy for the record industry should begin from the need to maintain a real plurality in popular music making.

NOTES

1 Nicholas Garnham, 'Concepts of culture: public policy and the cultural industries', paper given to GLC Conference on Cultural Policy, December 1983.
2 For a more detailed analysis of punk rock see my *One Chord Wonders*, Milton Keynes: Open University Press, 1985.
3 'The recording and rental of audio and video copyright material', HMSO Cmnd 9445.
4 Tony Haynes (with David Laing and Julie Eaglen), *Music in Between*, London: Gulbenkian Foundation, 1989.
5 Phil Hardy, 'The record industry: the case for public intervention', *GLC, Economic Policy Strategy Document*, no. 16, London, 1984.

11

'If you can't stand the heat, get off the beach'
The United Kingdom holiday business

GRAHAME F. THOMPSON

In the autumn of 1985 a fierce battle emerged between United Kingdom holiday firms in an effort to enhance their share of the 1986 summer holiday market. This involved in particular two 'market leaders', Thomson Holidays and Intasun Holidays. Each began to cut prices, implicitly challenging the others to follow in a tit-for-tat sequence. Anything between 30 per cent and 60 per cent was being cut from the price of holidays. Some of Thomson's holidays to Spain sold for only £25 a week or £35 for two weeks, and 500 Intasun Holidays were offered for £39 each. Partly as a protest at these 'irresponsible' price reductions NAT Travel, a smaller holiday firm, introduced a ten-day coach/camping holiday for £5 at one stage. People were seen queuing overnight outside travel agents to be able to cash in on a £20 holiday for four! The holiday sale season (some would argue 'silly season') was on. But behind these bravado tactics lay some intriguing and important features of the development of both United Kingdom holiday firms and of the United Kingdom economy itself. It is these features that are explored in this chapter. While the 1985/6 period forms the focus of my analysis this particular episode should not be seen as unique in the context of the United Kingdom holiday industry. In the early 1970s something of a similar competitive battle emerged in which a series of well known holiday firms at the time either collapsed or got into severe financial difficulties (Clarksons, Horizon Midland, Court Line amongst others). It was confidently predicted that some firms, particularly the smaller ones, would also go out of business as a consequence of the 1985 round of price cutting. (This was trumpeted under the holiday industry's unofficial motto 'if you can't stand the heat, get off the beach'.) Indeed, in 1984 some eighteen smallish tour operators failed and in late 1984 an important firm, Budget Travel (the tenth largest at the time) also suddenly went out of business. Pundits of the travel scene were heard suggesting (and exaggerating) that as many as 200 to 300 travel firms could go bankrupt if things went badly. In the following sections the components, structure, and tendencies involved with the firms making up the holiday industry are analysed; and recent competitive battles are reviewed.

THE STRUCTURE OF THE INDUSTRY

The United Kingdom tourist industry was worth £11 billion in 1986, half of which was spent on the 10.5 million overseas inclusive tour holidays taken and 7 million independently organized overseas visits. There were approximately 700 firms offering holidays of some kind to consumers in the United Kingdom in 1986. However, most of these were very small organizations only arranging a few hundred or perhaps a few thousand holidays a year. The twelve largest companies in mid-1984 are shown in Table 11.1. The two main rivals that began to emerge in the early 1980s were Thomson, the traditional market leader, and Intasun, a fast growing holiday and leisure group of companies. The growth of the top eight firms in terms of the number of air tours authorized by the Civil Aviation Authority (CAA) is shown in Table 11.2. Whilst the total number of holidays authorized increased by nearly 50 per cent over the period shown both Thomson and Intasun expanded by a greater proportion but with Intasun far outstripping Thomson's growth. In fact, 1985 was a rather bad year for the overseas travel trade despite a surge of late bookings in the autumn as the indifferent summer took hold. Two previous years of good domestic summer weather had depressed the anticipated number of overseas holidays and this is probably reflected in the low 1985 figures shown for a number of operators. The 1986 and 1987 figures show a rapid pick up for the larger firms in particular.

These figures include the number of authorized (or anticipated) holidays. They are not the same as the actual numbers arranged by each operator, but they do indicate the broad magnitudes involved. The shares of the market in terms of actual holidays taken (*ex-post* market shares) of four of the main operating groups are shown in Table 11.3.

This demonstrates clearly the importance of the two leading companies in their fight for market share. But the general implications of the table are also important since it demonstrates the relative concentration of supply. Four firms are responsible for 50 per cent of the market. Under many circumstances this would be looked upon with some suspicion – giving rise to accusations of severe oligopoly or even near monopoly. However, the industry is highly competitive, as suggested above. This is because of two main reasons which are closely linked and which will be considered in more detail later.

One of these involves the ease of entry into the industry. It is not difficult to set up a holiday firm and expand rapidly. The other is ease of exit from the industry, not just by a company if it gets into financial difficulties and is forced to leave, but also by any particular customer. There are many alternative types of holiday on offer and even within the package sector the provision of a financial bond by firms and other guarantees give particular holiday-makers a relatively firm assurance that they will get the holiday they want or one very nearly like it. However, this being said, the trend towards concentration of capital is very rapid in the industry and this is likely to increase in the near future. In addition, if widespread liquidations emerge as a result of recent intensified competitive pressure there could be more severe disruption of holiday plans. The collapse of Budget Travel, for instance, left some 20,000 holiday-makers without adequate holiday cover in 1984 (Table 11.1) and important companies continued to collapse – in 1987, for instance, Biggles and Jetwing collapsed.

Let us now return to Table 11.1 and look at the operational details and financial situation of the companies mentioned there in greater detail. As far as operational details are concerned perhaps the most interesting feature is the way tour operators are usually part of larger, more diversified, groups. Inclusive tour operation is thus just one, and sometimes a very small, part of the parent company's business. This was particularly so in the case of Thomson, British Airways Holidays, Rank Travel, Blue

Table 11.1 The United Kingdom's top twelve tour companies: operating and financial details

TOUR OPERATOR	Number of holidays authorized by the CAA (Summer 1984)	Associated airline	Parent company	Turnover £'000	Pre-tax profits £'000	Profit margin[b] %	Return on capital[c] %
Thomson	954,500	Britannia	International Thomson Organization	478,528 (end 1984)	23,046	4.8	14.8
Intasun	550,000	Air Europe	Intasun Leisure Group	240,733 (1984/5)	24,844	10.3	57.9
Horizon	544,000	Orion	Horizon Travel	151,944 (1984/5)	12,518	8.2	13.8
British Airways Holidays	533,600	British Air Tours	British Airways	97,500 (1984/85)	3,200	3.3	na[e]
Rank Travel	365,000	British Cal.[d] Charter	The Rank Organization				
Cosmos	300,000	Monarch	Cosmos Motoring Anslatt (Leichensteine)	97,604 (end 1983)	1,764	1.8	3.8
Blue Sky	219,610	British Caledonian Charter	Caledonian Airways	45,604	223	0.5	20.0
Thomas Cook	203,800		Midland Bank	261,940 (end 1984)	16,738	6.4	25.3

Company	Turnover	Parent	Net capital employed	Pre-tax profits	Profit margin[b]	Return on capital[c]
Global	174,000	Great Universal Stores				
Sunny Tours (Budget Travel)	130,000[a]					
Portland	128,400	Britannia	32,050 (end 1983)	−217	−0.7	−9.13
Holiday Club International	126,000	Bass	16,496 (end 1983)	−1,743	−10.6	−9.5

Source: ICC Keynote Report, *Travel Agents/Overseas Tour Operators* (1985), Appendix Table 2 and Company Reports (various years).

Notes: [a] Sunny Tours (Budget Travel) ceased trading on 24 October 1984.

[b] Profit margin = $\dfrac{\text{Pre-tax profits}}{\text{Turnover}} \times 100$.

[c] Return on capital = $\dfrac{\text{Pre-tax profits}}{\text{Net capital employed}} \times 100$.

[d] Rank Travel owns 50% of British Caledonian Airways (Charter) Ltd.

[e] Not extractable from consolidated account.

Table 11.2 Number of air tours authorized by CAA ('000) 1981–7

	1981	1982	1983	1984	1985	1986	1987	% change 81–7
All operators	6,662	7,000	7,900	8,623	6,847	9,840	na	47 [a]
Thomson	856	899	966	954	1,313	2,100	2,700	215
Intasun	359	353	509	550	880	1,200	1,800	401
Horizon	361	428	481	544	409	590	884	146
Rank	345	354	316	366	323	405	477	38
British Air Tours	444	na	na	534	269	391	478	8
Portland	76	na	na	128	233	176	223	103
Cosmos	276	350	300	300	225	250	250	−9
Blue Sky	148	261	na	219	219	150	— [b]	1 [a]

Source: ICC Keynote Report, *Travel Agents / Overseas Tour Operators* (1985, 1987), and *The Observer*, 19 July 1987.

Notes: na = not available.

[a] to 1986 only.

[b] Blue Sky sold to Rank, consolidated under Wings title at end of 1986, sold to Horizon, which was subsequently taken over by Bass in 1987.

Sky, Thomas Cook, Global, and Holiday Club International, these all being travel firms operated by large leisure-based parent companies or diversified conglomerates. Even the tour companies themselves include a range of different brand names under their umbrellas. Thomson Travel, for instance, includes the Thomson label proper, plus Portland Holidays, Britannia Airways and Lunn Poly the travel agent chain. Intasun includes the Intasun label, plus Club 18–30, Golden Days, Ski Scene, Lancaster Holidays as well as its own airline, Air Europe. In 1985 Intasun acquired Global Tours from Great Universal Stores in a further step in its diversification and concentration moves. In addition, Global itself included such names as Golden

Table 11.3 Tour operators market share (% volume by air)

	1981	1982	1983	1984	1985	1986 (est.)
Thomson	18	18	19	20	21	25
Intasun	10.5	11	12	14	16	23
Horizon	7.5	9	8	9	5	8
Cosmos	9	8	6	7	5	6 (British Air Tours)
Others	55	54	55	50	53	38

Source: ICC Keynote Report, *Travel Agents / Overseas Tour Operators* (1987), Table 13, p. 19.

Circle and Overland Holidays, as well as its own name. Rank Travel was made up of Wings and OSL in 1985, while British Airways Tours included the Enterprise, Sovereign, Flair, Alta (Speed Bird), and Martin Rook holiday names as well as its own airline company, British Air Tours. The more independent companies shown in Table 1 were Cosmos and Horizon. Cosmos has been losing market share and falls out of the top four companies in 1986 as British Air Tours takes over (Table 11.3).

The Horizon Company itself has an interesting history, being a firm that got into financial difficulties as Horizon Midland in the mid-1970s. When it collapsed, two 'public' bodies stepped in to effect a rescue, namely, The Greater Manchester Passenger Transport Executive (GMPTE), and Nottinghamshire County Council. These two bodies took a major stake in the company since Horizon, with its associated airline Orion, was one of the main users of Manchester Airport and East Midlands Airport. Its collapse could have had serious roll-on effects on the finances of these airports, and the relevant local authorities stepped in. This rescue operation proved reasonably successful, as shown by Table 11.4.

But with a declining profit margin and declining return on capital (particularly in 1985–6), and with the sale by the GMPTE of its shareholding at a considerable profit, Horizon needed a new injection of resources. To keep up with the competitive pressure put on it from Thomson and Intasun,

Table 11.4 Horizon Travel Ltd: financial results 1978–86 (£'000)

	1978–9	79–80	80–1	81–2
Turnover	31,269	50,179	72,577	96,833
Pre-tax profits	2,951	3,815	7,381	13,402
Profit margin[a]	9.4%	7.6%	10.2%	13.8%
Return on capital[a]	44.9%	40.0%	45.3%	36.4%
	82–3	83–4	84–5	85–6
Turnover	118,487	124,206	151,944	198,330
Pre-tax profits	14,368	12,564	12,518	4,590
Profit margin[a]	12.1%	10.1%	8.2%	2.3%
Return on capital[a]	28.8%	20.4%	13.8%	5.8%

Source: Company Reports.
Note: [a] Calculated as in Table 11.1.

Horizon was itself diversifying in this period. Apart from its original holiday retailing company, it has set up a chain of travel agencies, developed a flight training centre in connection with its Orion airline subsidiary, moved into holiday hotel development and even into selling holiday properties abroad. These later developments were aided by the Bass brewery group taking a 27 per cent stake in the company in 1985 – after it had been sought by Grand Metropolitan, another leisure grouping. This brought with it Bass's own Holiday Club International and Pontins Holidays. In addition, Rank Travel was consolidating its holiday interest by buying Blue Sky from British Caledonian (Table 11.1) along with the Arrowsmith company, and organizing these under its Wings Holiday label. Wings was subsequently sold by Rank to Horizon at about the same time as Horizon was itself purchased more or less outright by Bass for £90 million in May 1987.

Thus there has been some significant organizational development in the industry even since 1985 when Table 11.1 was drawn up. All this goes to show, however, the great uncertainty associated with the holiday industry. It exists on relatively thin and unstable margins, requiring the heavyweight financial resources of a larger group if it is to survive for long.

The other main operational feature that Table 11.1 highlights is the way most of the big firms are associated with an airline. This became an emergent feature of British (and other European) inclusive tour companies in the late 1960s as the expansion of charter non-scheduled activity gained momentum. It was pioneered by now defunct companies such as Eagle Airways, Court Line, and more recently, Laker Airways. It represents another arm of holiday firm diversification. Not all of each airline capacity is restricted to the holidays of its associated holiday company, however. The airlines also sell their capacity to those firms not operating an airline. Table 11.5 shows the main operators and their seat capacity in 1985.

Clearly the airlines' authorized capacity does not match up to the company market shares as shown in either Table 11.2 or Table 11.3. In addition there is a major charter airline shown in Table 11.5 which has not appeared before. Dan Air offered 22 per cent of capacity in 1985 but is not organizationally linked to any single tour operator and functions as a totally separate company.

Table 11.5 General Air Tours: major operators 1985

Holiday firm	Charter airline	% of charter seats
Thomson	Britannia	28
–	Dan Air	22
Intasun	Air Europe	9
Enterprise, Sovereign etc.	British Air Tours	12
Horizon	Orion	8
Cosmos	Monarch	9

Source: ICC Sector Report (1985), Table 6, p. 10 plus text.

The final four columns of Table 11.1 give details of the financial position of the companies as far as this could be discerned from published data. The first point to make here is that holiday firms are big business. Thomson Travel, for instance, had a turnover of nearly £500 million in 1984. Profit margins vary between the firms but are low relative even to the indifferent performance of British firms more generally. It would be useful to chart these trends over a number of years for each of these firms, rather like the analysis offered for Horizon in Table 11.4. Overall industry data of this kind are collected in Table 11.6, giving an indication of profitability for the industry as a whole. This goes to confirm that the figures shown in Table 11.1 are fairly representative of the industry more generally.

This table also confirms the seeming decline in overall profitability during the 1980s and particularly in 1986. Eight of the top thirty companies in 1986 recorded losses, amounting to £19 million (in 1987 six companies recorded losses totalling £14 million). While the top three or four companies now seem to be

Table 11.6 Profitability of top thirty operators[a] (£ million)

	1980	1981	1982	1983	1984	1985	1986
Turnover	906.9	1,019.7	1,299.5	1,407	1,799	1,840	2,130
Net profit	43.8	52.2	27.7	55.3	53.3	60.7	35.6
Profit margin[b]	4.8%	5.1%	2.1%	3.9%	3.0%	3.3%	1.7%

Source: ICC Keynote Report, *Travel Agents/Overseas Tour Operators* (1987), *Financial Times*, 28 May 1987.
Notes: [a] Top thirty are those with over 50,000 holiday sales per year.
   [b] Calculated as in Table 11.1.

in reasonable financial shape it is the medium-sized firms in the top thirty that are feeling the pressure. It is from this group that more collapses are likely or in which reorganizations and consolidations will occur.

GENERAL ORGANIZATIONAL TRENDS

Of the longer term organizational trends that have developed within the travel industry, diversification needs to be broken down into a range of separate forms.

In the first place the industry is typified by two types of integration, vertical and horizontal. Both of these imply the concentration and centralization of capital. Vertical integration refers to the way in which travel firms are increasingly organizing all the separate features of a holiday under a single organizational umbrella. This can involve both forward vertical integration and backward vertical integration. For instance, if a holiday firm buys into a chain of travel agents, which are traditionally separate retailing agents for holiday sales, this is a case of forward vertical integration since it brings the holiday firm 'forward' towards the consumer. On the other hand, if it integrates with the airline part of the holiday and begins to develop its own hotels and resort complexes this is a case of backward vertical integration, since in this case the holiday firm is pushing its liaisons further back into the supply network of the holiday.

Both of these tendencies were well underway by 1985 with nearly all the large firms included in Table 11.1. Thomson Travel includes an airline (backward integration) and a chain of travel agents (forward integration). Intasun and Horizon are taking backward integration even further by not only operating their own airlines but also developing or buying up hotels and holiday centres in the Mediterranean area. This has been done in the first instance through joint ventures with Ladbrokes and Bass respectively, though Horizon also owned and operated hotels in its own name. Thomas Cook is a slightly different case in that its origins are at the consumer end – as a travel agent chain – but it has now developed into the provision of holiday sector as well, thus generating backward vertical integration. On the other hand, a company like Virgin Airways has developed forward integration by setting up and selling its own holidays (to the United States). Most of the other companies included in the table are also developing or have already developed liaisons of this type.

The second form of diversification that is underway in the industry is horizontal integration. This appears when a holiday firm either itself generates, or is absorbed into a sequence of activities parallel to its own business. Here we might point to the way Holiday Club International has become part of the wider leisure services and manufacturing group Bass Holdings. Another instance of this would be Rank Travel (OSL, Blue Sky, Wings) and its integration into the diversified leisure activities of the Rank Organization (prior to its sale to Horizon/Bass). These two cases are examples of the centralization of capital; the way previously separate organizations are brought under a single centralized unit of direction (though they may actually be run rather autonomously in practice). A different example of the same basic process but one which involves the concentration of capital is given by Intasun's expansion strategy. This involves the original holiday firm generating parallel activities itself. Thus Intasun is diversifying into the United Kingdom hotel market. In 1985 it purchased the Grosvenor and Charing Cross hotels in London and entered into joint ventures with the large American hotel chain Ramada Inns to manage these hotels and others that it intends to buy. Other examples of this form of diversification would be Midland Bank ownership of Thomas Cook, this firm having traditionally arranged the travel requirements of Midland Bank staff (and those of other corporate institutions), and also being a major issuer of travellers' cheques (a money dealing activity).

What are the reasons for these kinds of diversification? This has been the subject of endless commentary within the economics profession since these sorts of trends have typified nearly all industrial and service sectors of capitalist economies (and some socialist ones, it might be added). Perhaps the two main sets of determinants can be summed up under 'economies of scale' and 'economies of scope'.

Economies of scale refer to the way average costs of provision can fall as the scale of output increases. This is a well known if perhaps exaggerated feature thought to typify the production of larger and larger levels of output. Certain necessary fixed costs of overheads can then be spread over a greater number of units of output thus reducing their incidence per unit of output, and also unit attributable costs might be lowered via bulk buying or the better management of production, and by strengthening of purchasing power. It is probably these potential economies of scale that are involved with elements of vertical integration in particular, and also with the increasing range of types of holidays being offered by firms as discussed below. Economies of scale are also a feature likely to be associated with the struggle for market share. The larger a firm becomes the more cost efficient it can become and hence prices can be kept below those competitors. Clearly, within the scale of output being contemplated by existing holiday firms they feel this potential advantage can give them a decisive competitive edge *vis-à-vis* their rivals.

Economies of scope refer to the potential cost advantages likely to arise via diversifying strategies involving horizontal integration in particular. In the case of holiday firms the main element here would seem to be the financial advantages of being part of a larger conglomerate grouping. Holiday demand is highly sensitive to changes in underlying economic conditions (it is relatively income-elastic for instance) which means it can be subject to rapid changes as the cyclical pattern of economic activity develops. This implies an oscillating financial performance for the industry as a whole.

Add to this the thin margins on which the industry has traditionally had to rely and a very unstable and uncertain environment for individual firms emerges. In this context the financial muscle associated with a more diversified grouping, where risks are spread more evenly, can serve to help weather the storm. It also offers the prospect of an easier means for raising finance when investment is needed.

In practice, of course, economies of scale and economies of scope are processes which are usually run together as any firm diversifies. There is also no guarantee that these 'potential' advantages will actually be realized in practice. Many a case can be cited where business strategies of this kind have utterly failed. But one general implication of these tendencies is the increasing concentration of capital. Thus, what were previously transactions between different organizational units become transactions internal to a single organizational unit. 'Externalities' are turned into 'internalities' and the 'market system' is increasingly being undermined by bureaucratic methods of internalized economic allocation within conglomerates or diversified firms.

Given these tendencies and features, what is the typical cost profile of a holiday company? Only a general indication of this can be given here. Table 11.7 lays out the main elements and their likely proportional magnitude.

One consequence of competitive price battles could be to raise the overhead and marketing cost element in any firm's budget. It is estimated that some 30 per cent of the overhead and marketing budget represents the cost of production and distribution of brochures. Some 40 million glossy brochures pack agents' racks advertising holidays each year. In the context of the late 1985 competitive battle to gain market share, 're-issuing' of the brochure became a commonplace as price reductions were instituted.

A further organizational trend underway in the tourist industry concerns an aspect of the internal organization of travel firms themselves. This involves the way these firms perceive their marketing effort. In particular, a strategy towards differentiation of the market is strongly underway. Specialist sectors are identified and firms either decide to concentrate on one or two of these or arrange their activities so that they cover the whole range of sectors. In the latter case a set of different brochures would be issued by any single firm. Table 11.8 gives a breakdown of the main sectors that can be identified and also the leading firms or 'names' in each sector.

These 'leading operators' need not be the ones holding the largest share of any particular market sector. That may still accrue to one of the main operators already mentioned. For instance, in the ski-ing category, Thomson is yet again the

Table 11.7 Air tour operators estimated cost

Overheads and marketing	5%–10%
Hotel or villa	35%–50%
Flight	25%–35%
Travel agents' commission	10%

Table 11.8 The differentiation of the market

Specialist sector	Leading operator
Direct sell	Portland, Martin Rook, Tjaebourg.
Ski-ing	Hotel Plan, Blue Sky, Neilson, Bladon Lines
Age-group	Over 50s: Saga, Golden Days, Golden Circle
	Youth: Club 18–30, Buddies, Freestyle
Self-catering	Canvas Holidays (Camping), OSL (Villas)
Coach tours	Wallace Arnold, Saga, Cosmos
Cruises	P & O, Royal Viking, DFDS
Long haul	Kuoni, T. Cook, Rank
'National'	Yugotours, Olympic (Greece), Sunmed (Greece)

leader with the highest share of this sub-market (around 20 per cent). But this is followed by the rather more specialist firms listed in Table 11.8, Hotel Plan (under the Inghams and Swan Plan labels), and Blue Sky which also specialised in this area.

The first specialist sector mentioned in the table is direct sell. This cuts out the travel agent and was pioneered in the United Kingdom by the Danish firm Tjaebourg (which also has its own airline, Stirling Airways). The idea is to reduce costs by cutting out the 10 per cent travel agents' commission (Table 11.7). The market here is probably around 500,000 holidays a year (5 per cent of the total volume of holidays). Although Portland (a Thomson subsidiary) and Tjaebourg itself seemed to be doing well, in 1985 the British Airways subsidiary Martin Rook was rumoured to be up for disposal, with an uncertain future. This sector of the market has not expanded as rapidly as expected.

In the age-group sector, the independent firm Saga is the market leader in the over-fifties category, followed by Intasun's Golden Days. Global's Golden Circle concentrates on the United Kingdom over-fifties market (now a part of Intasun). This sub-sector is an increasingly competitive one which all of the major firms have identified as a growth area. Saga pioneered this market and became a very large company on the basis of it. However, the firm made a mistake in buying up the Laker Holidays label and trying to revive it in an effort to diversify its operating base. The failure of this initiative set the firm back somewhat and it may find it difficult to recover.

At the other end of the age-group market is the 'youth' category, led by Intasun's Club 18–30. This sold 90,000 holidays in 1984 and claimed 45 per cent of the market. It was followed by Buddies (a Bass subsidiary). Thomson launched their slightly up-market version, Freestyle, in 1984. This sub-sector is recognized as another growing one and it has been further differentiated in recent years by the recognition of a specifically educational, volume travel market. Schools Abroad (95,200 authorized holidays in 1984) and School Plan (Intasun) lead in this market.

There is even a recognition of a specifically religious holiday clientele. Thomas Cook, for instance, sent over 5,500 pilgrims on holiday in 1985 through its Inter-Church travel firm subsidiary.

The other main sector of interest given in Table 11.8 is the long-haul category. True long-haul serves holidays to Australia, New Zealand, South America, Southern and Central Africa, and the fast expanding Far Eastern market. The recognized market leader here is the Swiss firm Kuoni, claiming 24 per cent of the market (40,000 holidays in 1984). This is followed by a number of others including Thomas Cook, Thomson's 'World Wide' label, and the more recent tobacco brand Silk Cut/Meon Travel's 'Far Away' entry. This is generally recognized as still an upmarket sector but is growing by about 5 per cent per year. Its long-term prospects as far as mass marketing is concerned are still uncertain and will depend upon the ability of airlines to keep their prices down and upon relative exchange rate movements, both of which disproportionately affect this sector. In 1984 the total holidays in this market sector were in the region of 170,000. Thus, whilst important, numbers here are still small relative to other areas. Table 11.9 shows Kuoni's top long-haul destinations in 1983–4.

Table 11.9 Top 15 long-haul destinations (Kuoni 1984)

Country	% change on 1983	Country	% change on 1983
1 Thailand	+ 37	9 Sri Lanka	− 26
2 Hong Kong	+ 31	10 Egypt	+ 3
3 Barbados	+102	11 Antigua	− 5
4 Kenya	+ 2	12 China	+ 34
5 Bali	+101	13 Brazil	+ 11
6 Singapore	+ 49	14 The Gambia	− 23
7 India/Nepal	+ 19	15 Seychelles	+246
8 St Lucia	− 29		

Source: Kuoni Report 1984.

This probably represents the situation in the sub-market as a whole given Kuoni's position as market leader (except for the Gambia which is beginning to appear strongly in short-haul brochures). The long-haul market is important however for another reason. It embraces the development of quite new holiday areas and is thus in the forefront of pushing the 'tourist experience' onto previously unaffected or relatively little affected people and cultures. It represents the spear-head of a possible 'tourist imperialism', with all the unsatisfactory consequences that this might engender.

OTHER COMPONENTS OF THE TOURIST INDUSTRY

Table 11.7 pointed out that 10 per cent of air tour operators' costs represented travel agents' commission. Travel agents are an important component in the organizational structure of United Kingdom overseas travel. Increasingly they are grouping themselves into multiple retail chains, as can be seen from Table 11.10. This sector of the industry has been characterized by an extraordinarily rapid series of takeovers and mergers in recent years to create the multiples shown. Thomas Cook is a wholly owned subsidiary of Midland Bank, Pickfords is owned by the National Freight Consortium (previously the National Freight Corporation until its de-nationalization in 1983 and 'buy-out' by management) and Lunn Poly is owned by Thomson

Table 11.10 Travel agency multiples (end 1984)

Outlets	Proprietor	Chains included
Over 300	Thomas Cook	Thomas Cook, Frames, Blue Sky
250–300	Pickfords	Harry Leek
150–250	Lunn Poly	Ellerman, Renwick
	Hogg Robinson	Wakfield Fortune, Blue Star
100–150	A.T. Mayers	Nain Travel
	W.H. Smith	(in store)
	National Travel World	
	Co-operative	(in store)
50–100	American Express	P & O Travel Agents
	Automobile Association	
	Exchange Travel	mainly in stores

Source: ICC Keynote Report, *Travel Agents/Overseas Tour Operators* (1984), p.8.

Holidays. Thus the main multiples in the table are also themselves smaller components of parent organizations.

There were approximately 12,000 travel agent outlets in 1986, 6,000 of which belong to the trade association ABTA (of these, the total of separate travel agent firms was 2,500). ABTA, set up in 1950, exists as a cartel. Since 1966 it has operated a set of rules known as the 'stabilizer' which has regulated the behaviour of tour operators and travel agents in the inclusive tour industry. This involves exclusive dealing and retail price maintenance in return for which consumers are guaranteed a degree of protection and recompense in the case of financial failure of a tour operator. Five hundred tour operators also belong to ABTA, effectively covering 90 per cent of holiday journeys. The stabilizer scheme creates a common fund to which members contribute according to their turnover. If an operator goes out of business the fund is used to rescue stranded holiday-makers or to provide alternative holidays. In addition to this fund there is a bonding operation supervised by the CAA against airline failure. The basic ABTA fund is financed by a 10 per cent levy on ABTA licensed members and 15 per cent on non-ABTA operators. The level of funding has proved inadequate on several occasions (Eros and Americana failures in 1983 and Budget Travel in 1984, for instance). A major issue in 1985 was the possibility of increasing the cover. The idea of the bond is both to demonstrate the financial security of the firm and to provide funds to rescue its clients if it goes out of business. But it can place a large burden on operators and travel agents and any increases in the size of the bond are seen as likely to further the pressures for rationalization in the industry. The problem in this area arises because of the advanced booking process in which customers commit their money or some part of it well in advance of actually taking their holiday and without 'seeing' the service offered. In 1986 the fund paid out £1.3 million to customers of fifteen failed holiday firms. A typical travel agent's income is made up of two-thirds from holiday traffic and one-third from business traffic. Approximate sales turnover in 1984 is shown in Table 11.11. The standard commissions on which the agents have relied for their income are shown in Table 11.12.

Two main problems face the travel agent sector of the market. In the first place, the march of the multiples and

Table 11.11 Travel agents' sales turnover 1984

	£bn	%
Holiday travel of which	2.15–2.6	67–75
Inclusive tours	1.72	44–60
Independent	0.43–0.88	15–23
Business travel	0.72–1.3	25–33
Total	2.87–3.9	100

Source: 'UK Travel Agents', *International Tourism Quarterly* (1984), no. 3, Table 3, p. 3.

diversification by travel operators themselves is likely to undermine the traditional relationships established between travel agents and operators. Lunn Poly and Thomas Cook are already part of larger groups. The multiples in particular are increasing their share of the market. But, as yet, concentration in the sector is quite low and market share remains fragmented. However, rapid changes are sweeping the sector and trends remain flexible.

The second and probably more serious problem for the sector arises in the context of ABTA remaining a cartel. The Office of Fair Trading already looked into this in 1982 and offered a judgement giving a guarded acceptance of the closed shop. But this was again investigated in 1985 and a less favourable

Table 11.12 Travel agents' standard commission (pre-1987)[a]

Travel product/service	Standard level of commission (%)
Inclusive tours	10
Air tickets	9
Rail tickets	7.5
Coach bookings	8
Shipping bookings	9 (19 for cruises)
Car hire	10
Accommodation	8
Theatre tickets	10
Insurance	30–40

Source: 'UK Travel Agents', *International Tourism Quarterly* (1984), no. 3, Table 3, p. 3.
Note: [a] The Monopolies and Mergers Commission Report (*Foreign Package Holidays*, Cmnd 9879, HMSO, London, 1986) recommended the dismantling of many of these commissions.

response emerged from the Monopolies and Merger Commission's Report issued in 1986. The report (*Foreign Package Holidays*, Cmnd 9879, HMSO: London, September 1986) recommended the end of resale price maintenance agreements. These effectively buttressed the sector against the kind of cut-throat competition raging amongst operators. However, one complaint already made by the travel agents is the impossibility of existing on the lower commissions implied by holidays of £25 and the like that came into existence at the end of 1985. All in all, these twin developments are likely to throw the agents into ever greater turmoil as we enter the 1990s.

DOMESTIC HOLIDAY SUPPLY FIRMS

So far, overseas holidays have formed the focus of my attention. But very large numbers of domestic holidays are also taken – about 30 million in 1986. Clearly in looking at the travel agent sector we have already been analysing something of the domestic arm of the industry since these agents also arrange domestic holidays or parts of them. However, the domestic holiday situation is much more fragmented than overseas tourism. The 'inclusive tour' is less well developed, for instance, and most holidays are independently arranged and are for much shorter periods. This makes for a radically differentiated supply structure, one not easily captured in a manageable set of statistics. Perhaps the most suitable starting point is to look at the major domestically based leisure groups, the activities of which are summed up in Table 11.13. This gives a breakdown of their main holiday-based activities and similar financial details are given for the holiday firms discussed in Table 11.1. Points to make in the context of this table are, again, the very large turnover involved and the fact that profit margins are healthier and more stable than in the tour operator case. Two of the organizations mentioned in the table are also prominently involved as parents in the tour operator case, namely Bass and, until recently, Rank. Most of the organizations involved are themselves again parts of large conglomerate groups with diversified interests, not necessarily just in the leisure services area. Grand Metropolitan and Rank, for instance, have wide ranging manufacturing and property interests, though the

Table 11.13 Major United Kingdom hotels, catering and leisure groups: operating and financial details (1983/4)

Group	Activity	Chains/brands	Turnover £'000	Pre-tax profits £'000	Profit margin[c] %	Return on capital[d] %
Trust House Forte	Hotels	THF, Post Houses, Little Chef,	1,148,600 (10–'84)	105,200	9.2	9.4
	Catering	Happy Eater Motorway Services, Airline Catering Industrial Catering (Gardner Merchant)				
Grand Metropolitan	Hotels	Intercontinental, Others	1,510,700[a] (3–'84)	99,300	6.6	9.6
	Catering	Berni Inns, Clifton Inns, Chef and Brewer, Industrial Catering				
	Holiday Centres	Warner[e]				
	Other Tourism	Travelscene,[e] Mecca Entertainments				
Bass	Hotels	Crest	571,300[a] (3–'84)	36,000	6.3	[b]
	Catering	Toby Inns, Old Kentucky				
	Holiday Centres	Pontins, Coral Bookmaking and Bingo				
Rank	Hotels	Rank (London)	334,000[a] (3–'84)	19,300	5.8	[b]
	Catering	Motorway Services				
	Holiday Centres	Butlins, Leisure Caravans				
	Other Tourism	Wings,[e]				
Ladbroke	Hotels	Ladbroke, Comfort	738,500 (3–'83)	35,100	4.8	[b]
	Holiday Centres	Ladbroke				
	Other Tourism	Casinos				

Sources: ICC Keynote Report, *Tourism in the UK* (1986) and Company Reports (various years).

Notes: [a] Leisure services divisions only.

[b] Capital employed in leisure services division not given in accounts.

[c] Profit margin = $\dfrac{\text{Profits}}{\text{Turnover}} \times 100$.

[d] Return on capital = $\dfrac{\text{Profits}}{\text{Net capital employed}} \times 100$.

[e] Subsequently sold in 1986/7.

others tend to be associated with at least the provision of leisure-based products in their diversified activities. Trust House Forte is probably the group most closely centred upon leisure and holiday based activities, being mainly a hotel and catering operation.

One other point to note from Table 11.13 is the ownership of 'holiday camps' by the companies listed. In fact holiday camps is a misnomer as these have recently been renamed 'holiday centres' or 'villages' in an effort to up-grade their market image. Large investments in this area also have been made in recent years, as indicated in Table 11.14. They have capitalized on the move towards self-catering by heavily introducing this element into their operations and have also benefited from the 1983 and 1984 slight trend back towards domestic holiday taking. In addition, these holiday centres are increasingly catering for second holidays – a few nights or a week or so spent off-season – taken in addition to the main holiday abroad. Thus the image of a Billy Butlin, Fred Pontin or Harry Warner (or Joe Maplin even!) coaxing their 'campers' into early morning collective exercises is long gone and unlikely to return, except on television.

As mentioned, domestic short-break holidays of three to four nights away from home are the fastest growing segment of the market. The Mecca Leisure Group has already set up its own travel company to cater for and organize this kind of holiday, and others are likely to follow suit. The 'holiday village' idea is being heavily marketed in the United Kingdom. A major development here was the Dutch company's Sporthuis Centrum Recreatie investment in a complete holiday village in Sherwood Forest, opened in 1987. This attracted the English Tourist Board's largest ever single development grant of £1.5 million.

Blackpool's Pleasure Beach still boasts the single most popular tourist attraction in the United Kingdom with an estimated 6.5 million visits in 1986. This was followed by the main London museums, headed by the British Museum at 3.6 million visits (*The Economist*, 1 August 1987). Of those attractions for which an entrance fee is charged, Madam Tussauds in London headed the list with 2.4 million visitors, closely followed by Alton Towers in Staffordshire with 2.2 million. The fastest growing attraction in recent years has been the 'Jorvik Viking Centre' in

Table 11.14 Leading British holiday centres 1984

Centres	Ownership	No. of centres	Estimated visitors	Nights spent	Investment
Pontins	Bass	30	850,000	5.2m	£30m (since 1981)
Butlins	Rank	6	815,000	5.0m	£9.5m (since 1982/3)
Ladbroke's	Ladbroke Group	16	500,000	na	£6m (since 1984/5)
Haven Holidays	English China Clays[a]	18	350,000	na	na
Warners	Grand Met.[b]	10	150,000	1.4m	£7m (since 1984/5)
Total			2,665,000		

Source: J.C.Holloway,*The Business of Tourism*, London: MacDonald & Evans, 1985, Table 4, p. 140, and newspaper reports.
Notes: [a] Sold to Rank in February 1986.
[b] Sold in 1986

Table 11.15 Hotel ownership (1985)[a]

Chain	Parent	No. of UK hotels	UK rooms
Trusthouse Forte Hotels	THF	208	21,000
Ladbroke/Comfort	Ladbroke Group[b]	50	6,200
Crest Hotels	Bass	60	5,700[c]
Thistle Hotels	Scottish & Newcastle	39	5,100
Mount Charlot Hotels	Mount Charlot Invest.	42	4,600
Queens Moat Houses	Queens Moat Hs.	57	4,500
Holiday Inns of America (UK)	Holiday Inns of Canada	17	4,100
Embassy Hotels	Allied Lyons	42	3,000
Swallow Hotels	Vaux Breweries	32	3,000
Grand Metropolitan Hotels (Intercontinental & Forum Hotels)	Grand Metropolitan	8	3,000
Viriani	Viriani Group	19	2,200
Rank Hotels	Rank	5	2,100
Reo Stakis Hotels	Stakis	24	2,000
De Vere Hotels	Greenhall Whitley	14	1,500

Source: Derived from ICC Keynote Report, *UK Tourism* (1985), Appendix Table 11, and *Accountancy*, January 1985.
Notes: [a] Does not include private consortium hotels: eg. Inter, Best Western and Prestige.
    [b] Ladbroke purchased Hilton Hotels in September 1987.
    [c] Beds.

York (0.9 million visits in 1986) owned by Heritage Projects Limited (for full details, see pp. 4 and 5 above). This company is planning more such ventures, notably 'The Pilgrim's Way' in a Canterbury church and 'The Oxford Story' in Oxford. It is the recognized market leader in this field.

Finally, we can look a little more closely at the main hotel groups operating in the United Kingdom. These are listed in Table 11.15 according to the number of rooms they operate.

In the case of United Kingdom hotels it is again the large diversified conglomerates that are heavily involved plus brewery groups (Scottish and Newcastle, Vaux, Greenhall Whitley, Allied Lyons, Bass). Surprisingly, perhaps, North American hotel chains are not strongly represented in Britain, Holiday Inns being the only one to appear in the table. But groups like Hilton and Sheraton were just hovering outside of the list, both with over 1,000 rooms in the United Kingdom. All this was poised to change rather rapidly by the late 1980s as these groups, plus the third largest American hotel chain Ramada, made a determined effort to increase their stake in London in particular, on the backs of the upsurge in American tourists coming to the United Kingdom largely because of exchange rate changes. It has already been pointed out above how Intasun had joined with Ramada to manage its new London hotel interests. In fact the world-wide Hilton chain was taken over by the Ladbroke Group in a £645 million deal completed in September 1987 (Ladbroke also owns the Texas Homecare d-i-y store chain). In addition, Intasun has pulled back from its initial moves into the hotel market. The company was returned to private ownership in mid-1987 in what was seen as a retrenchment and change in direction of its development. Things are thus still very unsettled in this area.

CONCLUSION

The United Kingdom holiday industry was in a period of rapid change and flux in late 1985 and this is likely to continue for some years to come. Indeed it could be argued that ever since the 1960s when inclusive charter holidays began to 'take-off' the United Kingdom industry has been in a continued state of flux. It is recognized to be one of the most 'dynamic' in the country. Failures, mergers, acquisitions, and diversification are the day-to-day diet of firms involved with the industry. Competitive pressures are intense and economic fluctuations are highly significant to the fortunes of companies. Add into this vagaries of the weather and a veritable hubbub of movement and change emerges. But this is itself dependent upon a number of rather more enduring features, perhaps the most important of which has been the continual growth in demand for overseas holidays despite the deep recession in the economy. It is the number of first-time overseas holidaymakers, 'new' consumers for this particular market that has remained surprisingly stable through the late 1970s and early 1980s, increasing by about 1 per cent per year. In effect this has meant approximately 400,000 new and inexperienced customers coming on to the overseas market each year, and it is this that has kept the traditional inclusive tour package alive. In this context there is always room for some sharp operator to move up the industry hierarchy of market share, although this is probably becoming more difficult as large

218

groups become consolidated and the industry generally matures. It has been estimated that the real cost of an average package holiday was 16 per cent less in 1987 than 1980, and this value for money is likely to keep the large groups well placed at the top of the market share listings.

However, competitive pressures can still be generated by another feature of the industry mentioned before – the relative ease of entry into and exit out of the big league. Amongst the hundreds of small firms expertise is continually generated and a taste for the big time engendered. It was the small firms who first spotted specialized market segments and exploited them, and they are encouraged in this by the ability to sub-contract most of the holiday provision to other operators. In particular, aeroplane seats can be contracted relatively easily and hotel beds booked cheaply. It is not even that difficult to set up an associated airline company given the leasing arrangements organized by financial institutions and the aircraft producers, and the developed secondhand market in airliners. A further advantage for holiday operators is the traditional nature of consumer booking arrangements whereby many millions of pounds are deposited with them several months in advance of the holiday being taken. This enables the operator to keep its own financial resources low and in effect secure commitments on the basis of the cash flow advanced to it by customers. These 'loans' (which is in effect what they amount to) can also be invested over the winter and spring period at considerable gain to the operator.

To some extent this latter advantage has been eroded in recent years by the tendency to go for late bookings, at least by the 'experienced' holiday-maker. Clearly, from the operator's point of view, one of the favourable elements to emerge from the competitive price battle of late 1985 was the reversal of this tendency, at least temporarily. One of the reasons that 'loss leaders' of £25 holidays could be easily tolerated, and even a more general price reduction installed, was the advanced booking this drew in. Thomson, for instance, was reported to have sold 400,000 1986 holidays in two weeks in November 1985 at the height of the price war, and other main operators probably did equally well. This was likely to produce an income of £16 million on the deposits advanced by customers.

The price war of autumn 1985 then was little more than an advertising exercise, though it did reduce the general price of holidays for 1986. However, tendencies in the economy and in the internal organization of firms were likely to have allowed this without too great an increase in risk to longer term financial viability for the larger operators. Inflation had slowed down in the United Kingdom to 5 per cent per year which produced a greater sense of economic security in terms of planning expenditures ahead. Added to this was the increase in real incomes of those still in work partly as a consequence of reduced inflation but also because of private sector wage rises running well ahead of inflation levels. Another contributory factor was the expected favourable exchange rate payments and downward pressures on hotel bed prices, particularly in Spain. As far as internal operations were concerned costs had been reduced by the extensive installation of computer technology, particularly with respect to booking and internal control procedures. Thus, all in all, a fall in the price of holidays would probably have emerged in 1986 largely because of these changes in underlying economic conditions, and need not have been accompanied by the razzmatazz of a full-blooded price war. However, this did serve to advertise the industry, create excitement, and generate a lot of early bookings that might not otherwise have come forward. A similar situation is very likely to be repeated in years to come.

*I would like to acknowledge the support of the Open University Faculty of Social Science Research Fund for financial assistance, and to Leon Martin for research assistance, in completing the analysis for this chapter.

12

Holidays for all
Popular movements, collective leisure, and the pleasure industry

ALAN TOMLINSON AND HELEN WALKER

In early 1986 Butlins celebrated the fiftieth anniversary of the opening of its first holiday camp in Britain. The Butlin version of the holiday camp prospered in a climate of campaigning for holidays with pay and in a period before packaging had been fully developed as the major way of selling holidays and travel. Butlins offered a comfortable exoticism, prioritizing pleasure for all. 'Hi di Hi', the collective address of 'Goodnight Campers' – these greetings welcomed millions to packaged mass pleasure and at the same time contributed to the growing marginalization of other practices in leisure.

The inter-war period offered increasingly cheaper possibilities in leisure. Between 1920 and 1938 the average real price of entertainment and recreation fell. Regularly employed working people had no problem finding the cost of a cinema, theatre or music hall seat, a dance hall or excursion ticket. Hire purchase was also available for new commodities such as bicycles. Generally speaking, and in spite of the Great Depression, for the employed inter-war working class, 'increased purchasing power led to an increase in total consumer expenditure on commercial leisure forms'.[1]

Some trade unions argued that free time was as important as – perhaps even more important than – money in the struggle for workers' rights. There was a lot of sense to this, with little point in earning more real income if there was no time available in which to spend it. Post Office unionists in the 1920s perceived a 'share out of leisure and a betterment of life' as 'more vital than money'. Printers expressed similar views, and painters argued for a package of extended pre-work education, a shorter

221

working week, and holidays with pay. This is not, of course, to say that workers would have been prepared to face long-term falls in real earnings. But it is a reminder that the labour movement has always addressed issues of the quality of life as well as of material pragmatics. And the period after the First World War was a watershed in the battle against oppressive hours of working. By 1920, 7 million workers had gained an average six and a half hour reduction in the working week – the equivalent, almost, of what we now see as a full day's work. The working week now averaged forty-eight hours, the model for the following two decades.

The Holidays With Pay legislation of 1938 combined with the rise in living standards and the shortened working week to produce a climate ripe for the leisure and consumer markets. The principle of holidays with pay had been extended to an estimated million and a half manual workers in Britain by the beginning of the 1920s, but the economic recession of that decade meant that this figure remained relatively static until the late 1930s. Some employers reneged on agreements once the slump set in; a few new agreements were made. Organized labour did not drop the issue though and some more enlightened firms continued to introduce private agreements. By 1937 a tripartite departmental committee of inquiry on the issue of holidays with pay was set up, reporting in favour of paid holidays in 1938. In the Committee's terms, the annual holiday could contribute to workers' 'happiness, health and efficiency', and be of 'benefit to the community'.

The 1938 Act covering statutory wage-regulating bodies was not a strong and wide-reaching one, ostensibly applicable to only 2 million workers. With its proposal for the granting of a maximum of three days consecutive holiday, it actually worsened some workers' conditions. But it was symbolically vital, as a recognition of the principle of the paid holiday. In 1937, 15 million people (one-third of the population) were holidaying away from home for a week or more. By 1939 4 million manual workers and another 4 million or so non-manual workers were receiving annual holiday pay, going on for half of the total occupied population. The Holidays With Pay Committee stressed happiness and health. Some voices within the labour movement stressed a blend of self-improvement, pleasure and health. Billy Butlin stressed fun, pure unadulterated, non-uplifting collective fun. The victory on paid holidays was achieved out of a mixture of motives, an amalgam of control and progressive reform. Its longer-term outcomes though were less ambiguous. It made the annual holiday more easily available to millions. These millions were ready for new forms of fun, or at least new combinations of familiar and proven elements. Seaside entrepreneurs had been feeding this appetite, building this market, for several generations already.

The seaside landlady figures prominently in the popular perception of the traditional British seaside holiday, but things were far from static in the inter-war period. In Blackpool – still stating its claims to be the biggest and the best in the 1980s, and countering the continental drift with slogans like 'Costa Notta Lotta' – there was a seven-fold rise in the number of private hotels between 1924 and 1938.[2] Clearly the holiday-maker was ready for more privacy, more comfort, more facilities and new arrangements in his/her main spell away from home. Blackpool guidebooks/brochures still feature photos of private toilet facilities very prominently.

Blackpool led the way with its aggressive conception of consumption, pleasure, and fun. The American inspired hi-tech thrills and spills of the pleasure beach became legend among holiday-makers. Yet traditional eccentricities on the seafront, the Golden Mile, could still draw millions. When the notorious Rector of Stiffkey – Reverend Mr Davidson – found that his encounters in London with 'at least a thousand' girls filled his Norfolk pews with scandalized but absorbed and voyeuristic worshippers in 1932, he soon found a less spiritual vocation. Convicted of several charges of indecency, this was the man for Blackpool. He found work on the promenade there, sitting in a barrel. Thousands of people rolled up to see this infamous figure in the summer of 1932. This was a peripatetic Diogenes of the masses though, and fined for obstruction he had to constantly seek new pitches: 'His barrel was sandwiched between a fasting girl and a flea circus. He sat in it for fourteen hours a day, hoping to get about £2,000 for all the appeals which lay before him.'[3] Via corpse-like appearances in glass cages the crazy parson ended up announcing a lecture-series for the 1937 summer season in a lion's cage at Skegness. The spectators got more than their money's worth on his first appearance, though little of his lecture. The Rector walked in on Freddie the lion and his sleeping mate. Freddie found this a bit intrusive or insensitive and killed him in front of the seaside spectators.

Through the 1930s such quirky turns were more and more discouraged in holiday venues. Local resorts wanted the respectable if unrestrained reveller. Guides of the time constructed an apparently more active leisure consumer, concerned with fashion, health, individual sports and style. Such ideals did not match all tastes though. The master tactician in the whole area was Billy Butlin, who a year before the Rector of Stiffkey's aborted lecture had opened up his first holiday camp, in Skegness. Maybe Billy himself set up Freddie the Lion to clear out the opposition in his own chosen patch.

Blending the bizarre with the familiar, Butlin took the established model of the British Holiday Camp by the scruff of the neck. In the late 1930s there were around 200 holiday camps, capable of taking 30,000 campers a week and often providing 'earnest all-in facilities' in the mould of the Holiday Fellowship.[4] Early holiday camps had been influenced by welfare considerations, educational ideals, political dreams of the collective subject, and the Social Darwinist spirit applied to the outdoor life. Camps had been founded by a range of organizations – the Co-op, the trade union, philanthropic or religious bodies.[5] Male youths experienced the idea of the camp in the Scouts too, but the boom in the commercial holiday camp in the quarter of a century after the end of World War Two was to dwarf the scale of these earlier models. Billy Butlin became the most successful entrepreneur in this explosive growth.

Billy Butlin's eye for the hedonistic package outstripped all competitors. The Butlins Empire has now had to market itself anew for the experienced package tourist; a move from wooden chalets to brick-built country suites, from the Minehead Camp to Summerwest World.[6] But in its pioneering way, and for several decades in the formative stage in the development of consumer culture, Butlins both represented and redefined core elements in working-class and mass leisure.

Roy Hudd, the comic and broadcaster, recalls being with 2,000 campers in the South Seas Coffee-bar in one of the camps, coping with flooding. One old boy, Hudd recalled, loved all this: 'It's marvellous – just like the war.'[7] With this sense of collective experience and shared pleasure the camps offered a commonality characteristic of working-class community. But they also offered a sense of the new. Butlin had previously provided large-scale seaside amusements throughout the thirties. Noting that landladies still hoofed boarders out for most of the day, Butlin saw how the holiday-makers would shelter in his amusement parks when it rained. What he spotted and exploited was a huge gap in the market – the provision of all-in accommodation and entertainment, the all-round holiday package.

When in 1936 the first Butlins camp opened up at Skegness the £500 spent on a half-page Daily Express advert in the early spring looked like money well spent. The immediate response to the advertisement for 'Butlins Luxury Holiday Camp' was virtually a full season's advance booking. The first campers, these pioneers of the British holiday industry, sat around the pool, ate the food, wandered around but looked bored, to Billy at least. On the third evening of the first week he sent one of his assistants into the dining hall and told him to get on the mike and chat to the campers/diners. This seemed to enliven them. Billy ordered his troops to get hold of brightly coloured blazers. Red was in the shops. It is in such accidental and unplanned ways that key historical decisions are made. The Redcoats ruled the roost in the world of the British holiday for many years, providing an apprenticeship for Roy Hudd, and a host of other showbiz dreamers.

Butlin of course wanted to keep campers in the camps. A range of regular routinized but riotous activities accomplished this, from the Glamorous Grannie to the Mr Knobbly Knees competition. The Butlin initiatives gave mid-twentieth century Britain some of its most enduring popular cultural events: dodgems, beauty queens, glamorous grannies, spaghetti-eating, knobbly knees, marathon walks, cross-channel swims. In and out of the camp Billy made sure that his camp and his model of the people's pleasures were always in the public eye. And he was ready to exploit the idea of celebrity. Listen to his biographer on this:

When Len Hutton scored his historic 364 runs against the Australians at the Oval in 1938, Bill phoned him a come-to-Skegness offer within twenty-four hours.

Len, the man whose aristocratic bat could practically score

225

runs without him holding it, was paid £100 for a couple of hours work, playing on stage at the camp theatre with a bat made of Skegness rock. Naturally, as it had to be the biggest show the town had ever seen, or nothing, so Bill hired the two brightest theatrical stars of the day to bowl to Len. His choice: Florence Desmond and Gracie Fields.[8]

Five thousand people paid a shilling each to see this show. These takings of a mere £250 more than covered the expenses but, more importantly, gave Billy Butlin the reputation of one of the country's leading showmen.

With his new blend, and showbiz entrepreneurial flair Butlin redefined the conventions of the British holiday industry. The Skegness Festival in 1938 had a Carnival Procession which took five or six hours to get through the town, the Rector of Stiffkey now forgotten. In 1937 Butlin had opened his Clacton camp with the brilliantly sharp slogan: 'Holidays with pay – Holidays with play. A week's holiday for a week's wage.' His finger on the pulse of the 'holidays with pay' movement, he reaped rich dividends with his new strategies for the packaging of popular pleasure.

The holiday pendulum swung unambiguously towards entertainment rather than worthiness, the just about respectably raucous rather than the recreationally rational. As millions flocked to Butlins, to other imitators and to other holiday resorts offering the packaged experience, older alternative forms of holidaying began to look more and more peripheral within the popular cultural practices of the British people.

The principal organizations promoting holidays for the working class in the early inter-war period were fired by motives very different from those of Billy Butlin. Postwar holiday consumption patterns in Britain indicate the rapid growth of package holidays in the 1950s, but the roots of this boom are located in an earlier period before the Second World War.

The early development of the annual holiday away from home in general, and the phenomenal growth of the inter-war outdoor movement in particular were influenced by popular movements and were important examples of class consciousness and class dynamics. 'Cyclists and hikers ... day excursionists, refugees from cursed towns' were prominent enough to provide fuel for the poetic pen of C. Day Lewis.[9] Holiday resorts, both inland and coastal, were expanding for new markets.

During the eighteenth and nineteenth centuries, the elite had maintained the view that sea water was an indispensable adjunct of health. With the development of the railway network the exclusivity of the cure had waned and many resorts were reshaped and redeveloped by commercializing forces, for the accumulation of profit. Changes in medical fashion and research led to the promotion of fresh air and sunlight as beneficial to health and the Victorian female's obsession with the maintenance of a pale complexion as a mark of class distinction gradually gave way in the early years of this century, to the pursuit of the sun, in search of a healthy tan.[10]

Through the period leading up to the Second World War rural England too was subjected, according to C.E.M. Joad, to an 'invasion of the untutored townsman'.[11] This mass discovery of the countryside was to some extent a car-borne movement, a consequence of a rapid rise in car ownership as prices fell with the application of mass production techniques to the manufacturing process. The unprecedented boom in the construction of private housing also seriously encroached upon the rural landscape. But there was another invasion of the countryside, noticeably quieter than that of the motorist but equal in terms of its impact. It was spearheaded by the rambling and cycling organizations and the movement as a whole included many thousands drawn from the older industrial areas or from the south of England with its new and expanding service and supply trades.

From the beginning of the century the young were attracted to these activities, and membership became increasingly dominated by individuals in their late teens and early twenties who, released from Victorian preoccupation with moral standards and propriety, rejected the values and fashions of the previous generation. For young workers such as H.G. Wells' Miss Milton and the draper, Hoopdriver,[12] who had money in their pockets and were without as yet the cares and responsibilities of family life, unchaperoned excursions in the countryside provided opportunities for encounters with the opposite sex. In the emergence of this 'young generation' of independent means lies the early identification of the sector of the population which was to be so effectively targeted by the market in the postwar era. By the 1950s and 1960s market researchers were chasing the 'teenager' as a major new figure in the world of consumerism.

In the late nineteenth century, the pastime of rambling through open countryside had been restricted to those who not only had time at their disposal but also the financial capability to travel into rural areas. Individual ramblers were drawn principally from the upper echelons of Victorian society, mainly aesthetes, academics and members of the legal profession.

The largely southern based and predominantly male rambling clubs were bastions of class exclusivity. The Polytechnic Rambling Club was formed in 1885, the London Federation of Rambling Clubs in 1901. The Federation scored an early triumph in the negotiation of concessionary fares (for the sole use of member clubs) with the Great Northern Railway Company, a forerunner in its early recognition of the commercial significance of the outdoor movement.[13] In the north of England there were fewer clubs but their class basis was as pronounced. One was the Sheffield Pennine Club, whose members were leading industrialists. Another, the Yorkshire Ramblers, was founded in Leeds in 1899. In Manchester one of the earliest clubs was the Manchester YMCA Rambling Club, dating from 1880. The club gained a reputation for undertaking strenuous walks frequently covering seventy miles between Saturday afternoon and Sunday evening. What went on on Saturday nights is less definitively documented! The Rucksack Club was founded in 1902, originally Manchester based but expanding into branches throughout the country. Its membership was exclusively middle class, and included an 'uncanny proportion of lawyers', together with large numbers of academics drawn from Manchester University. It was formed by members of the alma mater of climbers, the Alpine Club, founded in 1858. At the turn of the century a uniquely all-female climbing club, The Pinnacle, came into existence. The activities of the club, whose members were the wives and sisters of male enthusiasts, centred on North Wales and the Snowdonia region.[14] These outdoor pursuits, with roots in academia, included a self-improving dimension, emphasizing an interest in the botany, geology, archaeology and history of the districts visited.[15]

In the early 1900s, although there was a continued expansion of the traditional and more exclusive type of club, increasingly (and especially in the north of England), there were groups emerging whose members would not only challenge the middle-class monopoly of the countryside but who also expressed a commitment to the principles of socialism. For such groups leisure was an assertion of collective rights, not just a badge of exclusive status. The obtaining of access and maintenance of rights of way over Pennine moorlands, particularly in the Peak District, was fundamental to their activities. The denial, to the general public, of open access to the countryside led to an intensification of the fifty-year struggle for legislative changes culminating in the mass trespasses of the early 1930s.[16] One of the most remarkable of these early groups was the Sheffield Clarion Ramblers, established in 1900 and described by its founder as the 'first workers' Sunday rambling club in the north of England'.[17] The membership was drawn from the industrial conurbations of Yorkshire, and placed an emphasis on self-improvement and knowledge and understanding of the country-side.

Some individuals saw opportunities for social reform in leisure provision. One such was T.A. Leonard, born in 1864, educated in Germany in the 1880s, and committed to ideals of international friendship and socialism. On his return to Britain he entered the congregational ministry in the bleak Lancashire mill town of Colne where he was deeply affected by the social and economic conditions which industrial society imposed upon his flock. Appalled at the annual wakes week, with its general exodus to Morecambe and Blackpool, and what he saw as the mindless spending of hard-earned wages on inane amusements, Leonard proposed an alternative form of holiday. Within the ambit of the social guild work of his church, he planned a modest two-day holiday in Ambleside in June 1981 during which thirty men from his pastorate scaled the fells. From these beginnings Leonard founded the Co-operative Holidays Asso-ciation which was non-profit making and became popular enough for advertisements to be placed in *Christian World* in 1893, offering CHA run rambling holidays in the Lake District. For thirty shillings all found, accommodation was to be provided at Ambleside and Keswick, parties would climb Helvellyn and the Langdale Pikes, and visit 'the haunts of Wordsworth, Ruskin and the Lake Poets'. The appointment of a chaperone enabled four women teachers to accompany this early party which spent eight strenuous days completing walking climbs of twenty miles or so and evenings listening to lectures on Ruskin and places of interest. This element of self-improvement recurs throughout the accounts of working-class leisure organizations founded on principles of social concern and there is a clear overlap of membership with, for example, the Fabian Society and later in the century, the Workers' Educational Association.[18]

A retrospective account written in 1937 gives the occupational composition of these pioneering groups: they were in the main teachers and shopkeepers, representing both high and low church – essentially the lower-middle classes. Although during the early years of the century the CHA attracted an increasing membership, Leonard was concerned at its failure to fulfil its founding aims. The main criticisms focused on the lack of progress in the provision of international holidays but principally on the fact that despite its founding objectives, to improve the lot of the exploited labouring classes, the Fellowship was becoming 'rather middle class in spirit, and conservative in ideas. . . . We want [Leonard stressed], to bring holidays within the reach of poorer folks.' The Holiday Fellowship was set up in 1913. It represented a novel venture, owned, controlled, and administered by its members. Membership implied the taking up of one or more £1 shares and shareholders were paid interest fixed until 1932 at 5 per cent. Use of the Fellowship's centres was not dependent on membership but there were certain benefits including a reduction of 2s 6d on the weekly charge, priority booking facilities, eligibility for office, but more significantly, in the event of personal hardship, a subsidized holiday at off-season times of the year.

Success was rapid with 2,196 organized weeks of holiday taken in the first year of operation. Four centres were opened in Great Britain and, fulfilling the international element so desired by Leonard, one in Germany. Membership of the Holiday Fellowship continued to rise even through the war years, and by 1919 the total numbered 5,241 guest weeks. By 1926 eleven British and four continental centres had opened; in 1938, with assets totalling £100,000, 45,169 guest weeks were taken at the thirty British and twenty-two overseas centres which spread from Brittany to Poland and Czechoslovakia.[19]

Basic shelter and kitchen facilities were necessary for the many thousands using rural areas each weekend, and the role of the Cyclists' Touring Club (CTC) was significant in pioneering the provision of cheap overnight accommodation and other services for its members. Founded in 1878, the CTC flourished with the cycling boom of the 1890s, a time when bicycling captured the imagination of a wide spectrum of society. H.G. Wells describes how 'Spectators would fall a-talking of the fashionableness of bicycling – how judges and stock-brokers and actresses, and, in fact all the best people rode – and how that it was often the fancy of such great folk to shun the big hotels . . . and seek, incognito, the cosy quaintness of village life.'[20] From an original figure of 142 to 3,356 in 1880, and 6,705 in 1882, club membership rose to a record 60,449 at the turn of the century.[21] Workers employed in the mills and factories of industrial areas took to the bicycle as a principal means of travel to work. In 1932, a new Raleigh bicycle could be bought for under £5, or on the instalment system for 9s 7d per month without deposit. The Raleigh was regarded as the aristocrat; a Hercules cost less, approximately £4, and there were cheaper makes and predictably, a thriving secondhand market.[22]

So by the 1930s there were thought to be at least 10 million cyclists – ten times the number of private motorists. Clubs were affiliated to organizations ranging from church to political party. This cycling boom was a youth-based phenomenon too, spawning its own networks of cafes and modest bed and breakfast 'digs'. The CTC and the National Cyclists' Union held their own conventions and cycling was not immune from fashions and crazes. For those within 'the Movement', a week's cycling holiday using CTC accommodation was possible for £3 10s all in; organized excursions took in the Scottish Isles, the West of Ireland, and the Black Forest in Germany. Party fares, low hostel charges, and the availability of cheap, simple meals made a three-week continental cycling holiday in 1930 possible for approximately £15.[23]

The Holiday Fellowship also promoted the provision of cheap overnight accommodation. In its quarterly magazine (*Over the Hills*, spring 1929) Lakeland Tours were advertised, centred around three camps equipped with bedding and cooking facilities for eight individuals who, it was hoped, would cater collectively. Although an immediate success the Fellowship was concerned at its inability to keep costs below 32s 6d for members and 35s for non-members, figures which were not far short of standard charges at that time. T.A. Leonard argued the case through the columns of *Over the Hills* for Spring 1930, in reforming ignorance of the emerging Nazi appropriation of the Germanic pastoral dream:

> If only we had something of the social sense they had in Germany, we might manage to give our young people the experiences they ought to have . . . [in Germany] the rambling movement . . . . [has] reached enormous proportions – 2,500 hostels provide shelter for 6d per night . . . . We do not value our country sufficiently, we let any rich man enclose hundreds of square miles of gorgeous mountain, heath or forest and do not care what devastation arises from the growth of commercialisation . . . . The simplest accommodation is all that is looked for, just good clean sleeping rooms with blankets, somewhere to eat and a place to shelter from inclement weather.

The inspiration for the experiment was the German *Jugendherbergen* accommodation which had long been popular with English trampers and cyclists. The *Verband fur Deutsche Jugendherbergen* (DJH) had, by the end of 1929, some 700 British members including a block membership by the School Journey Association, an organization founded at the turn of the century to assist teachers responsible for taking parties of schoolchildren abroad. The German scheme of cheap overnight accommodation dated from the years prior to the First World War and had its origin in the central European tradition of 'wanderlust'.[24]

In 1930 a British Youth Council Committee with representatives from the major outdoor, youth, and holiday organizations investigated the viability of establishing hostels in north Wales. It was planned that the new accommodation would be furnished very basically and would offer at minimum charge, a camp bed or mattress, blankets, and basic cooking facilities on production of the membership card of a central organization. The choice of a name caused some division of opinion but it was agreed that the word 'youth' should be used, and as the Merseyside group had publicized 'youth hostels', this stuck.

By the end of 1930, £2,750 had been donated by the public, £10,000 promised by the Carnegie Trust and 170 individuals as a gesture of good faith had become members of the Youth Hostels Association (YHA). By Easter 1931, 4 hostels had opened with a total of 130 bed-spaces; a further 3 hostels opened that summer and an impressive total of 9,926 overnight stays were made that year. British membership now stood at 1,639 but the overnight total had been augmented by many European trampers, a trend which was widely welcomed as a sign of real internationalism: 'This summer our hostels housed a miniature League of Nations', claimed the Manchester and District Ramblers' Federation Handbook in 1932.

By the outbreak of war, there were 297 hostels with 10,689 beds, a membership of 83,417 and some 58,000 'overnights'.[25] Although the accommodation remained spartan with bunk beds arranged in segregated dormitories, nevertheless, at a cost fixed at 1s per night plus a shilling for breakfast, extended holidays in the countryside became for the first time a practical possibility for thousands previously denied them.

The press reported a hiking boom in 1931. If rambling was a leisurely walk in the countryside on a Sunday afternoon, hiking was altogether a more ambitious enterprise, frequently involving a trip further afield for a week or a fortnight's hard walking using map and compass, regarded as an indispensable accomplishment as the threat of war increased. According to Graves and Hodge, the term 'hiker' had entered vernacular use from the United States in about 1927 when in an article in the *Daily Express*, an official of the Camping Club stated: 'We have 3,000 members. Most of these are solitary "hikers" who carry all their kit with them.'[26]

A distinctive form of dress, essentially egalitarian, was adopted by both cyclist and hiker, consisting of an open-necked khaki shirt, a jacket finished with the newly invented zip fastener, short trousers and a Basque beret. This style was adopted by both men and women.

The enormous popularity of hiking can be seen not only as a consequence of the formation of the YHA, but also of the emergence of many new organizations and clubs which undertook to arrange hikes and negotiate concessionary rates for travel, accommodation, and refreshment for their members, and others engaged in agitation for reform of the access laws. The opportunities for commercial exploitation of the hiking boom were grasped readily by the railway companies who offered cheap day returns to hikers. Bank holiday specials ran from all the major towns not just to the big seaside resorts but also into rural areas. The Whit Monday trains offering a concessionary service into the Derbyshire Peak District from both Manchester and Sheffield offered the advantage of returning from a list of alternative stations and were resoundingly popular. On the morning of Good Friday in 1932, the GWR ran a 'Hikers' Mystery Express' from Paddington to an unpublished destination and back. So many people wanted to be transported to this surprise Arcadian spot that an extra train had to be put on. During summer months there were many such trips; 'Ramblers' Harvest Moon Specials' were run along the Thames Valley, and in July 1932 an unexpected 1,400 stalwarts expressed a desire 'to witness the sunrise from Chanctonbury Ring' as part of a Southern Railway Moonlight Walk.[27] The Southern Railway made guided rambling a regular service as had most of the railway companies by the outbreak of war.

Popular movements did not of course remain outside the influence of market forces. The movement inspired popular songs, but also the commercial ditty, 'I'm Happy When I'm Hiking'. Publishers were not slow to realize the potential of the new market, releasing a spate of books and magazines which were the successors to the elitist Victorian guide book and the predecessors of the glossy coffee-table number for contemporary leisure motorists. Newer volumes such as the Shell Guides and the Batsford series, illustrated with photographs by the newly developed cheap photogravure process, presented an idealised romantic image of rurality as well as extolling in their unpolluted wholesomeness the benefits of a holiday in the open air. Commercial interests were quick to recognize the scale of popular interest in the outdoors, but whilst the outdoors had become integral to everyday life in Britain by the Second World War, it continued to represent in some of its expressions a relatively uncommercialized leisure culture.

Overlapping the provision of the Holiday Fellowship and the

CTC, sharing the mood of internationalism current through the period and blurring the boundaries between quasi-philanthropism and commercial enterprise such as Thomas Cook and Billy Butlin, was the Workers' Travel Association (WTA). This was a major provider of not only walking holidays but also package holidays and holiday camps.

The WTA was founded in 1921 at Toynbee Hall, moving later to Transport House (at that time the headquarters of Britain's largest trade union, the Transport Workers, and also of the Labour Party). In its inception and philosophy the WTA embodied national anxieties over the future stability of Europe, stating in its objectives a committment to the promotion of a lasting international peace through the ideals of the newly formed League of Nations. Initially concerned with the advancement of these aims through the provision of low cost holidays abroad, rapid early success led to the extension of operations to the home market with publicity material stressing the proletarian nature of the enterprise: 'Trips for the workers; Holidays to suit all pockets'; 'What Cooks have done in the way of facilitating travel for the upper-middle and middling-middle classes, the WTA are arranging to do for the masses.' The promotional literature continues with an explanation of the deliberately spartan-sounding and self-denying WTA philosophy:

> But there are differences, the WTA is not going to work on 'de luxe' lines. It has behind it an ideal; it aims primarily at getting working men and women of this country abroad in order that the scales shall fall from their eyes through real comradeship with those who do the hard work in other countries. It aims more at political and peaceful penetration than at profit.[28]

From an initial 700 in the first season, bookings rose rapidly to 26,000 by 1931. The economic crisis and in particular the slump produced lower totals for the next two years, but by 1939, the number of holidays booked had risen to a substantial 62,500, comprising 29,500 holiday-makers travelling overseas, and 33,000 taking home bookings.

The WTA offered hiking, rambling or climbing holidays at home and abroad, centre-based holidays by the sea, mountains or in the tourist centres of Europe. In planning its programme the Association emphasized its international objectives advertising, for example, from as early as 1924, annual holidays at two centres in the USSR: a 'unique opportunity to experience the USSR's great natural beauty, priceless and world famous works of art, gigantic collective farms and the thrill of seeing in progress the greatest social experiment in the world's history.

The WTA matched the provision of its main competitors while undercutting their prices: holidays ranged from winter sports, world cruises (three months, 165 guineas by freighter from Marseilles), tours of Lapland and biblical sites in Egypt, to courses on political theory at the international college in Elsinore and the Second Workers' Olympiad held in Vienna in 1931. For the latter, the Association arranged the travel and accommodation for the fifty strong British contingent which included a National Workers' Sports Association team, a group of Clarion cyclists, and spectators. In 1934, the centenary of the arrest of the Tolpuddle Martyrs, the WTA organized a commemorative event. The commemoration (now annual) involved the setting up of over fifty camp sites in the Dorset countryside, complete with tents and catering services.

Extremely responsive to demand, a characteristic which was to be lost in the postwar period, it was inevitable that the WTA would become involved in the mid-1930s in the development of holiday camps. Careful to avoid the regimentation and overcrowding that characterized the camps of its competitors and anxious to compete in terms of cost, the Association opened the 500 capacity Rogerson Hall camp near Lowestoft in 1938. A joint enterprise with the Co-operative Wholesale Society, such was the prestige of the WTA's reputation and the skill of the promotional machine that 5,000 bookings were taken in the first year, at prices two-thirds those of Billy Butlin, who had opened his second camp at Clacton the previous year. Yet despite his prices Butlin could take 5,200 in his Skegness camp by 1939.

The tremendous extent of the WTA's organization was reflected in the nature of its advertising campaign. In 1933 more than 400 advertisements were placed in 90 publications ranging from provincial newspapers to trade union journals. There were posters on 700 railway stations, 300,000 booklets and programmes were printed, 100,000 leaflets and 12,000 posters distributed nationally. By 1938 the WTA's annual turnover was in excess of £595,000. An early equal opportunities employer, it offered union rates to all its employees at a time when pay and conditions in the travel industry were notoriously poor.

Postwar, the WTA declined in relative importance, opting to focus on tried and tested coach tours and specialist holidays, and losing its market share to the newer and more competitive tour operators who were promoting the package trade. The trade union rates so jealously guarded in the inter-war period by the Association became little more than the minimum wage of the 1950s, producing salaries insufficient to attract the ambitious tour operator and dynamic advertising manager and leading in turn to a failure to compete effectively.

The WTA like the Holiday Fellowship was rooted in a commitment to the work ethic and the progressive movement. Along with internationalism, these values were to have a steadily devaluing currency in a postwar Britain inclined more and more towards individualism and consumer sovereignty.

Cooperative ventures dating from the turn of the century became anachronistic. Conspicuous consumption became, for more groups, an important element in leisure culture. When combined with a newly emerging and financially significant youth culture sharing a common childhood memory of war-time austerity, and specifically targeted by aggressively competitive marketing, the package boom of the fifties was irresistible.

Not all the demobilized troops had seen service in the immediate European war zone. For some the Second World War was a time of extensive travel with tours of duty in, for example, North America or India presenting novel opportunities and providing the determination and individual confidence to repeat the experience in peace-time. The inter-war working-class holiday organizations had occupied a significant place, gradually introducing a previously untravelled sector of the population to the educative and recreative value of foreign travel while yet accommodating a more traditional pattern of holiday-making. Determined to break down chauvinism and confront the prejudice and suspicion of the unknown, the organizations also diminished the economic barrier to foreign travel by establishing the novel concept of the now standard, fixed price 'all-in' holiday which presented a defined objective to be budgeted for over a year. Postwar, the field lay open for entrepreneurial capitalism to woo this sector of the population and to create new markets to service its holiday needs. Consumption in leisure and holidaying became increasingly linked to the capacity of the individual consumer to make choices within the market. The new organizations catering for this were to be economically more efficient and culturally more bland than the popular movements of the first half of the century. The leisure and recreational movements generated from the grassroots or from the concerned philanthropist looking down from on high were to give way to a cultural and economic popularism which was to be progressively constructed by the new generation of market-orientated professionals. Even 'getting away from it all' was to become absorbed into the logic of the third stage in the development of Braverman's universal market, in which: 'a "product cycle" invents new products and services, some of which become indispensable as the conditions of modern life change to destroy alternatives'.[29]

Butlin himself was to be overtaken by further developments in the postwar holiday industry. His own excursion into foreign fields was an unmitigated disaster when his Grand Bahamas Island Vacation Village collapsed into a financial mess before it had really got started, in 1950. Butlin's blend maybe didn't look too modern for very long once chartered air travel offered a world of new possibilities to the British holiday-maker, and at the same time patterns of leisure were developing more privatized forms. But Butlin, in bridging the pre-affluent and the affluent phases of modern Britain, was truly formative in his contribution to popular culture and mass modes of consumption. As a 23-year-old, Stan Whittaker was one of Butlin's first clients in 1936, having met Butlin himself as a customer in the early thirties at Skegness Amusement Park. Stan liked Bill a lot, his savings from the Sheffield steelworks were ploughed, a little at a time, into Butlins Ordinary shares. In early 1962 his 50,000 one shilling shares were worth almost £50,000. Stan holds nothing back in his admiration for Billy: 'if the history of my generation is ever written, Butlin's name is going to rank along with Sir Winston Churchill's, Marconi's and Sir Alexander Fleming's'.[30] War, communications, medicine and fun. Maybe

Stan's got it right. Winning for Britain, the wireless, penicillin, and the packaged holiday. In Stan Whittaker's eyes it is perhaps good health and good fun that make the sacrifices of a fight against Fascism at all worthwhile.

As millions flocked to the seaside resorts and holiday camps of postwar Britain they cemented a growth of the holiday market and confirmed the conception of the organized pleasure-seeker, the packaged punter. This hedonistic surge to the seaside and the camp hailed a new phase of consumer capitalism far removed from both the collective initiatives of traditional working-class culture and the improving motives of the pioneering holiday organizations of the pre-affluent period.

NOTES

1 The details on holiday pay and the struggle over working hours is taken from Stephen G. Jones, *Workers at Play: A Social and Economic History of Leisure 1918–1939*, London: Routledge & Kegan Paul, 1986, pp.14–33.

2 Alun Howkins and John Lowerson, *Trends in Leisure, 1919–1939*, London: Sports Council/Social Science Research Council, 1979, p. 6.

3 Ronald Blythe, 'The Rector of Stiffkey', in *The Age of Illusion: England in the Twenties and Thirties, 1919–1940*, Harmondsworth: Penguin Books, 1964, pp. 156–78. The quotation is from p. 174.

4 Howkins and Lowerson, *Trends in Leisure*, p. 12.

5 Colin Ward and Dennis Hardy, *Goodnight Campers: The History of the British Holiday Camp*, London: Mansell Publishing, 1986.

6 Su Read recalls the guest-houses' 'bowl of hot water to wash in in your room', and then 'Along came Butlins' with an all-in entertainment programme and four meals a day for £3 a week (*Woman's Hour*, BBC Radio 4, April 1986). See Su Read, *Hello Campers!*, London: TVS/Bantam Press (Transworld Publishers), 1986. See too, J. Drower, *Good Clean Fun*, Twickenham: Arcadia Press, 1982.

7 In the Independent Television (Television South) documentary, 30 April 1986, *Hello Campers: Butlins 1936–1986*.

8 Rex North, *The Butlin Story*, London: Harrolds, 1962, p.59.

9 C. Day Lewis 'The magnetic mountain 32', in R. Kelton (ed.), *Poetry of the Thirties*, Harmondsworth: Penguin 1964, p. 50.

10 For a more detailed picture of the sea-side holiday see J.A.R. Pimlott, *The Englishman's Holiday* (1947), Hassocks: Harvester, 1976; J.K. Walton, *The Blackpool Landlady*, Manchester, Manchester University Press, 1978; J.K. Walton, *The English Seaside Resort: A Social History 1750–1914*, Leicester: Leicester University Press, 1983.

11 C.E.M. Joad, *The Untutored Townsman's Invasion of the Country*, London: Faber & Faber, 1946.
12 H.G. Wells, *The Wheels of Chance*, London: Dent and Son, 1914.
13 H. Hill, *Freedom to Roam*, Ashbourne: Moorland Publishing, 1980, p. 26.
14 ibid., p. 25.
15 E. Gaskell's *Mary Barton*, Harmondsworth: Penguin, 1970, p. 75, contains the line: 'There is a class of men . . . who know the name and habitat of every plant within a day's walk from their dwelling . . .' See also U.C. Knoeflmacher and G.B. Tennyson, *Nature and the Victorian Imagination*, Berkeley: University of California Press, 1977; and D.E. Allen, *The Naturalist in Britain*, London: Allen Lane, 1976.
16 See Hill, *Freedom to Roam*, and J.R. Lowerson 'Battles for the countryside', in F. Gloversmith (ed.) *Class Culture and Social Change: A New View of the 1930s*, Hassocks: Harvester, 1980.
17 *The Sheffield Clarion Ramblers Handbook* 1920–1921.
18 Some of these links are examined in J.F.C. Harrison, *Learning and Living 1790–1960*, London: Routledge & Kegan Paul, 1961.
19 *Over the Hills*, Journal of the Holiday Fellowship. Various years.
20 Wells, *The Wheels of Chance*, p. 221.
21 F. Alderson *Bicycling: A History*, Newton Abbot: David & Charles, 1972, p. 190.
22 N. Branson and M. Heinemann, *Britain in the Nineteen Thirties*, London: Weidenfeld & Nicolson, 1971, p. 262.
23 ibid., also C.L. Mowat, *Britain Between the Wars, 1917–1940*, London: Methuen, 1968; and, J. Stevenson, *British Society 1914–1945*, Harmondsworth: Penguin, 1984.
24 A youth movement known as *Die Wandervogel*, 'The Wanderbirds', had come into being in the early years of the century. Highly romantic and idealistic, eschewing alcohol, tobacco and conventional dress and determined to be at one with nature for the summer months, the *wandervogel* rambled through the countryside carrying the necessities of life on his/her back. D. H. Lawrence eulogized them as 'sturdy youths bearing guitars' observed, admired and joined by the fifteen-year-old Constance Chatterly and his sister Hilda on a visit to Dresden – 'They sang the Wandervogel songs and they were free.' See *Lady Chatterly's Lover*, Harmondsworth: Penguin, 1960, p. 7.
25 Annual reports of the Youth Hostels Association, also O. Coburn, *The Youth Hostel Story*, London: The National Council of Social Service, 1950.
26 R. Graves and A. Hodge, *The Long Weekend – A Social History of Great Britain, 1918–1939*, London: Faber & Faber, 1940, p. 277.
27 ibid., also Lowerson, 'Battles for the countryside'.
28 *The Travel Log*, Journal of the Workers' Travel Association; also H. Walker, 'The popularisation of the outdoor movement', in *The British Journal of Sports History*, 2:2 (September 1985).

29 In which, according to Harry Braverman 'the capitalist mode of production takes over the totality of individual, family and social needs and, in subordinating them to the market, also reshapes them to serve the needs of capital'. The universal market invades cultural spaces which might have previously been the terrain of the family, community or whatever. Braverman points to two earlier stages in the move towards and the creation of the universal market: first, the commodity form becomes the predominant mode of the production of goods; second, the range of services which are converted into commodities expands (leisure would be a good example here); See Harry Braverman, *Labour and Monopoly Capital*, New York: Monthly Review Press, 1974, pp. 271, 281; see too, Veronica Beechey, 'The sexual division of labour and the labour process: a critical assessment of Braverman', in Stephen Wood (ed.), *The Degradation of Work? Skill, Deskilling and the Labour Process*, London: Hutchinson, 1983, pp. 54–73. Beechey, in pp. 57–62, focuses upon Braverman's notion of the universal market, and develops a critical response to his theory of the family and its development in capitalism.

30 North, *The Butlin Story*, p. 125.

Index

This is a selective index. It does not aspire to total coverage of all the names, events and examples mentioned in the text.

Where authors are cited and named within the main text, they are usually indexed. Many authors, though, are cited and footnoted in the main text, but remain unnamed there. For full details of such authors, readers must consult the notes which follow the chapter.

This index includes references to the notes only where a substantial point is made, rather than just a reference given.